MW01166596

WHAT WILL I DO
with the
REST OF MY LIFE?

WHAT WILL I DO *with the* REST OF MY LIFE?

An Inspirational Guide
for Baby Boomers
Who Want to Finish Strong and
Leave a Lasting Legacy.

Happy Dane Publishing

by

DR. GREGORY M. PAGH

What Will I Do with the Rest of My Life © Copyright 2022 Dr. Gregory M. Pagh

All rights reserved. No part of this publication may be reproduced, distributed or transmitted in any form or by any means, including photocopying, recording, or other electronic or mechanical methods, without the prior written permission of the publisher, except in the case of brief quotations embodied in critical reviews and certain other noncommercial uses permitted by copyright law.

Although the author and publisher have made every effort to ensure that the information in this book was correct at press time, the author and publisher do not assume and hereby disclaim any liability to any party for any loss, damage, or disruption caused by errors or omissions, whether such errors or omissions result from negligence, accident, or any other cause.

Neither the author nor the publisher assumes any responsibility or liability whatsoever on behalf of the consumer or reader of this material. Any perceived slight of any individual or organization is purely unintentional.

For more information, email greg@happydanepublishing.org

15849 90th Street NE, Otsego, MN 55330

ISBN: 979-8-88759-384-5 (Paperback)
ISBN: 979-8-88759-500-9 (Hardcover)

Unless otherwise noted, Scripture quotations are taken from The Holy Bible, New International Version, NIV, Copyright 1973, 1978, 1984, 2011 by Biblica, Inc. Used by permission. All rights reserved worldwide.

Scripture quotations marked NLT are taken from the Holy Bible, New Living Translation, Copyright 1996, 2004, 2015 by Tyndale House Foundation. Used by permission of Tyndale House Publishers, a division of Tyndale House Ministries, Carol Stream, Illinois 60188. All rights reserved.

Scripture quotations marked ESV are taken from The ESV Bible (The Holy Bible, English Standard Version), Copyright 2001 by Crossway, a publishing ministry of Good News Publishers. Used by permission. All rights reserved.

DEDICATION

This book is dedicated…

… to my dear wife, Colleen, my life partner and best friend. You have walked with me faithfully through every twist and turn of more than 45 years of marriage, family and ministry, always encouraging me to trust Jesus and remain true to His calling. This was certainly the case when the Lord put this book on my heart in the summer of 2021. I am forever grateful for your love, understanding, prayers and encouragement.

…to my parents, Gary and Betty Pagh. You have been such faithful examples of living every season of life to the fullest. Your testimony and influence are referred to numerous times in my writing. It is unavoidable. Your legacy, by God's grace, is mine. Dad, you are greatly missed!

…to my Christ Church family in Otsego, Minnesota. It has been my profound privilege to serve as your pastor for more than 30 years. You are a faithful band of Christ-followers who have embraced a transformational lifestyle and are walking it out every day in your families, neighborhoods, workplaces and schools. I continue to be inspired and blessed by your partnership in the Gospel!

…to my friend, mentor and spiritual father, Dr. Ed Silvoso, the Founder and President of Transform Our World. You and your amazing team have always encouraged me to "go for it" in partnership with others, trusting the Holy Spirit to lead and empower. Because of your inspiring leadership I have also been blessed with a global family of transformers who are changing the world!

… and finally, to my children and grandchildren; Matt and Leah Pagh, Ella, Sam, Abby and Livia; Josh and Sarah Pagh, Mason and Micah; Sarah and Jason Flaspeter, Simon, Ethan, Hailey and Isaac. Although this book is directed at my generation, it is all about what Colleen and I hope to leave for you… a lasting legacy of faith and love. You are all our pride and joy!

FOREWORD

There is no escaping the reality that we are living in unusual and uncertain times in which it seems that everyone from individuals to nations are living in turmoil of one sort or another. That is why it is extraordinarily important for the Christian Church – the Ekklesia of Jesus–and all her generations to be **"strong in the Lord and in the strength of His might" (Ephesians 6:12).**

This is the age for modern day Calebs to rise up! When he was 85 years young he said to Joshua, "Give me that mountain." And when he declared his "dream," his daughters with vision said, "Father, give us the upper springs and the lower ones." When the younger generations see that their elders haven't given up but instead have chosen to conquer the next mountain, they will also rise-up with greater strength, wisdom and courage.

That's where this book finds its very important purpose and clarion call. Its challenge to the older generations has the potential to unleash the younger generations into greater vision and boldness. We desperately need this baton to be passed with love, faith and wisdom so that our children and grandchildren are not left floundering. Although addressed to the Baby Boom generation, in the end this book encourages every generation to ask the question, "What will I do with the rest of my life?"

With elegant prose, engaging anecdotes and sound scholarship, Dr. Greg Pagh pours decades of wisdom and experience into every page in this book, which flows from his role as the beloved pastor of a transformational church and as an apostle to the unreached. Read on and get ready to be re-fired in order to make the world a better place.

Dr. Ed Silvoso
Founder / President, Transform Our World
Ordinary people doing extraordinary
deeds to change the world

CONTENTS

INTRODUCTION

I'm a Baby Boomer, a member of that generation born between 1946 and 1964 that became the largest demographic in the history of the United States. As of the 2020 Census, there are currently 69.6 million of us still alive and kicking. By the year 2030, all Baby Boomers will be 65 years of age or older. With new medical advancements happening every year, many of us can expect to live well into our 90s. No wonder that millions of "Boomers" are asking, "What will I do with the rest of my life?"

Consider this! Many of us in the Baby Boom generation are right now effectively entering the 4th quarter of our lives, which in the world of sports is "crunch time." This is when most games are won or lost. If the good Lord gives us another 10, 20 or 30 years to live, what will we do with it? Will we rise-up or just ride-it-out? Will we re-fire or simply retire?

This book is for all of you who are passionate about living your best life and leaving a lasting legacy for the generations that follow. God is not finished with you yet! I welcome you to this journey because I believe with all my heart that when you are a follower of Jesus every day is a gift to be lived to the fullest and the best is yet to come!

Dr. Gregory M. Pagh
Elk River, Minnesota, USA
December 2022

CHAPTER 1

Take Stock of Your Life!

I'm not a runner! I like to say that I don't have the body type. However, when it comes to this thing called "the race of life" I desperately want to run well. I want to finish strong! And so it was that during the summer of 2021, a year when Covid-19 was ravaging the planet, I had a very good talk with the Lord.

My wife and I are campers. We have a travel trailer and have seen so much of this beautiful country over the years. The Grand Tetons just south of Yellowstone are our favorite. No foot hills, just one big beautiful mountain chain that explodes out of the ground. We're not friendly campers though. We will talk to our neighbors, briefly, but no inviting them over for S'mores at our campfire. You see, I'm already in the people business. I'm a pastor. I love people, I really do… but when we go camping we go to get away. Just me and my wife, Colleen, unless some of the grandkids are with us. We have ten but that's a whole different kind of adventure!

So one starry night I was sitting around just such a campfire at a beautiful RV Park near the little town of Sister Bay in Door County, Wisconsin. It was late. Colleen had already gone in for the night. Just me, there in my lawn chair, stirring the fire, thinking and praying. Over the years I've found that when I do get away from the challenges of day-to-day ministry I'm able to get the 30,000 foot view. It may take a week or two… but when that moment of quiet reflection comes it's a wonderful thing!

That's how it was that beautiful July evening. Just me and the Lord. As I said, we were in Wisconsin but you should know that we live in Minnesota – Elk River, Minnesota. I serve as the Senior Pastor of Christ Church in the neighboring community of Otsego. I'm also the President of a state-wide ministry called Bless Minnesota.

The Minnesota Miracle

While we were on this particular vacation I'd been reading a book by Pastor Dale Gilmore called "Minnesota: The Revival State."[1] It contained amazing stories and testimonies of how God had moved in such powerful ways over the past century and a half in this state I call home. One story in particular really spoke to me. It is verified by a number of historical societies.

It happened in the Spring of 1887. A locust or grasshopper invasion threatened the southern 2/3rds of Minnesota and there were no pesticides at that time to combat them. This infestation had been building for about two years… but that year entomologists were predicting disaster. You see, every Fall, female grasshoppers lay about 20 egg-like pods which hatch in the Spring and give birth to about 150 grasshoppers each. In other words, one female grasshopper will produce 3,000 more in just one year.

These Rocky Mountain grasshoppers had come from the drought stricken West looking for more food to eat. When swarms arrived, the whole sky would darken and it would look like a storm cloud hovering over the landscape. Thousands of grasshoppers would descend on a field or garden and devour everything in sight and then move on to the next area. The scientists figured that with the new hatch anticipated that April there would soon be 60-80 grasshoppers in every square yard… and not just in one area but covering a large portion of the state.

In both faith and desperation the citizens of Minnesota appealed to Governor John Pillsbury to establish a state-wide day of prayer and fasting. He agreed and set the date for Thursday, April 26, 1877. When the day came the streets were empty. Stores were closed. Theaters and bars went dark… but the churches were filled with people as never before. Other families gathered to pray in their homes with their neighbors. It was a beautiful warm Spring day. When this day of prayer came to a close the people said, "We have left it with the Lord; we can do no more." They waited to see what would happen next.

Shortly after midnight, in the early morning of Friday, April 27, the sky clouded over. The wind shifted and a cold front moved in from the North. Rain began to fall which soon turned into sleet and snow. All that day the storm raged covering the farm fields. This continued into Saturday the 28th, and then, when it finally stopped, the farmers hurried into their fields to see what had happened.

They discovered that the grasshopper eggs had all been frozen and destroyed just as they were beginning to hatch. The grasshoppers that did survive mysteriously rose-up and flew away as if to say, "We're gettin' outa here!" The farmers planted their crops and that Fall they were blessed with the most bountiful harvest ever in Minnesota's young history. And get this! Since then there has never been another serious grasshopper infestation in Minnesota. Newspapers across the country declared it to be a "Minnesota Miracle." Praise God!

A New Chapter

That night, as I sat around the campfire, I was praying and imploring God to do the same kind of miracles today… and more! I was asking for revival and transformation to sweep across Minnesota once again. I was praying for fresh revelation and an outpouring of the Holy Spirit when I sensed the Lord speaking to

"Greg, I'm about to write a new chapter in Minnesota's story. Would you like to be a part of it?"

me… not audibly, but with a word that dropped deep into my soul. He said, "Greg, I'm about to write a new chapter in Minnesota's story. Would you like to be a part of it?"

My immediate answer was "Yes, Lord. Of course. I'm all in!" But the more I stared into that campfire the more I realized that I shouldn't respond so quickly. To truly answer "yes" would require a new level of commitment in my heart and fire in my belly. I realized that I had better count the cost before being so bold. I should take time to consider carefully what my response would mean for me, my family, the congregation I serve and my wider ministry, before I truly answered "Yes! I want more!"

Over the next several weeks I continued to pray and seek the Lord. Clarity came. I realized that to follow this Call with all my heart would require asking one very important question. "What will I do with the rest of my life?"

At the time I was 68 years old. A lot of my pastor friends were retiring, many of them discouraged and burnt out. For so many people in our world today it seems that their primary goal in life is to retire as soon as possible and ride off into the sunset of leisure and personal fulfillment. By contrast, I had always somewhat cavalierly said, "There is no such thing as retirement in the Bible. We are called to serve the Lord with all our hearts for all our days!" Now, in those quiet moments it felt like the Holy Spirit was nudging me saying, "Do you really believe that… or did it just sound good?"

What is the right finish line in life? A lot of us run, and run hard, but don't know where we're headed or why. To some the right finish line is a modicum of success and the approval of family and peers. To others it's love or leisure, health or financial security. To those who are followers of Jesus, the Bible suggests there is a greater calling. In his letter to the Philippians, the Apostle Paul summarizes his personal commitment with the following statement: **"I press on toward the goal for the prize of the upward call of God in Christ Jesus" (Philippians 3:14 ESV).**

He's not talking about earning anything here, let alone salvation. Paul was very clear that forgiveness and heaven are free gifts from

God for all who put their faith in Jesus as their Savior and Lord. No! I think he was talking about finishing well. The "prize" is itself the "call of God" in our lives that doesn't end until the day we meet Jesus face to face. It's the journey of loving, pursuing and serving Jesus in a growing relationship for as long as He gives us breath. I believe that God is saying to each of us, and especially to my generation called Baby Boomers, "I'm about to write a new chapter in the story of your life, your family, your community and this world. Would you like to be a part of it?"

On the Way to the Dump

We can't truly answer in the affirmative until we first ask ourselves some important questions. "Honestly, how would I like to live-out my remaining days? Am I motivated to press on… or ready to just park it? Do I feel a Call to rise-up… or just ride-it-out? What do I still have to give and gain… or maybe lose?" The purpose of this book is to inspire you to consider your options, and I pray, answer in the affirmative, "Yes, God! I'm all in!" When we do, I'm absolutely convinced that this season of our lives can be the most fulfilling and impacting ever and leave a lasting legacy for generations to come.

My journey began in a Christian home where faith was real and an integral part of everyday life. I'm the oldest of four children; two brothers, Mike and Brad, and a sister, Lori. We are all "Boomers!" My mom and dad, Gary and Betty, came from a small town, were high school sweethearts and got married at age 19. I was born just one year later on June 5, 1953. Queen Elizabeth II had been crowned 3 days earlier at Westminster Abbey in London, England. That fact alone reminds me that I'm not a kid anymore!

> *Am I motivated to press on… or ready to just park it? Do I feel a Call to rise-up… or just ride-it-out?*

We lived in Eau Claire, Wisconsin, during my elementary school years. I was a Green Bay Packer fan and quarterback Bart

Starr was my hero. My dad was a salesman, selling everything from insurance to encyclopedias to pots and pans. When he got a job with the Pillsbury Company we moved to a small town in central Wisconsin called Stratford; population, 1,106. Small town life was great. You could be gone all day playing with your friends and your mom never worried about you. Perhaps ours should have! One day my brother Mike and I decided to hop a slow moving freight train as it came through town. Just one problem. It began to pick up speed and we managed to jump off into a ditch just in time to avoid ending up in the next town with no money in our pockets to make a phone call!

When I was in 7th grade we moved to Richfield, Minnesota, a suburb of Minneapolis. The Junior High I attended had more kids than the whole town I had just come from. I was like a fish out of water – my clothes, my haircut… nothing about me was cool! There were lots of talks with my dad which helped me through that first year. We joined a wonderful local church called Woodlake Lutheran with an awesome youth program.

When I was a 9th grader I experienced a weekend retreat that changed my life. A speaker named Herb Brokering helped me realize that God loved me just as I was and that I could love myself. In the years that followed I grew in my relationship with Jesus and developed lots of great Christian friends. In 1971 I graduated with a class of 960+, the 2nd largest high school graduating class in the history of the State of Minnesota. It was the peak of the Baby Boom generation.

I registered at the University of Minnesota and began a program in Pre-Dentistry, which for some reason I had decided was a desirable career path way back in the 8th grade. After two years I realized that I wasn't enjoying classes like Calculus, Biology, Zoology and Physics nearly as much as I was English, Speech, Sociology and Psychology. I took a year off to work and pray and figure out what I really wanted to do with my life.

During that time it became very clear that my calling wasn't to be a Dentist. We had a family friend who was a professor at a

Baptist liberal arts college called Bethel in Arden Hills, Minnesota. I switched schools and this decision became a huge blessing. I decided to major in Speech Communication. I loved my classes. I loved the daily chapel services. And best of all, I fell in love with a beautiful young woman named Colleen Shibrowski who would become my bride.

During the early 70s my spiritual life was also greatly impacted by two different events. The first was the 1973 Billy Graham Crusade at the Minnesota State Fairgrounds. It was reported that more than 16,500 people gave their lives to Jesus during that week-long crusade. I had always been a believer but the Gospel message shared so clearly by Dr. Graham totally grabbed my heart during those special nights. Many years later my life came full circle when I served as a counselor at one of Billy Graham's last crusades.

The second game changer for me was the International Conference on the Holy Spirit. It was held annually at the old Minneapolis Convention Center during the 70s and drew as many as 10,000 people a night for a week of worship, teaching, preaching and workshops. In addition to the "laying on of hands" and "the baptism of the Holy Spirit," I also received a prophetic word that came as a tremendous affirmation of my Call to ministry. It was during those formative years that I discovered what it means to live a spirit-filled life and experience God's power and presence every day. All I knew was that I wanted more!

To help pay for college, my brother Mike and I began a lawn service. We bought a used red Ford truck that was totally awesome along with the mowers and equipment we needed for our fledgling business venture. At one point we were taking care of about 40 residential and commercial lawns. The minimum wage at that time was a meager $1.60 per hour. We were clearing at least $5.00 an hour and thought we were quite the entrepreneurs!

One day I was taking a load of grass clippings to the county dump. As I was driving down 35W south I was praying about my future. As a 21 year-old I was asking that question, "What will I do with the rest of my life?" At that point I had been considering the possibility of seminary and pastoral ministry but wasn't sure. I had always been told by people that I would make a good pastor but had shrugged it off with a hint of rebelliousness. The only way I can describe what happened is that the overwhelming presence of the Holy Spirit filled that truck cab and filled me with peace and the confirmation I needed regarding my Call to pastoral ministry. It was such a powerful experience that I never looked back.

When I graduated from Bethel College in 1976 I enrolled at Luther Theological Seminary in St. Paul. My joke was that I thought the Lutherans needed me more than the Baptists, which is ironic, because I worked as a Youth Pastor at Woodbury Baptist Church for two of my four years at Luther. Colleen and I were married on June 11, 1977 after she also graduated from Bethel with a double major in Speech Communication and Elementary Education.

The third year of seminary involved an internship year in a congregational setting. We asked to be sent as far away as possible having both grown-up in the Midwest. We landed in Fairfax, Virginia at Lord of Life Lutheran Fellowship. It was a young, caring, rapidly growing congregation in a suburb of Washington, D.C. The founding pastor, Ron Christian, taught me ministry lessons that have served me well my whole life. During that year we took a group of 40 youth to a national youth convention in Kansas City, Missouri, performing a musical we had written at churches along the way. After internship year we returned to Minnesota.

Our first son, Matthew, was born during finals week of my Senior Year. He actually got me out of a couple of finals! We received a Call to be Associate Pastor back at Lord of Life in Virginia. Our second son, Joshua, was born there. After two more years we accepted a Call to First Lutheran Church in Portland, Maine, two hours north of Boston. Our daughter Sarah was born there. We decided that we shouldn't move to any more states! All tolled we lived and served on the East Coast for 12 years. Our family grew and so did we, making so many dear friends along the way!

In July of 1991 we moved back to Minnesota and began what is now a 31-year ministry at Christ Church. As I reflect on these years it feels like I've served at least three congregations as we've travelled various seasons of life and ministry together. I'm now performing weddings for kids that I've known their whole lives and baptizing their children. It's one of the great blessings of ministry to be able to go deep with people and grow together through all the ups and downs of life.

Yes, I like to tell people that I received my Call to ministry "on the way to the dump" and that it confirmed that "God Don't Make No Junk," which was actually a popular bumper sticker at the time. I've been privileged to serve the Church, capital "C," as a pastor for a total of 42 years now. I could retire and be very satisfied with the life I've lived and all that God has accomplished along the way. However, in my gut I know that God isn't finished with me yet. Will I be a parish pastor forever? No, probably not. Does God still have work for me to do? I think so! I know so!

Pause and Reflect!

During each step of my journey I've found it important to pause long enough to take stock along the way. When we were in Fairfax, Virginia, about 50% of the members and families of that congregation were career military. I came to realize that in the various military branches you must "re-up" every two years to continue. I love the parallel to living the Christian life. I have found that every year or two it is so important to re-examine my core beliefs and commitments and then ask the Holy Spirit to help me take the next step.

What is your story? Take some time right now to reflect on where you've been, experiences celebrated, lessons learned and roads travelled. Which have been the most meaningful? Which have been the most painful? In

> I could retire and be very satisfied with the life I've lived and all that God has accomplished along the way. However, in my gut I know that God isn't finished with me yet.

Romans 8:28 it says: **"And we know that in all things God works for the good of those who love him, who have been called according to his purpose."** When we choose to "re-up" in our relationship with Jesus, there is always another adventure, another step of growth awaiting us just around the next corner. Our God is so faithful and I'm excited about what He has in store for you! Won't you trust Him to surprise you again in this season of your life?

Walking Past Billy

> When we choose to "re-up" in our relationship with Jesus, there is always another adventure, another step of growth awaiting us just around the next corner.

I mentioned the impact of Billy Graham, the greatest evangelist of the 20th century, on me personally. I had always hoped to meet him. During his later years he often visited the famous Mayo Clinic in Rochester, Minnesota, for various forms of medical care. He had Parkinson's. Rochester is about 2 hours south of St. Paul, our capitol city. One time we travelled there for a weekend high school basketball tournament with our son, Joshua. We were crunched for time to check-in at the team hotel and make it to his first game. Josh had come down earlier with the family of one of his teammates.

We pulled up in front. I just ran in to get our keys. While I was waiting I happened to look around the lobby and noticed an old man standing near some couches off to the side reading a newspaper. He had a couple days growth of white beard, was wearing a cardigan sweater and looked somewhat disheveled. The thought crossed my mind, "He looks a little bit like Billy Graham… but it couldn't be."

We hurried off to the game. Afterwards we went out for pizza with the other players and families. As we were sitting at the restaurant my son, Josh, said to me, "Hey Dad, we heard that Billy Graham is staying at our hotel." The word had gotten around through some of the parents. I thought, "Oh no! That was him in the lobby! I had the opportunity to meet one of my real heroes, talk to him personally and thank him for the impact he has had on my life… and I missed it. I can't believe that I walked past Billy just because I was in a hurry!" I still regret missing that unexpected opportunity to this very day.

This is often our dilemma in life. We get so busy that we walk, or run right past opportunities that God places in our paths. We live with such tunnel vision when it comes to our own schedule and priorities that we miss what God intends to be huge blessings. Part of "taking stock" is to slow down long enough to think and reflect and see the people and opportunities that God is placing before us now, in this season of our lives.

A seminary professor of mine once said, "You can run the rat race your whole life and the best you'll ever end up is head rat!" That one stuck with me. The key, friends, is to run the race that God has called us to run! If we are willing to listen He will tell us when to walk, when to sprint and when to pace ourselves for the long haul. We can count on the fact that Jesus will be there at the finish line waiting with open arms.

Check Your Ingredients

I've titled this first chapter "Take Stock of Your Life." My intention is that every chapter in this book will help you consider the question "What will I do with the rest of my life?" There is no singular answer although in Chapter 20 I will share one

"You can run the rat race your whole life and the best you'll ever end up is head rat!"

verse from the Bible that comes pretty close! No peeking!

For us "Boomers," to take stock is to reflect and consider what we have to work with moving forward. When a company "takes stock" they count their inventory. When an investment banker speaks of "stock" they are referring to shares of a company. A "stock" can refer to the back end of a gun that is made out of wood or plastic.

"Stock," or bouillon in French, is also a word used in cooking. It refers to the broth obtained from simmering meat, vegetables or seasoning in water to create a foundation, for example, for adding other ingredients and making soup.

Right after my high school graduation my best buddy Scott and I went on a trip to the Boundary Waters on the border of Canada in northern Minnesota. It's a pristine area of woods and lakes that stretches for miles. A special permit is required to even enter it. We had my 17-foot Grumman canoe which we paddled and portaged several miles north on the first day. It didn't take long to get far from civilization. We had a tent and a large canvas "Duluth Pack" full of our clothes, food, collapsible fishing gear and other supplies.

There were plenty of bears in the wilderness, so at night you had to string your supplies high-up off the ground from a large branch of a tree quite a distance from your tent. We did! However, just our second day out we woke up in the morning, went to get our pack and found it laying on the ground ripped open. All our food was eaten with the exception of a bag of carrots and some Lawry's Seasoning Salt. I guess these bears weren't in the mood for vegetables that day.

No problem! We were hardy adventurers with five more days ahead of us. We would catch fish and live off the land. These were the "dog days" of summer, however. No fish were biting. We got hungry real fast! We boiled some water, added some of that seasoning, cut up our few carrots (why we had carrots along I'll never know) and made some soup. You could call it "soup stock." Just one problem. There was nothing else to add to it!

Somehow we made it for a week in the wilderness, both losing about 10 lbs. When we finally got back to the town of Ely, Minnesota we went to an "A & W Root Beer," pigged-out and slept in the car overnight both a little sick to our stomachs. Oh the misadventures of a couple of 18 year-old buddies!

As you enter this season of life what does your stock consist of, your foundation? What ingredients would you like to add to it? As you look ahead what will it take to not only survive these next years but thrive? You may have had your lunch eaten a few times in life too! I think we all have in more ways than one. Don't give up. Stick together. Find a way forward. There is more of God's creation to explore!

The Parable of the Twins

Colleen and I are now grandparents of 10 beautiful grandchildren. What a huge blessing! From oldest to youngest they are Ella, Sam, Mason, Micah, Abby, Livia, Simon, Ethan, Hailey and Isaac. They are all gifted and special in their own way. There are no twins among the group but I will never forget a story I came across one time about twin boys who were conversing in the womb wondering about what was coming next. It's called "The Parable of the Twins." Enjoy!

"Once upon a time twin boys were conceived. Weeks passed, and the twins developed. As their awareness grew, they laughed for joy, 'Isn't it great that we were conceived? Isn't it great to be alive?' As they grew the twins explored their world. When they found their mother's cord that gave them life they sang for joy, 'How great is our mother's love that she shares her own life with us.'

As the weeks stretched into months the twins noticed how much each was changing. 'What does this mean?' asked the one. 'It means that our stay in this world is drawing to an end,' said the other. 'But I don't want to go,' said the one. 'I want to stay here always.' 'We have no choice,' said the other, 'but maybe there is life after birth!' 'But how can it be?' responded the one. 'We will shed our life cord, and how is life possible without it? Besides, we have seen evidence that others were here before us and none of them have returned to tell us that there is life after birth.'

And so the one fell into deep despair saying, 'If conception ends with birth, what is the purpose of life in the womb? It is meaningless! Maybe there is no mother at all.' 'But there has to be,' protested the other. 'How else did we get here? How do we remain alive?' 'Have you ever seen our mother?' asked the one. 'Maybe she lives in our minds. Maybe we made her up because the idea makes us feel good.'

And so their last days in the womb were filled with deep questioning and fear and finally the moment of birth arrived. When the twins had passed from their world, they opened their eyes and cried, for what they saw exceeded their fondest dreams. And God's Word says, **'No eye has seen, no ear has heard, and no mind has imagined what God has prepared for those who love Him' (1 Corinthians 2:9 NLT)."**

Is there life after the kids are raised? Is there life after a successful career? Is there life after 65? Read on! God has more prepared for you in your 4th quarter than you can think or imagine. Open your eyes and experience a brand new world!

Questions for Personal Reflection or Group Discussion:

1. When have you had a good talk with the Lord? How did He speak to you?
2. If God were to write a new chapter in the story of your life, how would you like it to read?
3. Reflect on your life journey thus far. What have been among your most life-changing experiences?
4. What might God still have for you to do?

Notes:

1. Dale Gilmore, *Minnesota: The Revival State (Lulu Publishing Services, 2020).*

CHAPTER 2

Boom, Baby Boom!

W hen the Second World War ended, the Baby Boom generation began. During this 6 year global conflict from 1939-1945 more than 16 million men and women from the United States served in the armed forces. Another 3.5 million worked as federal civilian employees. Total military and civilian deaths were 418,000. The majority of those who served in WWII were just young adults between the ages of 18 and 25.

When Hitler's Nazi Germany, Hirohito's Imperial Japan and Mussolini's Fascist Italy were finally defeated, all these soldiers came home. Many carried such horrific scars from the war that they were never able to talk about their experiences, not even with family. They have rightly been called "The Greatest Generation" for their selfless sacrifice for our freedoms. Sometimes they are also called "The Silent Generation" because of their humility.

Rather than dwell on the past, they enthusiastically turned to the future. It was time to catch- up on life. These young returning vets soon got married and began their families. The GI Bill enabled millions to pursue further education, develop a trade, start a business or build a starter home. During the next 18 years, between 1946 and 1964, the largest generation in the history of the United States would be born. They came to be known as Baby Boomers, not only because of the amazing increase in population they represented but because of their tremendous influence on society. At their peak the "Boomers" numbered 76.2 million.

Flash forward. As of 2022, at this writing, Baby Boomers are now between the ages of 58 and 76. This means that by the year 2030 this historic demographic will all be 65 years of age or older. Even with this not too subtle reminder that life passes by more quickly than any of us might like, lifespans continue to increase. In 1946 life expectancy was just 63 years. Today it is 79. A high percentage of the Baby Boom generation, of which I'm a part, will live well into our 80s and 90s. Effectively, we are entering our 4th quarter. So where do we go from here? How can we take all that we have seen, experienced, learned and accomplished and leverage it, both for maximum fulfillment in our "golden years" and to leave a legacy that will impact future generations in a positive way?

> They came to be known as Baby Boomers, not only because of the amazing increase in population they represented but because of their tremendous influence on society.

Oh Baby!

Let's begin with a closer look at just who we are as "Boomers." In 1964, the last year of the Baby Boom, there were only 191.9 million people living in the United States. At that time we represented 40% of the entire population. Just imagine! That's a lot of crying babies! That's a lot of new schools! That's a lot of growing communities! The housing market exploded during the 50s and 60s with young "Boomer" families contributing to the rise of modern day suburbia.

Ever since 1964 our generation has technically been in decline although those immigrating to the U.S. over the years have not only offset our losses but contributed to gains. That's why In 2022 there are about 70 million Baby Boomers alive out of a current U.S. population of approximately 335 million. So, as I said, in 1964 we were 40% of the population. Today we are only 20%. As a matter of fact, according to the 2020 U.S. Census, Millennials have now overtaken the "Boomers" as the largest population segment in the country. It is projected that by the time the youngest Baby Boomers all turn 67 by 2032, and are able to claim full Social Security benefits, our numbers will have decreased to 58 million. By 2050 all surviving "Boomers" will be over the age of 85. Stats like this only serve to highlight the urgency of the question that is at the heart of this book! "What will I do with the rest of my life?"

It can be presumptive to tag any generational demographic with a definitive list of character traits or shared values. Baby Boomers are extraordinarily diverse, representing every race, religion, socio-economic level, political persuasion and world view. However, our generation has been marked by an extraordinary pace of change. In addition to our God-given "uniqueness stamp" called DNA, and the considerable power of faith and family to shape our lives, to a significant degree we are a product of our times. Historical events and societal shifts have had a huge impact on our development as "Boomers" because we have seen and experienced so much. So before we consider opportunities that await us in the future, let's reflect on the years we have already navigated.

Indelible Moments

For each of us there are moments and periods of time that are etched in our memory banks, never to be forgotten. These include milestone events like your wedding day or the birth of your children. For the moment, I'm thinking more broadly than that. Check-out this "decade by decade" list of key words and phrases. I'm quite certain they will trigger memories that are unique not only to you personally but are common to our shared generational experience. Of course, other generations have lived through some of the same years, on both chronological sides of us. However, ask yourself how these events, inventions and societal experiences have impacted your personal development and unique outlook on life today.

The 1940s
Nazi Germany, Imperial Japan, D-Day, Atomic Bomb, the Baby Boom, Israel, Radio, Big Band, It's a Wonderful Life, Flu Vaccine, Slinky, Polaroid Instant Camera, United Nations

The 1950s
Black and White Television, Korean War, Suburbs, Duck and Cover, Rosa Parks, The Wizard of Oz, Alaska, Hawaii, Elvis, X-Ray, Microwave Ovens, Mr. Potato Head, Velcro, Eisenhower, Seat Belts, McCarthyism, Mickey Mantle, Campus Crusade for Christ, Billy Graham Evangelistic Association

The 1960s
Color Television, John F. Kennedy Assassination, Cuban Missile Crisis, The Beatles, Civil Rights, Martin Luther King, Jr., John Glenn, I Love Lucy, Vietnam War, Moon Landing, Pele, Super Bowl, Shopping Malls, Hippies, LSD, The Sound of Music, Psycho, Cassette Tapes, Calculators, The Andy Griffith Show, Arnold Palmer, Youth With a Mission, Woodstock

The 1970s
Watergate, Nixon Resignation, Gas Lines, Interest Rates, Mideast Peace, Iran Hostage Crisis, The Rolling Stones, Voting Age Becomes 18, Charismatic Renewal, The Godfather, Three Mile Island, Roe v. Wade, Bill Gates, Steve Jobs, Heart Transplant, Happy Days, Cable TV, Recession, Birth Control Pill, Mobile Phone, Microsoft, Apple, Email, Walkman, Personal Computers, Jonestown, M*A*S*H, Mohammad Ali

The 1980s
Berlin Wall, Iran-Contra, Star Wars, Personal Computers, Michael Jackson, Miracle on Ice, Challenger, Back to the Future, Wayne Gretzky, Post-It Notes, Exxon Valdez, Camcorder, DNA Testing, Contact Lenses, HIV/AIDS, Cheers, Michael Jordan

The 1990s
World Wide Web, Amazon, GPS, Toy Story, Saving Private Ryan, DVD Player, Bill Clinton, Whitney Houston, Backstreet Boys, Dolly the Sheep, Persian Gulf War, Monica Lewinsky, Desktops, Google, Home Improvement, Seinfeld, Ken Griffey, Jr.

The 2000s
September 11, Desert Storm, Lord of the Rings, Eminem, Britney Spears, iPhone, Prius, Segway, Friends, George Bush, YouTube, Hanging Chads, Survivor, CSI, Iraq War, Hurricane Katrina, Stock Market Crash, Harry Potter, Euro, Laptops, American Idol, Digital Cameras, Osama Bin Laden, Tiger Woods, Global Day of Prayer

The 2010s
Siri, Terrorism, The Avengers, Netflix, Barrack Obama, Afghanistan War, Gay Marriage, Black Panther, Adele, Hover Board, TikTok, Justin Bieber, Affordable Care Act, Game of Thrones, Tom Brady, Donald Trump, Joel Osteen

The 2020s
Covid-19, Mask Mandates, Ruth Bader Ginsburg, Social Distancing, Vaccines, Joe Biden, Ukraine War, Kobe Bryant, Baby Yoda, Hulu, Beijing Olympics, Impeachment, Uyghurs, Vladimir Putin, George Floyd, Black Lives Matter, Inflation, Stephen Curry, Gas Prices…

Your Most Impacting Decade

There are a million more historical events and people that could have been mentioned but I chose these to get you thinking… and remembering. We Boomers have certainly lived through some interesting times! My contention is that we can't really look forward until we have first looked back. So which of these words and phrases took you back to a special place, relationship, experience or season in your life? Which decade of your existence would you say has most impacted you as a person? For me it was the 60s. Here are several of my most profound memories from that decade. I'm guessing that many of us who are among the older half of our Baby Boom generation will have several of these memories in common.

At the top of my list is the assassination of President John F. Kennedy in Dallas, Texas on November 22, 1963. I think that it was the first significant marker in my young life as it was for so many. I was 10 years old, and like most kids, was in school that Friday afternoon when the news of his death began to spread like wildfire. What made it so strange for me was that I had left a happy, busy classroom with a bathroom pass and when I came back a few minutes later everyone was in tears. I remember being so bewildered, like "What could possibly have happened?" I was totally shocked when my teacher told me why everyone was so downcast. I remember watching the funeral on TV and feeling so sorry for President Kennedy's young children, Caroline and John.

A fun memory from those early years of my life was of The Beatle's first appearance on The Ed Sullivan Show on February 9, 1964. They were the biggest thing since Elvis and their first trip to the U.S. came at a time when our country was in much need of a lift. We were at my Uncle Lloyd and Aunt Lorraine's house in St. Paul, Minnesota. They had just purchased something that was still quite novel at that time. It was a Color TV in a big wooden cabinet that included an AM/FM radio and stereo record player. It didn't matter though. The Beatles were in black and white. When they were announced to the deafening screams of hundreds of teenage girls in the audience… my older cousin, Marsha, screamed too. I remember the look on our parent's faces. It was like "Oh boy! What are we in for now?" Little did they know!

Being younger, I was somewhat sheltered from the full impact of the Civil Rights movement of the 60s. By the end of this critical decade I was still just 17. By then stories of Emmett Till, Rosa Parks, Ruby Bridges, Freedom Riders, Bloody Sunday and the March on Washington were settling into my consciousness and would have a much greater impact during my college years. As a young Christian, though, with a strong sense of morality, my heart was torn by the injustices I was seeing on television as coverage improved.

Martin Luther King, Jr.'s "I Have a Dream" speech given in front of the Lincoln Memorial stirred the whole nation. As painful as this season was it resulted in three significant pieces of legislation; the Civil Rights Act of 1964, the Voting Rights Act of 1965 and the Fair Housing Act of 1968, passed just one week after Martin Luther King, Jr. was assassinated on April 4, 1968. The impact of his death was certainly on a par for me with that of President Kennedy. I remember realizing the great sacrifice that often comes for those willing to stand-up for truth.

Another indelible memory from the 60s was the moon landing on July 20, 1969. I was 16. My dad was a space buff. We even had a model of the Saturn 5 rocket that stood 3 feet high. The night of the touchdown our whole family gathered in our living room to watch this historic moment. We were nearly breathless in anticipation as Neal Armstrong came down the steps of the moon lander and declared, "That's one small step for man, one giant leap for mankind."

The 60s were also deeply impacted by the Vietnam War and so was I. Every night there were body counts given on the news. The war slogged along for years and so did the protests. By 1971, my first year at the University of Minnesota, the anti-war sentiment was overwhelming. By then your eligibility for the draft was determined by a lottery system. The drawing for those born in 1953 like me was held on February 2, 1972. My closest friends and I gathered together to listen to the results. At that point none of us wanted to go to Vietnam. I was so relieved when my birthday, June 5, drew number 230 out of 365. They only took up to 95 that year. A good high school buddy drew #1 and went and enlisted in the Navy the next day.

Vietnam left a bad taste in my mouth when it came to the military. It wasn't until several years later that I had a change of heart, when, as I mentioned in Chapter 1, I did my seminary internship and then served two years as Youth Pastor at Lord of Life Lutheran Fellowship in Fairfax, Virginia. With so many members being career military I discovered that they were just ordinary people who had families, loved the Lord and loved their country. This was simply the career path they had chosen to follow. That bad taste disappeared for good.

Notice that my most significant memories occurred during the decade when I was between the ages of 7 and 17. What decade would you highlight from your life? What historical events stand-out the most in your memory? Reflecting further, what are your most significant childhood memories related to family, school, friends, first loves, personal achievements, disappointments and failures? There is no doubt that our formative years play a big part in the person we become. Even so, the most profound events in your life may have happened in your adult years. Whatever your story, it is unique to you! Now let's consider some identifying traits and shared values that many have suggested are common to our generation. See if they apply to you.

Traits and Values

In surveying the literature on Baby Boomers several traits were repeatedly identified. The first was optimism. Our generation grew up believing that anything was possible provided we were willing to

> *What decade would you highlight from your life? What historical events stand-out the most in your memory?*

work for it. Even with the challenges of the 60s and 70s, we remained hopeful of a better future and were willing to work hard to achieve it, both personally and as members of society.

A second trait, closely tied to the first, was a strong work ethic. It came from our parents, many who had grown up with very little in terms of material possessions and yet had been asked to sacrifice so much. They taught our generation to go after our dreams and be willing to work hard to achieve them. As a result,

"Boomers" came to be known as a generation dedicated to their careers, in many cases, to climbing the corporate ladder.

The 50s and 60s saw the birth and rise of some of the greatest corporations in American history; companies like Proctor and Gamble, IBM, General Motors, John Deere, General Electric, Disney, U.S. Steel, Kellogg, Coca-Cola, Boeing, McDonald's, General Mills, Pillsbury, 3M, Pfizer and Whirlpool, just to name a few. You may have worked for one of these companies because they employed millions. The economy flourished as Baby Boomers came of age and sought employment opportunities in pursuit of a better life. Corporations were king and largely responsible for growing the "Middle Class." Long-term employment in any of these well-known companies was considered a ticket to success and a comfortable retirement in the future. Trades of all kinds including carpenters, plumbers, electricians and truck divers were in high demand as well, and of course, the housing market was booming!

None of this came without a cost. The demands were great. Employees struggled to advance in their work environment and still maintain a work-home balance. Through the 60s at least, men were still the primary bread-winners for most nuclear families, often to the neglect of their spouses and children. Many considered dedication to their careers as a necessary sacrifice in order to secure "the good life" and advance in social standing.

Built for Competition

As a result, the Baby Boom generation was also known for being competitive. "Boomers" were built for competition whether in the workplace, on the sports field, in their hobbies or by the cut of their lawn. Our generation has always been highly motivated by goals, bonuses, sales quotas, degrees, promotions and titles. We even enjoy creating goals for ourselves and working to achieve them. New Year's resolutions have always been our thing. Boomers are independent and self-confident having grown up in a turbulent time in history. As a result, we aren't afraid to rock the boat, call out injustices and challenge the status quo. Baby Boomers share a unique blend of loyalty and rebellion.

Baby Boomers tend to be highly educated and visionary. It was in our generation that post-high school education began to flourish and many became the first in their families to achieve university and post-graduate degrees. The academic, cultural, political and industrial leaders of today are still dominated by Boomers. Examples include Presidents George W. Bush, Bill Clinton, Barrack Obama and Donald Trump, tech giants like Bill Gates and Steve Jobs, cultural and media influencers like Oprah Winfrey and Sean Hannity, explorers and entrepreneurs like Sally Ride and Jeff Bezos, music and entertainment legends like Michael Jackson and Tom Hanks, and sports legends like Michael Jordan and Wayne Gretzky. Most of the great inventions of the last 50 years have come from the creative minds of "Boomers." We were taught to dream big and indeed we have.

> *Baby Boomers share a unique blend of loyalty and rebellion.*

Family and Faith

Baby Boomers also value family and personal relationships. Most of us were born into traditional families; mom, dad, several kids and a dog; "Ozzie and Harriet" families they were called. This began to shift in the 60s as economic and societal pressures mounted and the divorce rate climbed. Many would argue that President Lyndon Johnson's "Great Society" programs, although well-intentioned, ultimately led to government dependence and a breakdown of the nuclear family. "Boomers" had to work extra hard to hold their families together, and today, continue to have that same passion as they often help care for aging parents, grown children and grand-children. We are referred to now as "the sandwich generation."

Faith has also been very important to Baby Boomers. In the 50s and early 60s evangelists like Billy Graham were becoming nationally known. Nearly every Christian denomination was growing. Even relationships between Catholics and Protestants were thawing with the election of John F. Kennedy, our first Catholic President, and the ecumenical pronouncements of Vatican II that came from Pope John XXIII. Church membership and attendance in the U.S. held at about 70% through our growing years. Most of us remember Sunday School, First Communion, Confirmation and regular worship attendance. There was no question in my house. On Sundays we went to church!

Through the turbulent 60s these numbers began to steadily decline. As of 2020 only 47% of Americans say they belong to a church, synagogue or mosque. Even that statistic highlights the great diversity that exists on the religious scene today. A new description of non-believers has crept into our vocabulary. Today we speak of the "nons" who have no church background and no desire for any religious affiliation. Churches across the denominational spectrum bemoan the fact that we are losing our youngest generations. As a result, "Boomers" often struggle to find meaningful and creative ways to pass on their faith to their children and grandchildren.

Optimism, vision, hard work, family, faith, these are qualities that have been, and remain, descriptive of the Baby Boom generation. Add to that, competitive, self-confident and even non-conforming in the face of injustice. Which of these qualities would you claim as your own? Are there also negatives that we are willing to admit? What about selfish, arrogant, overprotective, judgmental and even ruthless at times? There's a flip-side to every coin!

> *Will we continue to "Boom" as passionate difference makers in this world or will we "Bust" by abandoning our responsibility to the generations that follow?*

Boom or Bust?

Every Baby Boomer is unique in their own way and yet it's fascinating to reflect on the life experiences that have shaped our generation, note the commonalities of values that often characterize us, but then also ask, what will our identity be as "Boomers" in the years ahead? Will we continue to "Boom" as passionate difference makers in this world or will we "Bust" by abandoning our responsibility to the generations that follow? Let's press-on by considering our Home Base and who is influencing us as we run the bases of life.

Questions for Personal Reflection or Group Discussion:

1. Are you an older (1946-1951), middle (1952-1958) or younger (1959-1964) "Boomer?"
2. What decade or historical events stand-out the most in your memory?
3. Name some people from our "Boomer" generation that have had the greatest impact on your life from business, education, government, religion, sports and entertainment.
4. Which traits or values of Baby Boomers are most descriptive of you?

CHAPTER 3

Know Your Home Base!

If you ever played baseball you eventually learned that success isn't about where you start. It's about where you finish. Home Base represents both. In **Revelation 1:8** Jesus declares: **"I am the Alpha and the Omega... who is, and who was, and who is to come, the Almighty."** For the Christian, Home Base is Jesus. He is our Alpha and Omega, our beginning and end. He is both where we start and where we are called to finish in life.

When you understand Home Base, baseball becomes a great game. Whether it's driving someone in with a single or hitting a home run, it's all about crossing the plate and scoring for your team. The same is true when we play for Jesus. When we come to understand that He is our owner, manager and coach, the rules and opportunities that lead to playing well begin to come together. When we become passionate about reaching Home, we won't be content with just getting to First, Second or Third. We will want to "go all the way" by loving and serving Jesus with everything we've got... and we will know why! Without this knowledge and conviction we will be prone to a myriad of disappointments and unnecessary detours along the way. We may score runs in baseball but we will strike out in life. Who are you running for? What is your Home Base?

Teaching the Fundamentals

The Holy Spirit made this so clear to me many years ago on a beautiful summer day in Portland, Maine. It was one of those eye opening experiences you never forget. As I've shared, I served a church there called First Lutheran for 9 years. Our young family fell in love with the rocky coast of Maine, historic light houses, fresh lobster and so many dear friends.

It was 1987. That year I had volunteered to coach my son's T-Ball team along with several other young dads. My boys, Matt and Josh, were just little guys enjoying their first experiences with organized sports. Our line-up included both boys and girls, most of them 5 years old. Every game represented a huge learning curve.

One little boy will forever stand out in my mind. His name was Timmy and he struggled the most of any player on our team. I prayed for his protection in the field, that no line drives would be hit his way. When he was at bat I prayed for patience! Time and time again Timmy would swing and miss the ball or bump the rubber "T" just enough to see the ball drop to the ground. I would pick it up, set it back on the "T," line him up and he would swing again… and miss again. You may have been there with your kids, many of you. Not even my best coaching tips seemed to help.

One particular Saturday morning we were playing a team sponsored by Waste Management. With two outs, the bases loaded and Timmy due up at the plate it looked like we were the ones about to get wasted. Normally the rules allowed players to advance just one base at a time. On this day, near the end of the season, they could keep running.

I placed the ball on the "T" expecting the same routine… but much to my surprise Timmy connected with one. He sent the ball sailing out of the short infield and my eyes opened wide as saucers. A swarm of little defenders began to chase the ball and everybody on our team started to scream for our players to "Run, Run!!"

They did, and then, with a delayed reaction of total shock, Timmy ran too. He carried his bat most of the way to First Base, leaning a little to the right, running for dear life. He finally dropped the bat, stopped on First for a moment, and then with the emphatic encouragement of our First Base Coach, headed for Second. Unexplored territory! We kept on yelling and Timmy kept on running.

Go Home!

There was no stopping him now. He ran over Second Base and headed for Third, as the other three runners scored ahead of him. The kids from Waste Management finally began to un-pile in the outfield and I could see that one of them had the ball. I could also see that Timmy had a chance to go all the way. I started yelling "Go home, Timmy! Go home!!" Our whole team began to jump up and down and yell the same thing. Timmy ran for all he was worth. It seemed like an eternity but he finally crossed Home Base and was mobbed by the rest of the team. It was a Grand Slam for a kid who had hardly hit the ball 10 feet in the past.

A few minutes later, after things had settled down, I happened to look over at the bench. There was Timmy with his hat and glove on the ground between his legs and his hands partially covering his face with what appeared to be tears in his eyes. I couldn't imagine what had happened. I went over and knelt down by him and said, "Hey Timmy. That was a great hit… the best one of the season. What's the matter?"

I waited a few moments until he finally spoke softly through his tears, the way children do when they're both hurt and embarrassed at the same time. Sobbing, Timmy said, "Coach, when I hit the ball I ran as fast as I could. But then I heard everybody yelling 'Go home! Go home!' and I didn't think they wanted me on the team anymore."

I learned such an important lesson that day. I realized that no amount of screaming and yelling, no amount of high-fiving and back slapping, will encourage a kid who hasn't learned the fundamentals. All of my patient coaching and enthusiasm had fallen short that day because I had failed to teach Timmy about Home Base and the meaning of the words used by those of us cheering him on.

The reality is that so many of us are like Timmy. We're running for dear life, looking for success and purpose… but don't know where we're headed. In the process we're confronted with dozens of voices shouting for our attention and it can all be very confusing. Instead of celebration there are often tears. Friends, if we are to run successfully and eventually cross Home Base there is one voice that must be heard above all the others. It is the voice of Jesus, our Head Coach. As a matter of fact, hearing His voice will be life-changing!

Who are you, Lord?

About 2,000 years ago a man named Saul of Tarsus heard the Lord's voice loud and clear one day as he travelled to a city called Damascus in ancient Syria. His mission was to arrest Christians and have them thrown in jail. He had a letter from the High Priest in Jerusalem allowing him to do it. Those known as "followers of the Way" were already under significant persecution and Saul's reputation preceded him. The Bible says that he was **"…breathing out murderous threats against the Lord's disciples" (Acts 9:1).**

> We're running for dear life, looking for success and purpose… but don't know where we're headed.

Well, he didn't make it to his destination on time! As he neared Damascus he was struck down by a blinding light from heaven and a voice said: **"'Saul, Saul, why do you persecute me?' 'Who are you, Lord?' Saul asked. 'I am Jesus, whom you are persecuting,' he replied. 'Now get up and go into the city, and you will be told what you must do'" (Acts 9:4b-6).**

Talk about getting knocked off your high horse! When Saul looked up he couldn't see anything and something like scales covered his eyes. His men helped him into town. For three days he was blind and didn't eat or drink – call it an unplanned hunger strike. This must have been a great lesson in humility for Saul who was used to giving orders, not taking them.

There was a follower of Jesus in Damascus called Ananias. The Lord spoke to him in a vision and told him to go to a particular house in the city where he would find Saul praying. The Lord said that Saul had already seen a vision himself, that a man would come and lay hands on him and that his sight would be restored. What an interesting peek we are given into God's future plans for Saul in that he was already praying and receiving visions even before he really became a believer.

From Saul to Paul

Ananias was reluctant to go, given Saul's reputation as a persecutor of Christians... but he was obedient. When he found Saul he placed his hands on him and said: **"'Brother Saul, the Lord – Jesus, who appeared to you on the road as you were coming here – has sent me so that you may see again and be filled with the Holy Spirit'"** (Acts 9:17b). Immediately the scales fell off Saul's eyes. When he opened them, he could see. The Bible says very matter of factly: **"He got up and was baptized, and after taking some food, he regained his strength" (Acts 9:18b-19).**

From that point forward, Saul, who later was called Paul, became perhaps the greatest advocate for the Christian faith the world has ever known. Almost all those who heard him were amazed at his personal transformation. Some were so threatened by it that they even plotted to kill him. Paul became God's ambassador to the Gentiles and would go on to write 13 of the 26 books found in the New Testament. Some suggest that 6 of them may have been written by others using Paul's name or in partnership with him. Paul was a fearless witness for Jesus and suffered greatly for proclaiming the Good News, the Gospel of Jesus Christ. He was shipwrecked, beaten, jailed and publicly condemned... and yet I'm guessing that he never forgot the day he first heard Jesus speaking to him on the road to Damascus.

Do you remember a time in your life when God spoke clearly to you? How did He get your attention? What was His message? Did you have to go through some tough times to get from where you were then to where you are today?

State Your Credentials

Years later, on a pastoral visit to the Christians at Philippi, the Apostle Paul described the change that had occurred in his life as a result of hearing and following the voice of Jesus. He started with his former credentials as a Jew. He said: **"If someone else thinks they have reasons to put confidence in the flesh, I have more: circumcised on the eighth day, of the people of Israel, of the tribe of Benjamin, a Hebrew of Hebrews; in regard to the law, a Pharisee; as for zeal, persecuting the church; as for righteousness based on the law, faultless" (Philippians 3:4b-6).**

Paul was speaking of his attitude before encountering Jesus. What was his Home Base then? It was his status as a Jew, a "Hebrew of Hebrews." His identity was based on his credentials; a perfectionist when it came to keeping all the rules and an enthusiast when it came to persecuting Christians. The voice that was shouting at him the loudest back then was the Law. His goal was to keep all 613 commandments better than anyone else. His boasting indicates that he actually thought he had achieved it. He thought he was faultless. That's some ego! His confidence was totally in himself.

Few of us would display such blatant arrogance… but the truth be known, our confidence is often more in ourselves and our credentials than it is in God. "Boomers" have been raised to be rule keepers. It's the "great American work ethic" that has driven us to achieve. We're not likely to admit it but our identity is often firmly placed in our degrees, titles, accomplishments, homes, toys and bank accounts. Are we really so different than Saul? We may be running for Jesus now but the Law still has a grip, shouting "Keep the rules! Strive to be better than others! Achieve more! You are being measured by your success!" Until we break free we will never make it Home.

What's in a Name?

When Saul became a believer, and eventually took the name Paul, his Home Base changed and the contrast couldn't have been more dramatic. Scholars debate the reason for the name change. Some suggest that Saul became Paul for a very practical reason. Saul is Hebrew and Paul is Greek. The later would simply serve him more effectively in reaching the Gentiles, his assignment from God. My purpose at this point is not to digress into a theological debate. Instead, let's recognize that when anyone changes their name it is with great thought and intention.

Our name says a lot about our identity. Names mean something. Abram was called by God to be a "father of nations" so his name was changed to Abraham which means that. The same was true for Jacob who wrestled with God and had his name changed to Israel because it means that. Levi became Matthew.

> *"Boomers" have been raised to be rule keepers. It's the "great American work ethic" that has driven us to achieve.*

Cephas became Simon Peter, the rock, and yes, Saul became Paul. There are many more examples in the Bible. In every case, the reason for a name change had to do either with a personal encounter with the Lord or a specific assignment.

The legal steps that one must take to change their name today are significant. The most common example is in marriage, in most cases involving the bride changing her surname to that of the groom. It's a way to indicate the joining of two lives and the seriousness of the marriage commitment. Sometimes names change for religious reasons. For example, the great boxer Cassius Clay changed his name to Muhammad Ali when he became a Muslim. Some name changes today indicate a shift in sexual identity like when Olympian and reality TV star Bruce Jenner became Caitlyn Jenner. Others change their names to sound more contemporary, catchy or provocative related to their careers in show business or the music industry.

For example, Robert Allen Zimmerman became Bob Dylan. Reginald Kenneth Dwight became Elton John. John Roger Stephens became John Legend. Ralph Lifshitz became Ralph Lauren. Stevland Hardaway Morris became Stevie Wonder. Paul David Hewson became Bono. Illyena Lydia Vasilievna Mironov became Helen Mirren. Caryn Elaine Johnson became Whoopi Goldberg. The list of name changes goes on and on… and in many cases we can understand why!

Titles or Testimonies

I can't help but believe that when Saul became Paul it was also for "show business." His sole desire became to show the world that Jesus had totally transformed his life! His testimony continues in **Philippians 3:7-9**. He says: **"But whatever were gains to me I now consider loss for the sake of Christ. What is more, I consider everything a loss because of the surpassing worth of knowing Christ Jesus my Lord, for whose sake I have lost all things. I consider them garbage that I may gain Christ and be found in him, not having a righteousness of my own that comes from the law, but that which is through faith in Christ – the righteousness that comes from God on the basis of faith."**

Paul was no longer running for himself. He was running the bases for Jesus now. Anything that had given him a reason to boast in the past looked like trash compared to his new life in Christ. His identity was no longer found in religious titles or meticulous "rule-keeping" which leads to self-righteousness. Now his pursuit was "faithful living" which results in a righteousness that can only come from God. I define righteousness as a gift from God that allows us to "do the right thing for the right reason at the right time." This is only possible when we are connected to the only one who is truly righteous, our Savior,

> *Paul was no longer running for himself. He was running the bases for Jesus now.*

Jesus. Paul's purpose now was to serve… not be served. When Saul became Paul it was an expression of his total transformation, the same one that is possible for each of us today. The next section of his testimony gets even better because Paul shares what had become the predominant voice and driving force in his life.

In **Philippians 3:10-14** he declares: **"I want to know Christ – yes, to know the power of his resurrection and participation in his sufferings, becoming like him in death, and so somehow, attaining to the resurrection of the dead. Not that I have already obtained all this, or have already arrived at my goal, but I press on to take hold of that for which Christ Jesus took hold of me."**

And then he concludes: **"Brothers and sisters, I do not consider myself yet to have taken hold of it. But one thing I do: Forgetting what is behind and straining toward what is ahead, I press on toward the goal to win the prize for which God has called me heavenward in Christ Jesus. All of us, then, who are mature should take such a view of things."**

Let Go

When it comes to our call as Baby Boomers, I see three challenges laid out here. The first is to let go of the past. Many of us have been so wounded while running the bases of life that we are currently sitting on the bench, hat and glove on the ground with tears in our eyes. We have no passion or strength left to keep going. Many of us have been so defeated by past failures that any kind of risk today seems out of the question. Or on the other hand, many of us have been so enamored with our successes in life that we're willing to settle for what we have rather than go after what God still wants to give. The

> *Many of us have been so wounded while running the bases of life that we are currently sitting on the bench, hat and glove on the ground with tears in our eyes. We have no passion or strength left to keep going.*

reality is that a lot of us have just given up and stopped running altogether. But friends, the game isn't won by looking backwards and dwelling on the past. It's only won when we keep our eyes fixed on the right finish line, which is our Home Base, Jesus Christ.

Think of all the star athletes who compete every two years in either the Summer or Winter Olympics. What if that swimmer let up in his race in the last 25 meters? What if that gymnast failed to make her last tumbling run? What if that skier decided not to navigate the last two gates on the course? What if that golfer decided not to play the 18th hole? What if that figure skater decided not to go for the quad? What if that sprinter raised her hands in victory 10 meters before the 100 meter finish line? None would win the gold!

That's why I declare to you again: Life isn't about where you start. It's about where you finish! Saul's conversion to Paul led to a complete paradigm shift in his life from the Law to the Gospel. It changed everything! He started listening to the voice of his new coach who taught him that life isn't about being better than someone else. It's about being our best for Jesus!

In order to finish well we must first let go of the past. Only then can we accept our second challenge which is to take hold of Jesus and our future. Do you see Paul's passion in the verses above? Talk about declaring "I'm all in!"

Take Hold

Paul wanted more! He wanted to know Jesus personally; not through religion but relationship. He wanted to experience more of Jesus' resurrection power. He even desired to participate in His sufferings in order that he might more and more reflect the love and character of his Savior. But then we see such a beautiful statement. Paul says: **"… I press on to take hold of that for which Christ Jesus took hold of me" (Philippians 3:12b).**

What are you taking hold of in your life right now? Is it Jesus… or have the things of this world captured your greatest attention?

As I mentioned in Chapter 2, by the year 2030 Baby Boomers will all be 65 years of age or older. In other words, our generation is either currently or will soon be entering what has traditionally been thought of as retirement age, the "golden years." It's that time when work is supposed to transition to leisure and unspoken permission is given to make our remaining years mostly about ourselves.

But as I also said, I don't find the word "retirement" anywhere in the Bible. I can't find one scripture that suggests there comes a point in life where we are to disconnect from the world and make it mostly about ourselves, our past accomplishments, leisure, comfort and security. I don't believe there's any point in the Christian journey where we're to stop growing and just put life on "cruise control" until the day we meet Jesus face to face.

Here's an example of the disconnect. I've heard several people say recently, "I can't stand to watch the news anymore. It's so depressing. It's so political. I just don't want to know about all the bad stuff going on." When the Holy Spirit gives me the patience to respond in the right tone I will say, "Yes, but if you don't know what's going on in the world, how will you know how to pray… or vote… or help?" Remember the three monkeys, "See no evil. Hear no evil. Speak no evil?" I agree with the third one… but not the first two. This is still our Father's world and we must stay engaged or we jettison any chance we have of bringing transformation now, let alone leaving a better world behind for our loved ones who will follow us.

Think about it for a moment. Paul says, "I want to take hold of that for which Christ Jesus took hold of me." Just how has Jesus taken hold of you? Have you experienced His love? Has He been there when you've gone through really tough times? Has He provided for your needs often in the most unexpected ways? When Paul expresses his desire to take hold of Jesus he's really

> I can't find one scripture that suggests there comes a point in life where we are to disconnect from the world and make it mostly about ourselves, our past accomplishments, leisure, comfort and security.

describing an alternate path to success, satisfaction and purpose in life. He's saying, "I know now that I haven't arrived… not even close. I know now that there's so much more and I want it! I want to take hold of everything that my Savior has to offer and never let go!" Do you want it too, the kind of gifts that only God can give? There's only one way to claim these blessings.

Press On

Our third challenge is to press on! That's what this book is all about. Our Head Coach is calling for each of us to go for Second and then Third and then keep on running with every ounce of strength we have until we reach Home. What might this look like in your life right now? Do you need to press on in your marriage? Do you need to press on in your relationship with your kids or grandkids? Do you need to press on in this season of your work life? Do you need to press on to conquer a physical or mental health issue? And what about your personal faith? Where is God calling you to keep running no matter how confusing the shouts of this world might be?

Home Base is Jesus, our King of Kings and Lord of Lords. He is where real life starts and where it is meant to end – in His loving arms. When Paul discovered this fact it changed his life forever and he birthed a Holy Spirit empowered movement of God that continues to this day. I believe this to be the calling of our generation as well. Jesus is shouting to each of us, "I love you! I forgive you! I'm for you and with you! Go for Home because there is so much more we have yet to accomplish!"

Questions for Personal Reflection or Group Discussion:

1. What was your favorite sport as a kid? Any "glory stories" to share? What sport do you enjoy the most today… as a participant or a fan?

2. Were you raised to be a "rule keeper" like Saul? How did this impact your understanding of God?

3. What is something you need to "let go" of from your past in order to "take hold" of the much more that God wants for your future? What will this require of you?

4. Is Jesus your "Home Base?" Are you running hard? Do you know where you're headed?

CHAPTER 4

Get the 30,000 Foot View!

I take pictures of clouds out of airplane windows. I just can't help it. It's one thing to see them from the ground… but from 30,000 feet! Wow! The height. The layers. The colors. The shadows they cast on the ground. Breaking through the clouds to a bright blue sky waiting above is something I've always enjoyed when I'm flying. It reminds me that no matter how dark our world gets, the glory of God is just a little bit higher waiting to reveal itself.

At this juncture in our journey as the Baby Boom generation it would seem constructive for all of us to get the 30,000 foot view on life. You see, just a very few of us are real visionaries who see the future. Most of us deal with what is right in front of us on any given day or week, the things that we can see, smell, taste and touch. We love our spouses, take care of our kids and grandkids, do our jobs, tend to our health and finances, walk-out our faith and try to live in peace with others.

That's all fine and good… but these days we're living in, quite frankly, demand more! If we're going to answer the question, "What will I do with the rest of my life?" we need to take a second look at our view of the world from a higher, wider angle.

What is Your Worldview?

A worldview is defined as the overall perspective from which one sees and interprets the world. Our worldview shapes our unique "take" regarding some of life's most important questions:
- The existence of God
- The origins of the universe and human life
- The source of truth, morality and values
- The meaning of life and death
- The power of loving relationships
- Our very reason for getting up in the morning

Our worldview can change over time depending on what the predominant inputs are in our daily lives. Worldview is shaped by family, faith, culture and experience from the very beginning of life to the end.

Consider how a person's view of the world might develop differently if they grew up in inner-city Las Angeles, California versus rural Fargo, North Dakota? Imagine the different perspective that a graduate of Harvard Law School might bring to life compared with someone who is a high school drop-out? What about a young child growing up in Rwanda, Africa versus one growing up in your town or city? How might life look differently to someone raised in the church who says they have always believed in Jesus compared with a drug addict who has just had a radical conversion experience through Teen Challenge? And just imagine the difference in generational perspective between our parents and grandparents who grew up with the Sunday newspaper and Walter Cronkite versus a Millennial who has grown up with computers, the internet and cell phones? I often think of my Grandpa, Theodore Pagh, who owned a small-town shoe store. Oh how I would love to show him around the Mall of America! He'd be blown away!

> Worldview is shaped by family, faith, culture and experience from the very beginning of life to the end.

41

Sponge or Mixed Drink

Many people develop their worldview like either a sponge or a mixed drink. They absorb life by rubbing against it. In the process they pick-up the dirt, the bacteria, the messes, and if they're not rinsed out regularly, they can get "stinkin' thinkin'." Or, like an experimental mixed drink, they take a little of this and a little of that and invent a worldview that is a concoction of their own making. Both approaches lead to real confusion.

Based on my observations over the years as a pastor and somebody interested in how others reflect on life, I would estimate that about three-fourths of our fellow "Boomers" still have no consistent worldview that can be articulated to others with any sense of clarity. Like it says in **Ephesians 4:14**, we are often **"… tossed back and forth by the waves, and blown here and there by every wind of teaching and the cunning and craftiness of people in their deceitful scheming."**

Contrast this with a biblical worldview. The Bible teaches that truth is absolute. It is revealed through God's Word in the person of Jesus of Nazareth; his life, death and resurrection. It requires faith but is also rational and defensible. A secular worldview, one without God, will eventually lead to distortion, division, confusion and death. A Christian worldview, on the other hand, will consistently lead to clarity, unity, peace and life. Which path are you on?

In **Romans 12:2** Paul says: **"Do not conform to the pattern of this world, but be transformed by the renewing of your mind. Then you will be able to test and approve what God's will is – his good, pleasing and perfect will."**

To "conform" is to be a sponge or a mixed drink. To "be transformed" is to get the mind of Christ so that we are no longer divided in our thinking. We receive the mind of Christ when we put our faith in Jesus and the Holy Spirit fills us with His presence. As Paul says, instead of conforming to the patterns of the world, we are transformed and our minds are renewed. We come into alignment with the person of Jesus and become both representatives and conduits of His love, grace, truth and wisdom.

The Mind of Christ

Look at these three portions of scripture from **1 Corinthians 2**. Here Paul is introducing elements of a Christian worldview to some of the earliest believers. He says:

> **"We do, however, speak a message of wisdom among the mature, but not the wisdom of this age or the rulers of this age, who are coming to nothing. No, we declare God's wisdom, a mystery that has been hidden and that God destined for our glory before time began" (vs. 6-7).**

> **"'What no eye has seen, what no ear has heard, and what no human mind has conceived' – the things God has prepared for those who love him – these are the things God has revealed to us by his Spirit. The Spirit searches all things, even the deep things of God" (vs.9-10).**

> **"The person with the Spirit makes judgments about all things, but such a person is not subject to merely human judgments, for, 'Who has known the mind of the Lord so as to instruct him?' But we have the mind of Christ" (vs.15-16).**

To embrace a biblical worldview is to have the mind of Christ which is to live all of life in agreement with God's plans, purposes and promises for the world – to bring glory to Himself, to restore creation, to seek and to save all that is lost, to provide salvation to sinners and bring His kingdom from heaven down to earth. We have the privilege and responsibility to be a part of this ongoing mission.

Too many of us today just "go along to get along." That's why Paul implies that sometimes we need to get the 30,000 foot view in order to test and approve (for our lives more than others) just what the will of God really is. Why is this important? Because confused minds generally make poor choices… and poor choices derail the life Jesus intends for us to live.

Counter-Cultural

> *To embrace a biblical worldview is to have the mind of Christ which is to live all of life in agreement with God's plans, purposes and promises for the world*

To adopt a biblical worldview is to commit to a lifestyle that is completely counter-cultural. Jesus constantly pushed against the accepted spiritual and cultural norms of His day to introduce kingdom values. This approach should be very attractive to us as Baby Boomers. As we looked at "Traits and Values" in Chapter 2, I said, "'Boomers' are both independent and self-confident having grown up in a turbulent time in history. As a result, we aren't afraid to rock the boat, call out injustices and challenge the status quo. Baby Boomers share a unique blend of loyalty and rebellion."

Instead of conforming to the values of this world we can truly be transformed in both our thinking and acting, and in the process become world-changers for Jesus! What is problematic is that so many in our generation feel that life has already passed them by. Not true! Our 4th quarter can be the most meaningful and impacting of our entire lives.

> *Instead of conforming to the values of this world we can truly be transformed in both our thinking and acting, and in the process become world-changers for Jesus!*

Is there risk in committing to this journey? Yes, but what if we look at our remaining years as a new adventure that God is preparing for us to enjoy? How exciting the next 10, 20 or 30 years can be! Friends, of this we can be sure. We will never be alone! God's promise to Joshua in the Old Testament still rings true today: **"Be strong and courageous. Do not be afraid or terrified because of them** (your enemies)**, for the Lord your God goes with you; he will never leave you nor forsake you"** (Deuteronomy 31:6).

Why is this whole issue of worldview so important for our generation? My sense is that when we come to understand and then reclaim our purpose and mission, all of life will come into clearer focus and along with it the potential for great blessings in our 4th quarter.

New Lenses

A Christian worldview requires 20/20 vision. The World Health Organization estimates that there are 1.3 billion people in the world who live with some sort of visual impairment. In other words, about 1 in 5 people need glasses, contacts or corrective surgery in order to see again with 20/20 vision. I'm near-sighted. That means that as I sit here working on this chapter my bifocals are sitting on the table next to me. I actually see my laptop better without them. On the other hand, if I were to get in my truck and head-out on the highway I wouldn't think of leaving the house without my glasses. I'm good at seeing what is right in front of me… but not as good at seeing what is coming down the road.

When it comes to spiritual vision, the need for correction is 100%! Sin has caused all of us to be blind to the things of God. Jesus chastised the religious leaders of His day who were quick to point out the faults of others but not admit their own. In **John 15:14** He tells His disciples: **"Leave them; they are blind guides. If the blind lead the blind, both will fall into a pit."** Jesus is the only one who can turn spiritual blindness into spiritual insight and reveal what is coming around the next curve.

To evaluate our worldview is really like going in for an eye exam. It's like looking through a Phoropter. Do you know what that is? No, it's not the name of some ancient dinosaur. A Phoropter is that thick instrument with all the lenses and dials that your Optometrist uses to conduct an eye exam called a Retinoscopy. As you gaze through the Phoropter, the eye doctor flips different lenses in front of your eyes as you focus on the eye chart on the wall. Then he says, "Better or worse?" and through a process of elimination determines the perfect lens prescription to make your vision clear.

This is what God does when we're willing to subject our current worldview to an honest exam. He flips different lenses in front of us represented by His Word and asks, "Better or worse?" The eye chart contains words like faith, family, work, hobbies, money and society. God wants us to return from the blurred, cloudy state in which we live to 20/20 vision.

In **Proverbs 29:18** it says: **"Where there is no vision, the people perish."** I submit that lots of people in our world, including "Boomers," are perishing because their sight is set on all the wrong things. God is the only one who can truly bring our vision back into focus.

Paradigm Shifts

Getting the 30,000 foot view of life, and re-examining the core beliefs that are the foundation of our worldview, will necessarily require some "paradigm shifts." A paradigm shift is a fundamental change in approach or underlying assumptions regarding life. When a person makes a heartfelt commitment to trust Jesus and follow His teachings it often requires a "re-wiring" of long-held assumptions that have been based on wrong information, a lack of information or a flat-out rejection of the truth. When a permanent change occurs we call it a paradigm shift.

> *A paradigm shift is a fundamental change in approach or underlying assumptions regarding life.*

It's like when a new sibling is born. It may take some adjusting but there is no going back. Simon was just two at the time. He is the first-born of our daughter Sarah and her husband Jason. He stayed with us, Grandma and Papa, for four consecutive nights when his new baby brother, Ethan, was born. He didn't realize it yet but his whole world was about to change.

Ethan arrived on a Friday night. We took Simon to meet him at the hospital on Saturday afternoon. The elevator and the big brother stickers were fun but then he discovered this little object of great curiosity in his mother's arms. I could just read his mind! "It can't be too bad a thing. It gave me a new truck! It's fun checking out his hair, eyes, nose, ears and tiny feet hiding under the blanket. And here, I'll help feed him a bottle just like that baby doll at home. But wait? Why is he at our house now? Why is Mommy holding him more than me and giving him so much attention? He cries and makes other noises that kind of concern me too. Let's see, maybe I won't take my nap today. I don't want to miss anything. I'd better watch him closely, this new baby brother. He might try to touch my toys. What can I do to let mom and dad know that this is still my world regardless of this new addition to the family?" Simon was really good… but so goes the circle of life and the challenge we all have of dealing with change. Paradigm shifts are never easy!

Spiritual Awakening

To shift paradigms from a secular worldview to a biblical worldview we first need to experience a spiritual awakening. In a genuine conversion the light goes on and we begin to see Jesus as more than our ticket to heaven. He becomes the center of our very existence.

One time I was doing pre-marriage counseling with a young couple. I shared the Gospel message of God's personal love for us through His Son, Jesus. I talked about how this love is the essence of the "unconditional love" we all need in our marriages. I could see that the bride-to-be was especially listening intently. I asked, "Is this making sense to you?" She looked at me and said, "Pastor, that is the most amazing thing I've ever heard. I didn't know that God loved us that way!" She had a spiritual awakening and it changed her life forever.

In Minnesota we do have some pretty cold winters. We usually have snow on the ground from late November until early April. During January sometimes temperatures can fall to -30 degrees Fahrenheit. That's what we call cold! Furnaces operating at full capacity are therefore very important. Even one night with a malfunction can cause water pipes to freeze and rupture even in a well-insulated house… let alone the family inside.

Before furnaces all became electronic there used to be pilot lights; tiny flames that stood at the ready until a signal was received from the thermostat, gas began to flow and the larger burner ignited. If your pilot light went out you were in trouble. I'm afraid that this is what has happened to so many of us. That small flame of faith that may have existed in our lives at some point went out. Now, even when we receive a signal from God, we are incapable of "firing up" and burning for Jesus. We need a spiritual awakening.

Spiritual Awareness

To shift paradigms and operate with a biblical worldview we also need spiritual awareness. Two friends were walking on a busy downtown street in a big city one afternoon. One was a biologist. All of a sudden he stopped and said to his friend, "Did you hear that? Crickets!" His friend said, "Are you kidding me? Here in the middle of the city?" Sure enough! As he began to tune-out the street noise and tune-in to the sounds of nature he heard them. The biologist said, "We all hear what we have trained our ears to hear. Let me show you." He took some change out his pocket and tossed it up in the air. When it hit ground about 10 people immediately stopped and turned in his direction. He said, "See what I mean? We hear what we are trained to hear."

Spiritual awareness means that we are tuned-in to Jesus. It's like the radio waves that are always all around us in the air. We can't hear them unless we have a tuner. The tuner God has given us is the Holy Spirit. When we train our ears to listen for His voice, we begin to hear and see things that we couldn't hear before. It might be the beauty of God's creation. It might be the pain in

> "We all hear what we have trained our ears to hear. Let me show you."

someone's life. It might be that "still small voice" the scripture talks about nudging us to go this way or that. What are your ears trained to listen for?

Spiritual Action

There's more! To truly shift paradigms, spiritual awakening and spiritual awareness must be accompanied by spiritual action. Good works don't save us but they are certainly an indication that faith is real. The Apostle James makes this argument: **"What good is it, my brothers and sisters, if someone claims to have faith but has no deeds? Can such a faith save them? Suppose a brother or sister is without clothes and daily food. If one of you says to them, 'Go in peace; keep warm and well fed,' but does nothing about their physical needs, what good is it? In the same way, faith by itself, if it is not accompanied by action, is dead" (James 2:14-17).**

By spiritual action I mean our willingness to respond to the needs we have come to see through our heightened spiritual awakening and spiritual awareness. That action might be directed towards our family, friends, neighbors, coworkers or others God puts in our path. One of my greatest concerns in respect to our Baby Boom generation is that we have become so absorbed with our own lives that it seems a great bother to respond to the needs of others. We shouldn't try to do more than God asks… but we should never be afraid to do exactly what He asks.

> We shouldn't try to do more than God asks… but we should never be afraid to do exactly what He asks.

Why? Because God has promised to fill us with His presence and power to accomplish every good thing.

Our outstanding Youth Pastor at Christ Church, Sean Nelson, calls it SANFANIJN. It means "See a need, fill a need, in Jesus name!" He teaches it to our youth and adults every year as they go on an annual Mission Trip. They have discovered that the best ministry on these trips is rarely found on the scheduled itinerary. It takes place when eyes and hearts are open to opportunities to be "the hands and feet of Jesus" along the way. It was true throughout Jesus' ministry and it is true for us today.

I was talking to a young father recently about his two boys, ages 7 and 10. I asked him what he was noticing in terms of their personality development. I said, "How are they different?" Of his second son he said, "I think he's more sensitive. He notices if someone's feelings are hurt and goes quickly to give them a hug." That's pretty sweet, isn't it? As we shift to God's agenda in life our eyes will be open to see the needs of those around us and we'll be ready to get our arms around them too!

A long-time member of Christ Church Otsego, and dear friend, Mark Lucas, has often said to me, "Pastor Greg, I think that at least twice a year you should just remind our church family why we're here and what we're called to do." He has been right! Vision leaks, even spiritual vision! Worldviews get distorted and need refreshing over time. We all need reminders of what we believe and why… and what we are called to do… and to what end. It's so easy to get caught up in all the day-to-day stuff and lose sight of the big picture… even in the Church.

Paradigm shifts are like looking through a new set of lenses. They change our perception of reality. As I've shared, this shift happens when we begin to see the world through the eyes of our heavenly Father *(Awakening)*, respond to the world with the love and spiritual sensitivity of Jesus *(Awareness)*, and act in the world with faith and obedience empowered by the Holy Spirit *(Action)*.

> *Vision leaks, even spiritual vision! Worldviews get distorted and need refreshing over time.*

Better Questions

When this change happens our questions about life will shift as well. Instead of asking "Where does God fit into my story?" we will ask, "Where does my life fit into God's mission?" Instead of asking, "What parts of the Bible can I selectively apply to my life?" we will ask, "How can I apply my life to all of the Bible?" And where we have tended to ask, "What kind of mission does God have in mind for me?" a better question becomes "What kind of me does God want for His mission?"

20/20 Vision

20/20 vision is a beautiful thing because there is so much beauty all around us to see! Sometimes Jesus restores our sight physically but he always wants to give it to us spiritually. Which is really more valuable?

One day as Jesus went on his way he saw a man who he discerned had been blind from birth. His disciples parroted the false assessment of the Pharisees regarding his condition. They asked: **"Rabbi, who sinned, this man or his parents that he was born blind" (John 9:2)?**

Jesus' response probably blew their old paradigm out of the water! He said: **"Neither this man nor his parents sinned, but this happened so that the work of God might be displayed in him. As long as it is day, we must do the works of him who sent me. Night is coming, when no one can work. While I am in the world, I am the light of the world" (John 9:3-4).**

Do we realize that any deficiency we have in our own lives provides an opportunity for God to do a miracle? If we truly believed this we wouldn't complain like we do. Who is the light of the world? It is Jesus! Who is to do the works of God the Father? We are… in Jesus' name… and the time is short!

Jesus healed the blind man that day. His neighbors didn't believe it and the Pharisees caught wind of it. They even called that young man's parents to verify that he was their son and had in fact been blind from birth. His parents confirmed it and still the religious leaders pointed to Jesus and publicly berated Him. They said: **"We know this man is a sinner" (John 9:24b).** That's when the now formerly blind man declared: **"Whether he is a sinner or not, I don't know. One thing I do know. I was blind but now I see" (John 9:25)!** That encounter with Jesus resulted in both physical sight and spiritual insight for this new disciple. As the dialogue continued with the Pharisees this man gave a clear testimony regarding his belief that Jesus was sent from God. His worldview expanded. His paradigms shifted and undoubtedly his life was never the same again!

Divine Perspective

As busy and full as life can be, I have found that when I'm able to get a break and get some distance, the Lord always speaks to me with comfort, encouragement and new revelation. Fellow Baby Boomers, if we're going to live meaningful lives during our 4th quarter and leave a lasting legacy for those who follow, we must be willing to pause in our lives long enough to get the 30,000 foot view. We must be willing to re-examine "what we believe and why" if we are to have any hope of communicating biblical faith and values to others. As the Holy Spirit leads, we must be willing to change paradigms and look through a different set of lenses in order to see the world as God sees it and love the world as God loves it. We need Jesus to open our eyes and give us 20/20 spiritual vision. Won't you call on Him to do that miracle in your life today? Our Savior is the one who makes the blind to see!

Questions for Personal Reflection or Group Discussion:

1. Where or when do you find that you are able to get the "30,000 foot view" in your life?

2. Worldview is shaped by family, faith, culture and experience. Which of these areas has been most influential in the formation of your worldview?
3. If God were to give you an eye exam today, would your current life look "better" or "worse?" What would you like to see change?
4. What do you sense is most needed in your life right now... a genuine spiritual awakening, greater spiritual awareness or more purposeful spiritual action?

CHAPTER 5

Dream Big Dreams!

D o you still dream? I don't just mean when you're sleeping. I mean do you dream about life? Are you dreaming today about what you would like to do with the rest of your life should God bless you with another 10, 20 or 30 years? Someone once said, "When we stop dreaming, we die." To no longer dream is to give up on life. Dreams are stories or images that our minds create or God plants while we are both "day-dreaming" and "night-dreaming." They can be entertaining, fun, romantic, encouraging, envisioning, frightening and sometimes really bizarre. Dreams can provide insight into our deepest desires, highest hopes and greatest fears.

Throughout the scriptures God speaks to people both when they're awake and when they're asleep. The Bible is filled with dreams and visions. In the Book of Genesis, Joseph is called a "dreamer" by his 11 brothers. Turns out he was just hearing divine revelation. God eventually used Joseph's dreams, and his God-given ability to interpret the dreams of Pharaoh, to save a whole country from famine and starvation. None of the astrologers and sorcerers could match him because he had received his insights from God.

In the New Testament Book of Matthew, Chapter 1, we read of another Joseph and another dream that involved supernatural revelation. You know the story. Mary announced her pregnancy, attributing it to "the power of the Most High." Joseph is both embarrassed and confused and offers to divorce her quietly. And then we read: **"An angel of the Lord appeared to him in a dream and said, 'Joseph son of David, do not be afraid to take Mary home as your wife, because what is conceived in her is from the Holy Spirit. She will give birth to a Son, and you are to give him the name Jesus, because he will save his people from their sins'"** (Matthew 1:20b-21).

Two dreamers! Two Josephs whose obedience changed the world! What if we were to "day-dream" about the Call of God in our lives today? What if we were to go to bed at night asking Jesus to download His plans and purposes for us even while we're sleeping? Instead of tossing and turning over shattered dreams of the past or the worries of the day we would begin to receive what I referred to in the last chapter as "the mind of Christ." The Bible also calls it "secret wisdom" and the "deep things of God." God wants to reveal His plans and purposes to us so that His life might shine through us!

> *What if we were to go to bed at night asking Jesus to download His plans and purposes for us even while we're sleeping?*

In **Acts 2:17** the Apostle Peter quoted a prophetic word from the Book of Joel that was being fulfilled on that Day of Pentecost: **"In the last days, God says, I will pour out my Spirit on all people. Your sons and daughters will prophesy, your young men will see visions, your old men will dream dreams."**

I've always been a bit puzzled by this verse. Prophecy, yes. God desires that we all prophesy (See 1 Corinthians 14). However, it makes more sense to me that young men and women would "dream dreams" and old men and women would "see visions." After all, those in their youth dream of adventure, love, marriage, family and career achievements. Those who are older see visions of the past and the future, even visions of heaven. So why the reversal? My hunch is that God is telling us to keep dreaming no matter what our age!

When I was younger I used to sleep walk quite a bit. One summer when I was 13 I was working on my Uncle Wayne Ford's dairy farm in Wisconsin. I was a city kid but I loved spending summers milking cows, cleaning the barn, driving tractor, baling hay, chopping wood and whatever else needed to be done. There were perks for the hard work. My Grandma Ford's cooking and baking was the best. I would put my order in every morning and by lunch or dinner there it would be; cake, cookies, pie along with fresh strawberries, raspberries or blueberries from the garden to top off a big bowl of ice cream. You name it. She spoiled me!

One day we had been baling hay from morning until night. I loaded and stacked something like 6,000 bales of hay that summer. I was dog tired. In the middle of the night my grandma heard me sleep walking. She came out of her room to see what was going on. There I was standing at the top of the stairs of their big farmhouse holding my pillow crossways with my arms underneath it. She said, "Where are you going, Greg?" I said, "I'm taking this bale of hay out to the barn." She said, "Why don't you put it back on your bed for now. You can take it out in the morning." I did and went right back to sleep. That's when you know you've put in a good day's work! My grandma loved that story!

It didn't get much better after Colleen and I got married. She will tell you how one night she woke up and there I was trying to climb up our bedroom closet folding door. I don't remember why. Maybe I was seeking a higher position in life! Another night she woke up with me sitting on top of her with my hands around her neck pulling up on her. No, I wasn't trying to cash in early on an insurance policy. I was trying to save her from the waterfall she was going over! Really! Colleen must have thought, "What in the world have I gotten myself into!"

I still dream a lot today. Sometimes my dreams are just plain silly or perhaps they reveal some deep-seated fears. By the way, pastors have dreams that are unique to our profession. One time I dreamt that I was standing in the lobby at church about to start a wedding ceremony when I looked down and realized I was missing my shoes. The wedding party stood there while I searched for them all over the church. I don't think I ever found them because I woke up. The wedding party is probably still standing there in dreamland wondering where I am!

One Sunday I shared this dream with my congregation. I dreamt that I was preaching a great message in front of a packed sanctuary but my introduction took so long that by the time I got to my main points I was already 45 minutes in. As I continued on people just got up and started to leave. Even so, I couldn't bring my message to a conclusion. I just kept talking and talking. After the service a good friend said, "Pastor, that wasn't a dream. I was here that Sunday!"

Thankfully, more often than not my dreams today come with comfort, encouragement or greater revelation. It might be a message God is giving me to share, insight into an impending decision, better understanding of a person I'm ministering too or a renewed vision for the future. Some of my dreams are so detailed that I get up in the middle of the night and write them down although I'm able to remember most of them. Sometimes I experience the overwhelming love and presence of the Lord in a dream and wake-up feeling so blessed and encouraged that I can hardly stand it. Sometimes I flash back to family gatherings where my grandparents or dad are there, for example, and have wonderful conversations with them. It reminds me that one day I will see them again in heaven. One time I had lost something very valuable and the Lord showed me where it was in a dream. My point is simply this. I want to keep dreaming dreams until the day I meet Jesus face to face! How about you? What kind of dreams are you having these days?

Whether awake or asleep, you might be dreaming about a vacation you've always wanted to take or checking another item off your "bucket list." You might be dreaming about living long enough to see your grandchildren grow-up, get married and live happy lives. Perhaps you're dreaming about celebrating a 50th or 60th wedding anniversary with your spouse, family and friends. There are so many wonderful dreams to dream, all in the context of living every day to the fullest for as long as God gives you life and breath. I quoted **1**

Corinthians 2:9 in Chapter 1. It is worth repeating here: **"No eye has seen, no ear has heard, and no mind has imagined what God has prepared for those who love Him" (1 Corinthians 2:9 NLT).**

Dream Big

We always tell our children and grandchildren, "Dream big! You can grow-up to be whatever you want to be!" Since you are still a child of God today I believe He is saying to you, "Keep dreaming! I still want to accomplish more in your life than you can even think or imagine!" The problem is that the world beats us down over time. Satan himself is a dream killer. He constantly whispers in our ears, "You can't do that. You're a failure. You've got nothing left to give. Look at what happened to your dreams in the past. Don't even try getting excited about something new!"

But "Boomers," I'm asking God to release in our generation the ability to dream again. And not just little dreams that might temporarily satisfy our own needs, but big dreams, big enough that God would use us to make a real difference in the lives of others. God is no respecter of status or position. He wants to reveal His plans and purposes to young and old, men and women, rich and poor no matter what our situation in life. God wants us to dream big dreams for Him!

If you could accomplish anything for God, and knew in advance that you could not fail, what dream would you still dream? What would you dream of accomplishing in the remaining years of your life? What would it look like for your dream to come true? Friends, God is not finished with you yet! When you ask Him to show you the way forward He will not only meet every need but fulfill every dream He has placed in your heart. However, to dream a big dream for God you must be willing to get out of your comfort zone, take a risk and trust Jesus every step of the way. A

> *"Boomers," I'm asking God to release in our generation the ability to dream again.*

God-sized dream is one that can only be accomplished with Him! Let's consider several aspects of life that may require adjustment in order for you to fulfill your dreams in this next season. First…

Get Out of Your Boat

Have you ever been out on a lake or the ocean in rough water? Not only can it be dangerous but it's downright scary! We know that here in Minnesota, the "Land of 10,000 Lakes." That was the experience of Jesus' disciples one night on the Sea of Galilee, which by the way is 13 miles long and 8 miles wide and is famous for quickly kicking up some big waves. It was dark. It was late in the night. The disciples had rowed several miles across the lake. That's when the wind began to blow and the waves got rough. Many of these men were seasoned fisherman. They knew the dangers. All of a sudden they saw the shape of a man walking toward them on the water and they were spooked. Were they having a dream or hallucinating? Some even thought it was a ghost. Then that ghost spoke to them! Jesus said: **"Take courage! It is I; don't be afraid" (Matthew 14:27).**

Peter, the bold and sometimes even cocky leader of the group responded: **"Lord, if it's you, tell me to come to you on the water" (Matthew 14:28-29).** Jesus simply said: **"Come."** Peter got out of the boat and began to walk on the water toward Jesus. Imagine his amazement. He had undoubtedly dreamed of doing miracles like Jesus but I'm sure never imagined it happening that night. Talk about exhilarating. He was doing something that to my knowledge no human being had ever done before or has ever done since. He was walking on water! Things were going great until he made one critical mistake. He took his eyes off Jesus and began to focus instead on the wind and the waves. That's when he started to sink like a rock. He cried out: **"Lord, save me" (Matthew 14:30b)!**

Immediately, Jesus reached out His hand and caught him. He said: **"You of little faith, why did you doubt" (Matthew 14:31)?** As they climbed into the boat together the wind let up and the seas became calm. The other disciples in the boat worshipped Jesus, saying: **"Truly you are the Son of God" (Matthew 14:33b).** Peter was probably still sitting on the deck with his heart beating out of his chest! However, I imagine that he never went out on that lake again without recalling this amazing experience!

To dream big dreams for God means not only recognizing Jesus as a "water walker," but having the faith and courage to get out of the boat ourselves and walk towards Him. The fishing boat in this story represents our places of security in life. What are those for you? Your home, your family, your job, your pension or bank account? When we keep our eyes on Jesus there is no doubt we can do the impossible. However, when we lose our focus we can sink just as fast.

> To dream big dreams for God means not only recognizing Jesus as a "water walker," but having the faith and courage to get out of the boat ourselves and walk towards Him.

To fulfill a new dream in your life will require step by step faith and obedience. That's why so many of our hopes and dreams fall by the wayside. There is initial enthusiasm which is great but it must be followed by the hard work of trusting Jesus even in the midst of life's storms. Where is Jesus calling you to get out of your boat today? Can you identify an area in your life where you need to risk more and trust more to see your dreams fulfilled? Go for it and keep your eyes on the prize! Second...

Work for Impact

Many of us in the Baby Boom generation have "worked to live." I'm suggesting that from this time forward we "live to work." Let me explain starting in the Book of Genesis. Did God have to work when He created the world? Look at **Genesis 2:1-3**. It reads: **"Thus the heavens and the earth were completed in all their vast array. By the seventh day God had finished the work he had been doing; so on the seventh day he rested from all his work. And God blessed** the seventh day and made it holy; because on it he rested from all the work of creating he had done."

Isn't that fascinating! Creating this beautiful world is described as work three different times. And when God finished with this most amazing job of all He rested. And then in **Genesis 2:15** it says: **"The Lord took the man and put him in the Garden of Eden to work it and take care of it."** Yes, we were created to work as partners with God. From the very beginning of time work was considered a blessing. But when sin came in... everything changed!

Also in Genesis we read how Adam and Eve ate the forbidden fruit from the tree of the knowledge of good and evil. This is symbolic of our desire to do life our way rather than trust in God. They were banished from the garden with these words: **"Cursed is the ground because of you; through painful toil you will eat of it all the days of your life. It will produce thorns and thistles for you, and you will eat the plants of the field. By the sweat of your brow you will eat your food until you return to the ground, since from it you were taken; for dust you are and to dust you shall return"** **(Genesis 3:17b-19).**

Here's what I want you to note. From this point forward until the cross and resurrection, work was largely perceived to be a punishment for sin with both physical and spiritual implications. In other words, as a result of sin, people now had to "work to live" when God's original design was that we "live to work" as caretakers of His creation.

What is your attitude towards work? Baby Boomers were raised with a strong work ethic but still many find work to be a necessary evil rather than a blessing, a drudgery rather than a joy. The attitude is "Life is tough. You have to work to put food on the table and survive in this world." Work becomes a means to an end. You work to earn a paycheck. You work to get to the weekend so that you can party... or you work to get to retirement so that you can stop working and really enjoy life.

For some people who operate with this mindset work actually becomes an obsession. We call them work-a-holics. Your work becomes your identity but not in a healthy way. You are driven at your job or career to prove yourself over and over again in order to be successful, make money and win the admiration of others. It's never enough and there is little joy in the process. This "work to live" attitude has led to phrases in society like "Sorry! I've got to go to work today," or "Another day, another dollar," or "Thank God it's Friday!"

This is a pretty discouraging assessment of work but I'm afraid it's the one too many of us have adopted. What might it look like to "flip the script" and return to God's original intentions for work? When Jesus paid the ultimate price for sin through His death and resurrection He not only redeemed us… but He redeemed work. Because of Jesus we can once again "live to work" as co-laborers with Christ rather than just "work to live."

In **Colossians 3:17** it says: **"And whatever you do, whether in word or deed, do it all in the name of the Lord Jesus, giving thanks to God the Father through him."** Rather than seeing work as a necessary evil, isolated and separated from the rest of life, we can now see it as integral to the fulfilling of every hope and dream. It's the difference between jumping out of bed in the morning and enthusiastically saying, "Good morning, Lord!" or falling out of bed and despondently saying "Good Lord, another morning." Which of these responses would most describe your attitude toward work?

> *It's the difference between jumping out of bed in the morning and enthusiastically saying, "Good morning, Lord!" or falling out of bed and despondently saying "Good Lord, another morning."*

Paul continues his teaching about work in **Colossians 3:23** when he says: **"And whatever you do, work at it with all your heart, as working for the Lord, not for men."** When we adopt this mindset our work can actually become an expression of worship. It can also become an important part of our witness and have a tremendous impact on others. Attitude matters! Jesus is your real boss and He's a "hands-on" kind of guy, like in the TV show "Undercover Boss." He has come down from the boardroom of heaven to get His hands dirty, to experience our world and walk with us through all the nitty-gritty places of life.

He chooses to do it by partnering with us and working through us to reach people with His love, no matter where we are or what we're doing. Paul is saying that your work is an important part of your ministry. You are called to serve Him when you go into the office, make a sales call, drive a truck, pour concrete, work as a cashier, take care of kids or flip burgers. When you do your work with the attitude of serving God and not man your impact will grow exponentially!

What are you doing for work today? Are you still in your career for a few more years or have you stepped away? Are you working in a different field now… or in a part-time job to help pay the bills? I understand that many "Boomers" are tired but still need to work. Most of us have worked hard our whole lives, like 40 or 50 years. We've paid our dues. We deserve to sit-back, celebrate our accomplishments and enjoy the good life. Unfortunately, that's not the Call of God.

Yes, there are seasons of life. Yes, we will probably not do the job we're doing right now forever… but just dream with me. When we recognize our Call to work with excellence and urgency for the Lord no matter what we're doing, what might God do through us in these important remaining years to bless others in Jesus' name? It's the difference between "working to live" and "living to work." Third…

Relax On Purpose

Many Baby Boomers are transitioning right now from work to leisure. Our generation will have more free time on our hands than any generation before us. The question is how will we use it? The "big lie" prevalent in culture today is that leisure time is "me time." The Bible

> The "big lie" prevalent in culture today is that leisure time is "me time." The Bible suggests something different. It calls us to "relax on purpose."

suggests something different. It calls us to "relax on purpose." The real purpose of leisure is to not only rest from work but in the process be renewed in body, soul and spirit. Call it a spiritual spa with the healing hands of Jesus serving as our masseuse. If we ignore any of these three parts of our being we may experience short-term rest or diversion but our lives will likely remain unsatisfied and out of balance.

This was the purpose of the Jewish Sabbath from the very beginning. It was not only a day of rest with strict rules accompanying it. It was a day of spiritual renewal when individuals were challenged to draw close to God and others. It was meant to contribute to "Shalom" or true peace both in one's heart and with the world. Because we don't approach our leisure time holistically, even good things can actually draw us away from God. It can be a hobby like golf, travelling to your favorite destination, enjoying a concert or just sleeping in. When our attitude and priorities are mixed up we pay for it with a tired restlessness that never seems to be satisfied. There is a better way!

In **Matthew 6:33** Jesus says: **"But seek first his kingdom and his righteousness, and all these things will be given to you as well."** The "all these things" refer to our deepest needs in life, those that truly lead to resting in the Lord and experiencing His peace.

How do "Boomers" spend their leisure time today? Not surprisingly, a lot of us spend it in front of a screen, i.e. television, computer, tablet or phone. Surveys show that those 60 or older, particularly those transitioning toward retirement, spend an average of 4 ½ to 6 hours a day utilizing technology. That's half or more of our available leisure hours. Baby Boomers also spend their leisure time with family, sleeping, exercising, shopping, volunteering, worshipping, traveling, dating, attending concerts, listening to music, eating out and pursuing a variety of hobbies from gardening to woodworking. In other words, we spend our leisure time like most people do… but with our own unique generational preferences and tastes.

What if we learned to "relax on purpose?" What if we took time to evaluate how we spend our leisure time according to the contribution any particular activity makes to the renewal of our whole person; body, soul and spirit? What if we were to also consider our leisure activities based on whether they provide an opportunity to bless others… and not just ourselves? Here's what I would suggest. In the years to come, if a particular activity or hobby draws you closer to God and others, build on it. If it takes you away from God and others, cut back on that activity or give it up altogether.

Take golf for example. I call it "Psalm 23 ministry!" You know… green pastures and still waters… except when my ball splashes down! I love golf because it's a sport where I can constantly work to improve my skill and score. It provides a lifelong challenge. I think I need two lifetimes! At the same time, what I enjoy even more is the fun and fellowship with my playing partners, be they family or friends. And then I really do love the beauty of a golf course which allows me to celebrate God's creation. I think it goes back to my lawn service days in college. So golf for me is a holistic experience that touches body, soul and spirit. I'm not kidding! When I keep this in perspective I find that golf is a hobby that is a blessing even when I slice my ball into the woods!

Or take travel. I love to visit new places and see the world. How about you? As I mentioned in Chapter 1, Colleen and I are campers. Oh the beauty of our state and national parks! We've also been blessed to visit other countries both for vacation and ministry and we've learned not to separate the two. When we travel we enjoy our rest, our relationship and the surprises that God always has in store for us along the way. It might be a discovery or experience that wasn't on our agenda. It might be an encounter or conversation with a person that allows us to provide encouragement or be a witness for Jesus. Again, I recommend a holistic approach to travel. "Me time" becomes "Thee time!" When you learn to relax on purpose you will discover that God has so many blessings waiting for you. Take a few moments right now to reflect on the different ways that you spend your time!

The Baby Boom generation has an opportunity to model something really important to the generations that follow us. Will our leisure time lead us to selfishness or selflessness? Will we use it to kick-back and do nothing or rise-up and do something? In the end it's about seeking Jesus first in every part of our lives. I love His invitation in **Matthew 11:28-30**. Jesus says: **"Come to me, all you who are weary and burdened, and I will give you rest. Take my yoke upon you and learn from me, for I am gentle and humble in heart, and you will find rest for your souls. For my yoke is easy and my burden is light."**

May your burden be light and all your days blessed as you use the time God has given you to "relax on purpose" and be a blessing to others! Fourth…

Make Your 4ᵗʰ Quarter Your Best

There is a major demographic shift happening right now in the United States. Approximately 70 million Baby Boomers are entering their senior years and turning 65 at the rate of 10,000 per day. Some call it the "gray tsunami." As we've noted, by 2030 all "Boomers" will be 65 years of age or older. This shift has enormous implications for the job market, health care, housing and decisions about retirement. Of those currently 65 or older approximately 40% are no longer in the workforce.

Part of this decision process is financial. The estimated median retirement savings for "Boomers" is only about $200,000. Many are concerned about having enough saved for retirement. Retirement income for Baby Boomers will be a combination of savings, investments, pensions, inheritances, Social Security and work. Will our generation be able to make this last season of life our best? I think that depends on how we view the word "best." It's a "quality of life" question in a "quantity of life" world.

If retirement income is your primary measuring stick you may be in for some disappointment. On the other hand, if your approach to these years is measured by family, friendships, faith, celebrating life and leaving a lasting legacy, there is no question that your 4th quarter can be your best. The key is to discover your passion in life and then go for it as you dream some new dreams for God! Will you still have the energy you had when you were 20 or 40? Probably not. Instead you have the wisdom and experience gained over a lifetime.

> *Will our generation be able to make this last season of life our best? I think that depends on how we view the word "best." It's a "quality of life" question in a "quantity of life" world.*

In 2007 Jack Nicholson and Morgan Freeman starred in a movie called "The Bucket List." Here's the summary. Fate lands two men in the same hospital room for cancer treatment. They are both terminal – one a billionaire and the other an auto mechanic. They discover they have two things in common; a need to come to terms with what they have done in their lives and a desire to complete a list of things they want to see and do before they die. Against their doctors wishes they leave the hospital and set out on the adventure of a lifetime including skydiving, racing a Shelby Mustang, getting a tattoo, seeing the Himalayas and kissing the most beautiful girl in the world. It was a fun movie that I'm sure many of you enjoyed back in the day!

What's on your bucket list today? If you need suggestions there are hundreds of examples online for you to consider. A few of them even have to do with helping others! I suggest that you firm up your list. Make it part of your dreaming and begin to check-off the items that are most important to you. In the process I have a hunch that God will toss a few other ideas into your bucket, that in the end, you will find to be the most rewarding of all.

Get Unstuck

In order to dream big dreams for God we have to be prepared to adjust some things in our life that may currently have us stuck. It will take a renewed faith in order to step out of our boat of comfort and trust Jesus for amazing new experiences. It will take a shift in priorities to "live to work" not just "work to live." We will need some new-found creativity and discipline to learn how to relax on purpose so that our whole person can be renewed and we can be a blessing to others. Yes, in order for our 4th quarter to truly be our best we will need to re-examine our "bucket list" through the lens of "quality of life" rather than "quantity of life." My prayer is that God will bless you with the ability to keep on dreaming until that day when you meet Him face-to-face. What a glorious day that will be!

Questions for Personal Reflection or Group Discussion:

1. Do you dream? Share a dream you can remember. How did it speak to you?
2. If you could accomplish anything for God, and knew in advance that you could not fail, what dream would you still dream?
3. Where are you at in your work life? Are you currently "working to live" or "living to work?" Explain the difference in your own words.
4. What is still on your "bucket list" today? What's the next item you would like to cross off?

CHAPTER 6

Mend and Tend!

Much of answering the question, "What will I do with the rest of my life?" has to do with relationships. When your relationships are solid, starting with your Creator and extending to those He has given you to love, everything else in life comes in a distant second. On the other hand, if relationships are broken with God, your spouse, children or extended family, life can be lonely and miserable. That thought can be expanded to include neighbors, friends, coworkers, church members and more.

In this chapter I'm going to encourage you to reprioritize your relationships. I'm going to challenge you to "mend" those that are broken and "tend" to those that especially call for your love and care. To "mend" relationships requires forgiveness and reconciliation. To "tend" relationships requires unconditional love and consistent effort. When these Christ-like qualities are present in relationships, those that have been broken can be healed and those that are already good can become even better. Let's explore the power of relationships to contribute to a long and fulfilling last season of life, but first, the story of someone who desperately needed both forgiveness and unconditional love years after a traumatic childhood experience.

Many years ago a dejected, disheveled middle-aged man came in to the church office at First Lutheran in Portland, Maine, the congregation I served for 9 years on the East coast. He told Jolene, my office assistant, that he was looking for a pastor and needed help. She brought him to my office door. The story usually goes something like this: "I'm just one week away from my next paycheck and am trying to get to my Uncle's funeral in Georgia. My wife and kids are out in the car. We just need money for a hotel room for the night and some food and gas and we'll be on our way."

I've learned to sit down with people, listen, ask some questions and try to discern if their request is legit or what the deeper need might be. Today we have some excellent community partners that work together to respond to special requests like this… but man have I been burned! One time during my early years of ministry I helped a couple who had a compelling story and seemed to be sincere. The next morning I saw them buying lottery tickets at our local grocery story with the money I had given them. My heart sank but I was so embarrassed by my own gullibility and lack of judgment that I didn't have the courage to confront them. Another time I let a homeless guy stay in our church building overnight. Big mistake. It turned out he had Tourette's syndrome and sometime during the night he punched several holes in the wall in the room where I had told him he could sleep. Can you hear me trying to explain that one to the Church Council!

This guy was different. Mid-40s, I guessed. He wasn't looking for help. He was looking for a friend. He shared that he had struggled with alcohol his whole adult life. He explained how recently he had lost another job and that his wife and kids were so frustrated they had kicked him out… maybe for good. After listening for about 20 minutes I felt led to ask him a question. I said, "And where do you see God in all of this?" Without any hesitation he said, "I don't! I'm sure that God gave up on me a long time ago." I responded, "And why would you think that?" He told me this story.

"When I was a kid, like 2nd grade, I got invited to go to Sunday School by a friend in my neighborhood. I began to hear about Jesus for the first time. I also learned that there were things that Christians weren't supposed to do… like drink or smoke or dance or even go to movies. I know now that it was an ultra-conservative church but I didn't know the difference back then. So one Sunday morning I got up my courage and asked my Sunday School teacher, 'Why? Why aren't Christians supposed to go to movies?' She said, 'The Bible tells us that Jesus is going to return again someday and we have to be ready. If you're in a movie theater, he won't come in… and you'll be left behind.'" As a pastor, my heart sank as I listened.

He continued, "Several weeks later a friend from school invited me to his birthday party. As part of his party we were going to go to a Disney movie at the local theater. Remembering what my Sunday School teacher had said I was torn. I asked my mom if she thought it would be OK and she said, 'Yes. Go and have fun with your friends.'

That day I remember standing outside the movie theater unsure if I should go in. At the urging of my friends I finally did. I couldn't even tell you the name of the movie. All I remember is leaning back in my seat, looking up at the ceiling and wondering if Jesus had come and left me behind." That's when he hung his head and said, "Pastor, after all I've done, I'm quite sure that if Jesus returned today he would still leave me behind."

That sad and maddening story opened the door to personal ministry, a treatment program and a relationship that continued for several years until he moved to another state. He got sober, got a job and the marriage somehow survived. I wish every story turned out that way. I'll never forget the image he described of himself as a young boy sitting in that movie theater, looking up at the ceiling and wondering if Jesus had returned and left him behind. It strengthened my resolve to share the true Gospel, the one that sets people free from fear and guilt and invites them into a personal relationship with Jesus.

We Baby Boomers have dealt with a lot of stuff in our lives, haven't we. We've all struggled. We've all made our mistakes. We all have stories to tell and many are not happy ones. Sometimes even our notions of God are skewed by the difficulties we've faced in life or the misguided things others have said. Often the first relationship that needs "mending and tending" is the one with our Savior. Do you know Him? Are you walking with Him? I want you to know that no matter where you're at in life, Jesus will always come and find you. He will never leave you behind!

Don't let past failures keep you from future successes. When we come clean, God is in the business of turning "set-backs" into "set-ups." The very relationships that feel so broken and impossible can be restored to something so good that we never imagined it possible. I've seen it happen time and time again. It really is the grace of God at work!

Marriage

If you are married, "mending and tending" has to start with your spouse. Hurtful words, disappointments and neglect can leave a lot of scar tissue over the years. If emotional wounds are allowed to build-up in a marriage they will lead to bitterness, loneliness and isolation in the one relationship that is intended to be the most intimate and satisfying. If there has been abuse, an affair or an addiction, the layers of scar tissue will go even deeper. Lovers become friends, friends become strangers and strangers eventually get divorced.

> *Don't let past failures keep you from future successes. When we come clean, God is in the business of turning "set-backs" into "set-ups."*

The Baby Boom generation continues to have the highest divorce rate of any living generation of marriages. There is much written about the pull factors causing the older generation to consider divorce as a preferable option today. Some have suffered through un-loving marriages for years waiting for the empty nest. They apparently think that sharing the news of divorce is easier with children who are 25 or 35 than it is with those who are 5 or 15.

A second factor influencing "later in life" divorce is that women today have the freedom and financial independence to leave a marriage by initiating a divorce much easier than in past generations.

Regardless of age this phenomena is being called the "the walk-away wife." She suffers for years but when she finally decides she wants out, that's it. No discussion. End of story! Another key factor is that both aging men and women are looking at the next 20 or 25 years of life and are simply not willing to stay stuck in an unhappy marriage. In most states, "no fault divorce" makes the whole process simpler. The kids are gone. Just divide up your stuff and move on!

Recent statistics provide even more cause for alarm. Between 1990 and 2010 the divorce rate for people 55-64 doubled. For those older than 65 it tripled. According to the 2020 Census the growth of "gray divorce" continues this trend. Of all the divorces reported in 2021, 34.9% of them were of couples 55 and older, far outpacing other demographics. Another recent factor was the Covid pandemic. The isolation of those two years caused many older couples to re-evaluate their marriages and find them wanting. Is it possible to reverse this trend? Let's hope so because more than 60% of second marriages also end in divorce.

The ingredients of a marriage turn-a-round begin with honesty, humility, forgiveness and a solid game-plan going forward. With the support of a qualified pastor, priest, rabbi or marriage counselor, couples can address the hurts and wounds of past years and work toward healing. In my experience, the willingness to confess sin and ask the other for forgiveness is absolutely vital. Too many of us have said "I'm sorry… it won't happen again" a thousand times. How many have truly said, "I'm sorry… will you forgive me?" The difference is as wide as the Grand Canyon.

True forgiveness comes from God and is meant to be shared with one another. In **Colossians 3:12-14** Paul says: **"Therefore, as God's chosen people, holy and dearly loved, clothe yourselves with compassion, kindness, humility, gentleness and patience. Bear with each other and forgive one another if any of you has a grievance against someone. Forgive as the Lord forgave you. And over all these virtues put on love, which binds them all together in perfect unity."**

In the same way that God forgives us, we are to forgive one another. This is true of every relationship in life but doubly true in our marriages. It's the difference between sweeping issues under the rug and dealing with them straight up. The "mending part" comes when we're first willing to extend spirit-empowered forgiveness and then open our hearts to the possibility of a brand new beginning. The "tending part" follows as we work together on changing attitudes and behaviors that lead to rediscovering our first love… or finding a new love altogether.

Can you be honest right now? If you are married, where does your relationship need "mending and tending?" Have you given up? Are you hiding your true feelings or just going through the motions for the sake of the kids and grandkids… or appearances? Don't settle for less than God intends for your marriage, family and legacy. Pray about it. Come clean with your spouse. Do it in a way that is loving and honoring but honestly shares your frustrations and hurts. Talk openly about what it would take on both of your parts to make things better. Humility goes a long way.

One day a wife complained to her husband, "You never tell me you love me anymore!" The husband responded, "I told you I loved you the day we got married and if something changes I'll let you know!" Ouch! It doesn't work that way, does it? Healthy marriages need love expressed and walked-out in hundreds of little ways every day. When you shared your vows on your wedding day "to have and to hold from this day forward, for better and for worse, for richer and for poorer, in sickness and in health, to love and to cherish for as long as we both shall live," you were committing to a life-long process, not a once and done event.

What would you like to see God do in your marriage in the next 10, 20 or 30 years? Share some hopes and dreams with your spouse and listen to theirs. Get back to envisioning your future together and working as a team. There is no such thing as a perfect marriage. Like all couples, Colleen and I have had our share of struggles too. When we've been willing to be honest with each other and do the hard work of fulfilling those marriage vows, with God's help we've always found a renewed love and a new beginning for our life together, now celebrating 45 years and counting. I pray this same blessing for you!

Family

There's a direct correlation between the health of our marriage relationships and those with our children. Kids, no matter what their age, always have their antennae up regarding what's going on in the home, especially with mom and dad. If they sense stress or conflict, guess what they will manifest? If they sense loneliness, isolation and a lack of love, guess what they will internalize? A professor of "marriage and family" once bluntly called them "crap detectors." Our children can sense what's going on a mile away!

That's why these same Christ-like qualities of "forgiveness" and "unconditional love" must permeate the whole family system in order for there to be health and happiness. Parents, it isn't "what you say" nearly as much as "what you do" that will speak the loudest to your kids and grandkids. Take a moment and take stock right now. What is your current relationship like with your grown children, including son-in-laws and daughter-in-laws, as well as the next generation coming behind them? Are there hurts and wounds that need to be "mended?" Are there aspects of your relationships today that need to be "tended?"

> Parents, it isn't "what you say" nearly as much as "what you do" that will speak the loudest to your kids and grandkids.

One of the great crises of the Baby Boom generation has been the growing number of absentee fathers in society. We laid the foundation that has now become epidemic. Stats show that something like 8 or 9 out of 10 of those who are incarcerated today in our prisons did not grow up with a father in the home. As we raised our children the reason for neglect often had to do with our commitment to work and career. Fathers rationalized their absence in terms of a desire to build a better life for their kids than the one they experienced growing up. As more and more mothers also entered the workforce, childcare centers grew exponentially and children were often left in the arms of a surrogate for as many as 8-9 hours a day. Add to this the growing divorce rate in those years and we can understand why there is work to be done today to "mend" and "tend" in our families.

It's easy to look at our children as a group. I encourage you to consider their needs as individuals. When you know you've caused them pain, "fess-up" in humility and ask for forgiveness. Express your desire to move forward and build your relationship in a more loving, healthy way. If often takes time and patience but every ounce of effort is well worth it. If you need professional help, get it!

I have never met anyone who on their death-bed asked for someone to bring in their diplomas or trophies or bank statements. No! Everyone says, "Please get my family." That's who we want to surround us during our last days on Earth. If we want to go out in peace with "everything said that needs to be said," why not start now?

> *I have never met anyone who on their death-bed asked for someone to bring in their diplomas or trophies or bank statements. No! Everyone says, "Please get my family."*

With God's help, that which has been broken and missing can be forgiven and restored. There is no greater blessing than to experience love and unity in our families!

Extended Family

Do you know what breaks my heart? It's when I hear someone say, "Yeah, I haven't talked to my sister in years," or "My brother and I just don't get along," or "I'll never forgive my family for what they did when mom and dad passed away!" And yet, these responses are far too common. Was there really something in your parent's estate, including money, which was more important than your life-long relationship with your siblings? Is one wrong from the past worth spending the rest of your life mad? You can probably count 20!

In every extended family system there are unique individuals! That's a nice way of saying "hard to get along with, weird and even crazy." Still, the love of God compels us to love them and do our best to be a sincere Christian witness. Sometimes appropriate boundaries must be established to protect ourselves and others physically, emotionally and spiritually. Barring abuse, however, our calling is to work for love and peace in our extended families, loving even the unlovable. Why? Our families provide a training ground for doing the same with other relationships in this world.

Who is on your "extra grace required" list? Is your dislike of this individual a product of their personality or actions or an even deeper wound? What would it take on your part, or theirs, to begin to work towards reconciliation and healing? Will you take a first step and trust God to go with you? When we hang on to anger, bitterness and resentment, in the end we only hurt ourselves. We can't choose our families. They come with the territory. However, we can choose how we respond to them and the kind of relationship we would like to have with them. As you intentionally "mend" and "tend" my hope is that your extended family relationships will be full of love, peace and deep fellowship!

Friendships

What I've been describing is a series of relationships in life that are like concentric circles, with the one in the center permeating them all. That's your relationship with God. Next is your spouse, then your children, then your extended family and then your friends. If your relationship and time spent with friends is taking precedent over the others, trouble is on the horizon.

Friends come in lots of different categories these days. There are best friends, life-long friends, co-worker friends, neighborhood friends, hobby or club friends, church friends, Facebook friends and hundreds of others who are really acquaintances with whom you are friendly. The old saying goes, "If you want to have a friend you need to be a friend." Meaningful friendships take time and attention like any other relationship. They are like a garden that needs to be cultivated and watered if it's going to produce something of value. Take a few moments and just run through in your mind how your various friendships fit into the above categories of friends. Would you say that you have lots of friends or just a few? How much time do you devote to "mending" and "tending" to these various relationships?

Jesus had friends. We know of his 12 closest friends called disciples, including the inner circle of Peter, James and John. We read about others like John the Baptist, Mary Magdalene, Lazarus, Mary and Martha. We can only assume there were many more. Why? In **Matthew 11:19** it says: **"The Son of Man came eating and drinking, and they say, 'Here is a glutton and a drunkard, a friend of tax collectors and sinners.'"**

Perhaps this Bible verse led to the saying "You will be known by the company you keep." Jesus, however, didn't care about the rumors or accusations of others. He cared about people. That's why the night before He was crucified He said: **"I no longer call you servants, because a servant does not know his master's business. Instead, I have called you friends, for everything that I learned from my Father I have made known to you"** (John 15:15).

Therein lies one of the secrets of building lasting friendships. It's called transparency. When we are willing to share our lives with others we generally find that they will be willing to reciprocate by sharing their lives with us. Friendship requires vulnerability. Sometimes we get burned… but isn't true friendship worth the risk? Let me ask you another question accompanied by a hypothesis. How many great friends have you made and kept from the first 25 years of your life, the second 25, and since then? I would propose that you have new friendships to be made in your 4th quarter that will be every bit as special and valued as all the others.

> *When we are willing to share our lives with others we generally find that they will be willing to reciprocate by sharing their lives with us.*

According to my Facebook account I have hundreds of "friends." Which of these could I call in the middle of the night in a moment of real crisis? Maybe 2 or 3! As a pastor I'm also blessed with hundreds of relationships in the church and community, many of whom I would consider friends. And yet there are but a handful with whom I can completely bare my soul! In other words, real friends are a precious commodity! They require nurture and care.

We did a sermon series at Christ Church one time called "Text a Friend." I taught on friendship, beginning with our relationship with Jesus and then extending to others. In the middle of one service I had everybody pull out their cell phones and actually text a friend. Most messages were short and sweet. Others said something like, "Hi! I'm here at Christ Church this morning and the Lord brought you to mind. I want you to know that I love you and appreciate our friendship and am praying for you today!" Just imagine the impact? There were many reports of people being deeply touched.

I've learned that when someone comes to mind right out of the clear blue I accept it as a nudge from the Holy Spirit to give them a call, or send a text, or even arrange to get together. I've been amazed at how many times that person gets back and says, "Your note of encouragement came at just the right time. I am really dealing with something." There are lots of ways that we can "mend" and "tend" friendships in our lives that share the love of Jesus. Just having one or two close friends in this world is a huge blessing. Identify the friends that are most important in your life and take a moment to let them know how much they are appreciated!

Enemies

Yes, Jesus was a "friend of sinners." We all fall into that category but so did those who were his enemies, even those who hung him on the cross. Among the most revolutionary of Jesus' teaching was the fact that we are to love our enemies. Imagine for a moment the crowds of people who had followed Jesus from Galilee, the Decapolis,

Jerusalem, Judea and the region of the Jordan and were now seated before Him on a hillside for what we know as the Sermon on the Mount. Well into His message Jesus declared:

"You have heard that it was said, 'Love your neighbor and hate your enemy.' But I tell you, love your enemies and pray for those who persecute you, that you may be children of your Father in heaven. He causes his sun to rise on the evil and the good, and sends rain on the righteous and the unrighteous. If you love those who love you, what reward will you get? Are not even the tax collectors doing that? And if you greet only your own people, what are you doing more than others? Even the pagans do that. Be perfect, therefore, as your heavenly Father is perfect" (Matthew 5:43-48).

None of us are perfect… but Jesus is lifting up the high standard of being a child of God. My paraphrase would be, "Loving those who love you is relatively easy. How about loving your enemies who hate you and want to destroy your life?" We all know what a tough challenge that is! In this politically charged environment today, it is in fact very easy to justify hating those who hate us. Pray for the President? No way! Pray for those who are such militant haters of America? How could I! Pray for those who support abortion right up until a baby is born? Impossible!

But what can change a human heart? Is it returning hatred towards those who hate us as Christians and the values we stand for… or is it the love of Jesus? We know the answer to that question. Now we need the strategy for accomplishing it. How do you "mend"

> But what can change a human heart? Is it returning hatred towards those who hate us as Christians and the values we stand for… or is it the love of Jesus?

a fence with someone who likes the fence? How do you "tend" to a relationship that doesn't exist? The clue comes in Jesus' words. The starting point is prayer! When we bring our enemies before the Lord in prayer He will not only work in their lives but in ours.

I'll speak more about it in Chapter 17 on the topic of "Share Your Faith."

When we begin with prayer for our enemies, our hearts will soften to the point where we can speak blessings over them instead of curses. In other words, we can begin to pray for what God wants to see happen in their lives. Next, God will give us a heart to build relationships even with people who are very different than us and with whom we vehemently disagree. In that context He will reveal not only their "felt needs" but their "deeper needs." That's when the Holy Spirit will open doors for us to respond to those needs with the love of Jesus and see answers to our prayers. It's only in this context that we can declare the Good News of Jesus and see it received by others. As my good friend, Pastor Jay Bunker once said: "You can't clean the fish before you catch them!" Even loving our enemies must be grounded in relationship. Just shouting at each other gets us nowhere!

Mend and Tend

At the beginning of this chapter I shared that my goal was to encourage you to reprioritize your relationships starting with your relationship with God. Then follows marriage, family, extended family, friends and even enemies. Most often "mending" requires forgiveness and reconciliation. Most often "tending" requires unconditional love and consistent effort. What are the next and most important steps for you? When we Baby Boomers are asked about what makes life most fulfilling, we nearly always answer, "family!" Friendships! Relationships! They all take work but oh the blessing of walking in fellowship with God and others!

Questions for Personal Reflection or Group Discussion:

1. If you are married, how would you describe the current season of your relationship? What are the blessings? What are the challenges?

2. On a scale of 1 to 10, 1 being poor and 10 being excellent, how would you rate your current relationships with your children and grandchildren? Which of them needs mending? Which of them needs tending? Next steps?

3. Is there a broken relationship in your extended family? Who or what caused it? What would it take to repair it?

4. What do you find to be the most challenging about Jesus' admonition to "love your enemies and pray for those who persecute you?"

CHAPTER 7

Go Deeper!

It was September of 1975. I was 22 years old when I walked into a Group Communication class at Bethel University and took my seat for the start of a new semester. The chairs were arranged in a circle around the outside of the room all facing the center. My eyes began to scan this new collection of classmates to see if I knew anybody. That's when I saw Colleen for the first time. I thought to myself, "What a cute girl! I've got to meet her and get to know her!" I did and I'm still enjoying getting to know her better all these years later.

I've used a pre-marriage resource called Prepare/Enrich[1] for many years as a tool for helping couples identify strengths and growth areas in their relationship as they prepare for married life. One of the statements in the survey under the "Marriage Expectations" category is this: "I believe I've already learned everything there is to know about my partner." Engaged couples get to react on a scale from 1-5, from strongly disagree to strongly agree, not only to this statement but 149 others. I've only had one future husband out of about 300 couples share that he thought he already knew everything there was to know about his future wife. I would love to have listened to their conversation on the way home!

Just as we know that couples must continue to learn and grow together in order to have loving and fulfilling marriages, we also intuitively know that we must do the same when it comes to our relationship with Jesus. The problem is that a lot of us only date Jesus. We call Him when we need a friend or companion, someone to make us look good to others, or when we have an emergency and need His help. In reality, though, our relationship with Jesus is only superficial. It's "user friendly" and we're the user.

There are also many of us who made a sincere commitment to Jesus once upon a time, probably as a child or young adult, but for a variety of reasons our relationship with Him has never grown deeper. When it comes to our faith, the farthest we got was a baptism certificate, a Sunday School pin for good attendance or a Confirmation celebration. No matter our age, there is so much more to learn and experience. For those who sense this calling to go deeper, what must we do?

> *The problem is that a lot of us only date Jesus.*

Know Him Better

This must have been an issue even during the first-century Church. In his letter to the Christians at Ephesus, the Apostle Paul encouraged them with these words: **"I have not stopped giving thanks for you, remembering you in my prayers. I keep asking that the God of our Lord Jesus Christ, the glorious Father, may give you the Spirit of wisdom and revelation, so that you may know him better" (Ephesians 1:16-17).**

To know Jesus better! He knows everything about you and still loves you. As a matter of fact He likes you. He calls you friend! Doesn't that make you want to get to know Him better too? It's never too late to go deeper in your relationship with your Savior! But how? Through religion? No. It's way more than that. Paul says that God has given us a "Spirit of wisdom and revelation" to help us. That is what's needed for us to get to know Jesus personally... to not just date Him but make a real commitment.

Fellow "Boomers!" For our generation to not only live fulfilling lives in these later years, but have the wisdom needed to leave a lasting legacy to the generations that are following us, we need our knowledge and experience saturated with revelation from God. We need Him to reveal truth in this day of such great confusion! We need the light to go on in our heads and hearts in order to understand what we believe and why we believe it. Only then will we really be able to break through!

Claim Amazing Grace

If you grew up around the Church you may remember your pastor beginning messages with this phrase: "Grace and peace to you from God our Father and from our Lord and Savior Jesus Christ." It's a compilation of the greeting offered at the beginning of many of our New Testament books. When it comes to pursuing a deeper relationship with Jesus, grace is always the best place to start. Grace is a word that means "the unmerited love and favor of God." An old pastor friend once gave me this acronym for GRACE: "God's Riches at Christ's Expense."

If you Google "most popular hymns," Amazing Grace, is always in the Top 5 all-time. Did you ever ask yourself, "What is grace and why is it so amazing?" Did you ever think that identifying yourself as a "wretch" that needed saving was just a little over the top? There's a back story! The year was 1748. John Newton, the author of Amazing Grace, was only 22 years old when a storm in the North Atlantic Sea hit his sailing ship called the Greyhound and nearly took his life. The ship's captain had shouted, "We're sinking! All hands on deck!" Newton had leaped from the bunk where he had been sleeping and scrambled to the upper deck without even stopping to put on his heavier clothes.

Just as he did, one of his ship-mates was swept overboard by a huge wave. Seconds later the main mast on the ship split and the hull began to take on water. The ship tossed and rolled and Newton believed they were about to sink. He and the other men continued pumping water in vain. It seemed they were all headed for a burial at sea, including their cargo below. No! It wasn't gold or silver or spices from the Far East. This was a slave ship, and John Newton, even at his young age, was already one of the most notorious slave traders of his time.

The ship traveled from England to Africa to the West Indies and back again, exchanging trinkets, spices, rifles and other merchandise for black slaves. John Newton was a rebel and an exile from the British Royal Navy. He was a proud, arrogant and self-proclaimed atheist whose foul language and total disregard for morality were already legendary. Even human beings were nothing more than a commodity to him.

After this long night of staring death in the face, at one point Newton shouted to the Captain, "If our efforts will not due, then Lord have mercy on us." The Captain was amazed to hear such words coming out of Newton's mouth and John himself realized that he had just unintentionally uttered a prayer. He thought, "If there is a God, what mercy could there possibly be for me? What mercy?"

They survived the storm and this experience began a faith journey that ultimately transformed John Newton's life from an immoral, unbelieving slave trader to a committed follower of Jesus Christ. Thirty years later, during the height of the Revolutionary War in America, he would serve as the pastor of a congregation in an English town called Olney, and one night, write the hymn Amazing Grace for their evening prayer service. "Amazing Grace, how sweet the sound, that saved a wretch like me. I once was lost, but now am found, was blind but now I see."

What makes grace so amazing? In reality we are all like John Newton. Only God can save us from ourselves, our sins and the storms of life. God does it by the merit earned on our behalf through the death and resurrection of his Son, Jesus. In **Ephesians 2:8-9** it says: **"For it is by grace you have been saved, through faith – and this is not from yourselves, it is the gift of God, not by works, so that no one can boast."**

To truly grow deeper in our relationship with Jesus we must claim the gift of amazing grace. We can't earn it and we don't deserve it. It is the free gift of God for all who believe and receive Jesus as their Savior. Grace is mentioned 114 times in the Bible. As much as these passages remind us that

> *"Amazing Grace, how sweet the sound, that saved a wretch like me. I once was lost, but now am found, was blind but now I see."*

we are "saved by grace," they also encourage us to "live by grace." Maybe you've been carrying the pain and guilt of a past life, one when you were far from God. Let Him take it now so that those memories no longer have any power to hold you. It's only when we live "by grace through faith" that we can truly conquer the sin in our lives, both past and present.

Be on Guard for the Sin Deception

Sin is often described as "missing the mark," like an archer missing the bullseye on his target. I had a recurved bow when I was a kid. Now I have a nice compound bow that I don't shoot nearly as much as I would like. I'm not a hunter unless you count the neighborhood cats. Just kidding! Do you know what a "Robin Hood" is in archery? It's when you intentionally split a wooden arrow already on the target with another arrow shot from the same spot.

Some like to split hairs when it comes to sin. In other words, make a lot of excuses for it. When we're honest we can't deny that at the heart of every sin is rebellion against God. We want to do life our way! This is what keeps us from growing deeper. Sin is more than just breaking a commandment. It's a condition that has a hold on our very lives from which only Jesus can set us free.

> *When we're honest we can't deny that at the heart of every sin is rebellion against God. We want to do life our way!*

We can sin in thought, word and deed, not only by what we say and do

87

but also by what we don't say and don't do. If someone is trapped in an abusive marriage and we don't help them find a way to be safe, we are in essence supporting the abuse. If a family member is stuck in addiction and we don't arrange an intervention to get them help, we are really co-dependent in their addiction. If an injustice is taking place in our community or our workplace and we don't speak up about it, we are complicit in the injustice. This may sound harsh, but a Christian worldview doesn't allow us to sit passively on the sidelines. We have to be engaged in our daily interactions with people and for the broader sake of the world. No excuses. Sin is both thinking and acting outside the will of God.

Why is sin so pervasive in our lives today, even the lives of those who confess Jesus as their Savior? The Bible actually has a lot to say about it.

First, we are ignorant.

Ephesians 4:17-18 says: **"So I tell you this, and insist on it in the Lord, that you must no longer live as the gentiles do, in the futility of their minds. They are darkened in their understanding and separated from the life of God because of the ignorance that is in them due to the hardening of their hearts."**

When we harden our hearts and turn away in rebellion against the things of God we inherit futility and ignorance. Futility is frustration. Ignorance is darkness. Jesus, the light of the world, has been rejected. The light of His truth and wisdom can no longer penetrate our stubbornness and we effectively cut ourselves off from His wisdom and blessings.

Second, we are deceived.

Romans 16:17-18 says: **"I urge you, brothers and sisters, to watch out for those who cause divisions and put obstacles in your way that are contrary to the teaching you have learned. Keep away from them. For such people are not serving our Lord Christ, but their own appetites. By smooth talk and flattery they deceive the minds of naïve people."**

Any false or misleading teaching becomes a stumbling block to our growth both as human beings and as Christians. It may tickle our ears for a time… but if all we're looking for is somebody to flatter us we will become even more susceptible to manipulation and lies.

Third, we develop the wrong priorities.

Philippians 3:18-19 says: **"For, as I have often told you before and now tell you again even with tears, many live as enemies of the cross of Christ. Their destiny is destruction, their god is their stomach, and their glory is in their shame. Their mind is set on earthly things."**

I understand that "stomach part" having grown up in a family where food and love were very close to the same thing. But seriously, if we choose to live as enemies of the cross rather than friends, life can get out of whack in a hurry. We trade a destiny of blessing for one of destruction. Think the "seven deadly sins."

Fourth, we develop a religious spirit.

2 Timothy 3:1-5 really tells it like it is. This admonition could have been written this week rather than 2,000 years ago. **"But mark this: There will be terrible times in the last days. People will be lovers of money, boastful, proud, abusive, disobedient, unholy, without love, unforgiving, slanderous, without self-control, brutal, not lovers of the good, treacherous, rash, conceited, lovers of pleasure rather than lovers of God – having a form of godliness but denying its power. Have nothing to do with such people."**

> But seriously, if we choose to live as enemies of the cross rather than friends, life can get out of whack in a hurry.

What is a religious spirit? Its definition is found there in the second to the last sentence of this text. It's having "a form of godliness but denying its power." It's acting religious on the outside but being far from God on the inside. It's religion without relationship. It's like the time that Jesus chastised the religious leaders of His day when He said, **"Woe to you, teachers of the law and Pharisees, you hypocrites! You are like whitewashed tombs, which look beautiful on the outside but on the inside are full of the bones of the dead and everything unclean"** (Matthew 23:27). He wasn't pulling any punches and I can't help but think that if Jesus were visiting many of our churches today He might very well preach the same sermon!

And fifth, we become blinded.

In **2 Corinthians 4:4** we read: **"The god of this age has blinded the minds of unbelievers, so that they cannot see the light of the gospel that displays the glory of Christ, who is the image of God."**

It's the difference between having physical sight and spiritual insight. Satan's goal is to have us go through life deceived by the things of this world and blinded to the truth of Jesus and its implication for the choices we make. Paul knew firsthand! Remember the scales on his eyes?

I hope these verses have provided some helpful perspective on why so many of us continue to struggle with sin at the expense of going deeper with God. To put it bluntly, but no more than the scriptures, we are ignorant and deceived. We've adopted wrong priorities and religious spirits. The values and temptations of this world have caused us to become blind to the things of God. Sin is at the root. In one way or another we have all missed the mark of God's intentions for our lives. The good news is that through Jesus there is not only forgiveness and the promise of eternal life… but there is help available right now for us to re-prioritize and re-engage.

Re-Visit the Great I AM

When God spoke to Moses from a burning bush and called him to lead the Israelites out of slavery in Egypt, Moses asked:

"Suppose I go to the Israelites and say to them, 'The God of your fathers has sent me to you,' and they ask me, "What is his name?" Then what should I tell them?' God said to Moses, 'I AM who I AM.' This is what you are to say to the Israelites: 'I AM has sent me to you'" (Exodus 3:13-14).

During His three years of public ministry, Jesus made 7 different "I AM" statements that are all recorded in the Gospel of John. Do you recognize these well-known descriptions <u>of</u> Jesus and <u>by</u> Jesus? Each one of them reinforces Jesus' claim to be the Son of God and the Savior of the world.

- **John 6:35 "I am the bread of life."**
- **John 8:12 "I am the light of the world."**
- **John 10:7 "I am the gate for the sheep."**
- **John 10:11 "I am the good shepherd."**
- **John 11:25 "I am the resurrection and the life."**
- **John 14:6 "I am the way and the truth and the life."**
- **John 15:1 "I am the true vine."**

These statements got Jesus into a lot of trouble with the religious leaders of His day because of the historical and religious significance of the phrase, "I AM." In making these statements Jesus was unequivocally declaring Himself to be the Messiah, the promised one of God. Jesus not only claimed that His message was from God but that He pre-existed with God before all time. In **John 8:58-59** we read: **"'I tell you the truth,' Jesus answered, 'before Abraham was born, I am!' At this, they picked up stones to stone him, but Jesus hid himself, slipping away from the temple grounds."**

> *Jesus was unequivocally declaring Himself to be the Messiah, the promised one of God.*

If we are to grow deeper in our relationship with Jesus would it not be helpful to re-visit these "I AM" statements and decide if we believe them to be true for us? If He is "the way and the truth and the life," we can do some soul searching and ask, "Is Jesus *my* way and *my* truth and *my* life?" If so, then Jesus is more than worthy of our life-long quest to "Know Him better." The Bible will show us the way!

Re-Discover the Owner's Manual for Life

My good friend, Scott Powell, is the owner of Cornerstone Auto in Elk River, Minnesota. He has several other car dealerships scattered around the Twin Cities. Scott is a dedicated Christian businessman and has found a unique way of being a witness to his customers. Cornerstone places a small Bible in the glove compartment of every car they sell. When the new owner comes in for delivery of their vehicle the salesman will pull out the owner's manual and make sure they understand all of the car's features. Then they will say, "We have another owner's manual we'd like to give you as a gift. We call it the 'owner's manual for life,'" and they present the Bible. The response has been amazing with very few exceptions.

If we are going to "go deeper" with Jesus we all need to "dig deeper" into the Bible, the inspired Word of God. In **Psalm 119:105** it says: **"Your word is a lamp for my feet, a light on my path."** When Colleen and I are camping I often use one of those head-lamps with elastic straps. What a difference it makes to have light on your path if you are walking in the dark. What a difference it also makes to have light on your path when you are trying to live for Jesus. This is what God's Word provides.

Friends, the Bible is far more than a book of rules. It tells the story of God's amazing love for the world and everyone in it. Its most important verse is **John 3:16**. We read: **"For God so loved the world that he gave his one and only Son, that whoever believes in him shall not perish but have eternal life."** I call this The Great Promise. It is the message of salvation encapsulated in one beautiful sentence.

In Matthew 22, one of the religious leaders of Jesus' day asked Him to name the greatest commandment. Jesus highlighted two. He said: **"'Love the Lord your God with all your heart and with all your soul and with all your mind.' This is the first and greatest commandment. And the second is like it: 'Love your neighbor as yourself'" (Matthew 22:37-39).** These verses are often referred to as The Great Commandment. For those of us seeking to "go deeper" they provide the train tracks of life. Love God and love others, starting with yourself. When we make this our goal we will never get too far off track!

And then in **Matthew 28:18-20** we get our marching orders. Just before his ascension to heaven Jesus gathered His disciples together and said: **"All authority in heaven and on earth has been given to me. Therefore go and make disciples of all nations, baptizing them in the name of the Father and of the Son and of the Holy Spirit, teaching them to obey everything I have commanded you. And surely I am with you always, to the very end of the age."** These verses are called The Great Commission. We go as witnesses but we don't go alone. We go with the authority, message, power and presence of Jesus.

God's Word is alive and active. When the Holy Spirit illuminates it, it will equip us for every good work we have been called to do in Jesus' name. The Bible invites us to go deep and discover more and more of Jesus, the "bread of life." Fast food won't do!

Avoid Drive-Through Christianity

During the Covid years all churches got creative about delivering their product, namely inspiring worship and relevant messages that communicated the Gospel of Jesus Christ. Nearly everyone offered online worship services through Facebook Live or YouTube. This technological leap for Christianity not only met the needs of homebound church members but became a vehicle of outreach to the community and beyond.

The challenge now has been getting people to come back! Many have found that they like worshipping in their pajamas over breakfast. My grandma used to call them "bed-side Baptists." I think the term applies to all denominations today. One time a mother called for her son to get out of bed and get ready for church. He said, "Mom! I'm tired! I don't want to go to church today!" She said, "Don't give me that business! You get up and get ready right now! We're leaving

> *Many have found that they like worshipping in their pajamas over breakfast. My grandma used to call them "bed-side Baptists."*

93

together in 30 minutes!" Her son rolled over and pulled the covers over his head with another huge sigh. His mother said, "And besides, you're the pastor and people are expecting you to be there!"

Someone suggested that a good intermediary step to draw people back to corporate worship might be to add a drive-through window to the side of our church facility. After all, this has been a "fast food" world since we "Boomers" were kids! A friendly server trained in hospitality would say, "Good morning and welcome to the Christ Church drive-through. May I take your order?"

The person in the car would respond, "Good morning! Yes, I'd like four donuts, two coffees, two juices, a sermon lite, two children's messages including the coloring pages, two Holy Communions, one short group prayer and hold the offering please." The host would respond, "Coming right up! Can I interest you in a service opportunity as well? We have several specials today!" The person in the car would say, "No thanks. Super busy time in my life right now." And off they would go. Another happy customer.

There isn't much that can't be picked-up at a drive-through window these days ranging from burgers to chicken, coffee to ice cream and groceries to prescriptions. Why not a weekly worship service with all the bells and whistles? Catholic congregations could even offer an incense option. This may seem far-fetched but it is essentially how many Christians view their faith commitment today. Take what you need and keep moving!

Do you agree? Fast food is good... but not so good when you make it your steady diet. There is a more helpful path. If the Baby Boom generation is going to leave a lasting legacy of spiritual health, not just physical wealth, we must re-engage with a local congregation of our choosing and sincerely model what a faithful Christian commitment looks like in every season of life. The next generations are watching; our families, friends, neighbors, coworkers and especially those who don't yet know Jesus.

The writer of the Book of Hebrews certainly understood the importance of congregational life, even in its most infant form. He challenged some of the very first believers: **"Let us hold unswervingly** to the hope we profess, for he who promised is faithful. And let us consider how we may spur one another on toward love and good deeds, not giving up meeting together, as some are in the habit of doing, but encouraging one another – and all the more as you see the Day approaching" (Hebrews 10:23-25).

Who might God be calling you to "spur on" toward love and good deeds today? You may no longer be serving as the President or a Board Member of your congregation but you can certainly encourage and counsel those who are. You may no longer be a key leader in the Women's Ministry but in what ways can you still encourage and mentor the younger women and moms in your local fellowship? You may no longer be leading a high school small group but how can you still acknowledge and affirm the youth in your church and offer your wisdom and support along the way?

Have we mistakenly come to think that active involvement in a local church is just meant for those who are younger than 65? Can you retire from the church just like you do from a career? The reality is that the Christian Church needs us "Boomers" today… our life experience, service, mentoring, encouragement, witness and financial support. If we abandon the family of God during our 4th quarter the game may well be lost. Let me challenge you to get off the "fast food" circuit and become a great church member; not one who "use to be" but one who "is today." I think it's time for drive-through Christianity to come to an end! I will share more later about being the Church, the Ekklesia, outside the four walls.

> If we abandon the family of God during our 4th quarter the game may well be lost.

Experience the Manifest Presence of Jesus

For most of my life I knew that the continent of Africa existed… but it seemed so far away. I had learned about it in geography and history classes. I knew the names of the leaders of several African countries and the political situation in places like South Africa. Finally, in my 50s I was able to visit Africa not once but four times. The tiny country of Rwanda was where Africa became manifest to me; real, visible, personal. And not just in a general sense but as I put my arms around two young children named Simon and Joselyn who Colleen and I would sponsor through World Vision for the next dozen years.

The definition of Manifest includes "… to be seen clearly, to be understood, to be displayed, to be made evident and experienced in a personal way." Isn't this what we all want when it comes to our relationship with Jesus? True seekers of God, true Christians don't just want to know about Jesus. We want to know Him personally. We want to experience His "manifest presence."

A.W. Tozer, in his classic book, "Experiencing the Presence of God" writes: "Within every human breast rages this desire, driving him forward. Many a person confuses the object of that desire and spends his or her entire life striving for the unobtainable. Very simply put, the great passion in the heart of every human being, who are created in the image of God, is to experience the awesome majesty of God's presence. The highest accomplishment of humanity is entering the overwhelming presence of God. Nothing else can satiate this burning thirst."[2]

The Psalms have a wonderful way of communicating this desire for a deep, personal relationship with God. **Psalm 16:11**, for example, says: **"You made known to me the path of life, in your presence there is fullness of joy; at your right hand there are pleasures forever more."** We can also see this longing described in **Psalm 42:1-2a. "As the deer pants for streams of water, so my soul pants for you, my God? My soul thirsts for God, for the living God."** How do we experience the manifest presence of Jesus? We allow Him to come close and put His arms around us.

I have a friend named Rosie Elizondo. She's a grandma, a prayer warrior and a wonderful Christian woman who really has a heart for lost souls. About a year ago Rosie moved to St. Cloud, Minnesota to help a young couple who had a child and were really struggling. Their little girl is now almost three years old and her name is Shaylin. She's a beautiful, loving, sweet little girl.

Their apartment complex is right next to a large city park. Almost everyone living in this area is Muslim and African American. It's a high crime area but Rosie has claimed it as her mission field. She often takes Shaylin to the park to play, and in the process, has befriended several Muslim women. One day she noticed a young girl, about 12 years old, sitting all by herself on the steps to the slide looking very down and discouraged. She wasn't crying but was definitely struggling. No one was talking to her. Shaylin was climbing up the steps and going down the slide over and over again as children will do, right past this young girl.

At one point little Shaylin noticed how sad this girl looked. She stopped and sat down on the step just above her on the slide. She just sat there but the girl didn't turn to look at her or say anything so Shaylin slid down a step and sat right next to her. Still there was no response. Next, something quite remarkable happened. Shaylin, not yet three years old, snuggled in to this young girl, laid her head on her chest, and said sympathetically, "Ooooh."

Rosie watched this in amazement. Now this girl had to react. She looked up at Rosie as if to say, "What should I do?" Rosie said, "I think she wants you to hug her." Slowly the older girl put her arms around Shaylin and hugged her and immediately her countenance began to change. You could see it in her eyes. Her sadness turned to love as she hugged this little girl who in that moment had become for her the "manifest presence of Jesus."

You see, that's what God does for us. He meets us right where we're at. He draws near but He's not pushy. God comes down to our level and snuggles in, and if we will respond and put our arms around Him, everything will change. That is the "manifest presence of Jesus." When we invite Him to come closer to us that's when we are able to go deeper in our relationship with Him. That's when real growth begins!

> God comes down to our level and snuggles in, and if we will respond and put our arms around Him, everything will change.

Know That the Father Goes With You

In this lifelong process of spiritual growth it is so important to know that God our Father goes with us. No matter what difficult situation or challenge we are facing, we're never alone. One Native American tribe had a unique way of training its young "braves." On the day of a young man's 13th birthday he was blindfolded and taken on horseback miles away to a dense forest to spend the entire night alone. Until then he may have never been away from the security of his family, village and tribe.

When he was left alone and took off his blindfold he found himself in the dark in the middle of thick woods with no weapon or provisions and a long night ahead. With every twig that snapped he visualized a wild animal ready to pounce. Every time the wind blew he wondered if evil spirits were coming his way. This was a terrifying test for many a young man who felt far less than the "brave" he was meant to be.

One boy described his experience. "After what seemed like an eternity, the first rays of sunlight entered the interior of the forest. As I woke from a restless sleep I stood to my feet and looked around. I saw trees and wild flowers and the outline of a path. Then to my utter astonishment I saw the figure of a man standing some distance away armed with a bow and arrow. It was my father. I realized that he had been there all night long protecting me from unseen dangers."

And friends, this is how our Heavenly Father works. We might not be able to see Him with our eyes but He is with us at all times, protecting us, loving us and enabling us to face life's most difficult obstacles with confidence. Through faith in God we know that we are never alone. Like King David, we can say: **"The Lord is with me; I will not be afraid" (Psalm 118:6).**

Grow Until That Day

Our calling is to keep growing deeper with God in every season of life. We know very little about Jesus' early life. It starts, of course, with the Christmas story of His humble birth in a barn in Bethlehem. We know that Mary and Joseph were warned by an angel to flee to Egypt because Herod was killing all the babies 2 years of age or younger in that region out of paranoia of this "newborn king." We know that after two years they returned to their hometown of Nazareth where Jesus grew up.

After that we have just one story when Jesus was 12 years old and went with His family to Jerusalem for Passover. His parents had travelled a day's journey on the way home before they realized that Jesus wasn't with them. They went back to Jerusalem and after three days of being worried sick they found Him sitting among the teachers in the temple courts, listening to them and asking questions. The Bible says that everyone who heard Jesus was amazed at His understanding of scripture and the answers He gave.

Somewhat upset, Mary said to Him: **"'Son, why have you treated us like this? Your father and I have been anxiously searching for you' 'Why were you searching for me?' he asked. 'Didn't you know I had to be in my Father's house'" (Luke 2:48b-49)?** They didn't understand Jesus' response but left together for home. This story concludes with a statement that in effect covers the next 18 years of Jesus' life. It says: **"And Jesus grew in wisdom and stature, and in favor with God and man" (Luke 2:52).** The next account of His life takes place when He is 30 years old and goes to the Jordan River to be baptized by John.

Perhaps when we get to heaven we can ask Him, "What did you do for fun when you were 15 or 18? Who were your best friends? Did you travel anymore? Did you ever have thoughts of marriage? What did you and your dad specialize in making in your carpentry shop? What were your thoughts about your Heavenly Father during those growing up years? Were you conscious of who you were and what your calling was to be?" All fascinating things to wonder about!

Of this we can be sure! Jesus was growing during those years both physically, emotionally and spiritually and that never stopped. Every time Jesus studied the Word, God was teaching Him. Every time He prayed, God was downloading greater revelation. Every time He interacted with people, God was teaching Him more about the human condition. We will never fully understand this amazing intersection between the human and the divine but we see this hunger in Jesus' entire life and ministry to go deeper.

In the same way, God is preparing us for all that lays ahead. Oh the privilege of being His disciples! Friends, it's time to "get growing." Only then will we be equipped to "get going" and truly make a difference in this world! You can talk to Jesus right now. Say something like… "Jesus, I want more! I want to experience your manifest presence. I want your Spirit of wisdom and revelation to fall on me so that I can know you better, and as a result, understand my calling in this world in these later years of my life. I want to continue to grow in my relationship with you until I meet you face-to-face." Baby Boomers, let's get after it, you and me! Our Heavenly Father has been standing watch this whole time!

Questions for Personal Reflection or Group Discussion:

1. How have you personally experienced the grace of God in your life?
2. Which aspect of sin has most held you back in your relationship with Jesus? Has it been ignorance of the truth, the deception of the enemy, wrong priorities, a religious spirit or spiritual blindness? Where do you feel most stuck today?
3. In what ways are you guilty of "Drive-Through Christianity?" Is this approach helping you grow in your relationship with Jesus to the degree you would like? Is it time for a change?
4. What is a question you would like to ask Jesus someday? You can start right now!

Notes:

1. Prepare/Enrich, PO Box 130039, Roseville, MN 55113
2. A. W. Tozer, *Experiencing the Presence of God* (Ventura, CA: Regal Books, 2010), p. 17.

CHAPTER 8

Survive the Swirl!

I've often admired storm chasers, although perhaps like you, I think they're half nuts! I mean who in their right mind hears about a dangerous weather system dropping tornadoes and goes looking for them? Have you seen the vans they drive? They're like storm bunkers on wheels with an extraordinary array of high tech weather equipment on the roof. They remind me of the "Ghost Busters" vehicle, Ecto 1, but that was actually a converted '59 Cadillac Ambulance. Here's the thing, though. Most of us don't have to go looking for storms… or ghosts. They have a way of finding us!

A former Chaplain to our Minnesota State Legislature, Pastor Lonnie Titus, was sharing a message here at Christ Church one Sunday morning. He said something to this effect: "In my experience, people from all walks of life generally deal with some sort of significant crisis every three to four months." That seemed like a lot to me. I thought, "I guess I've been pretty blessed," but then I reflected further on his observation.

I think Pastor Lonnie is right. It's not at all unusual for the storms of life to hit us when we least expect them, like tornadoes suddenly dropping out of the sky. Sometimes we've heard the sirens and are prepared in our basements or shelters. At other times we're totally surprised and experience significant damage not only to our property but to our lives.

Here are some examples:

- A good friend from work is diagnosed with cancer.
- A loved one passes away unexpectedly.
- A perfect grandchild gets in trouble at school.
- A job is lost after a sudden lay-off at work.
- A marriage that you thought was happy suddenly ends in divorce.
- A beautiful home is destroyed by a fire.
- An unexpected medical bill sinks a retirement account.
- A leader we trust has an affair.
- A safe community erupts in violence.
- A war breaks out after peace negotiations break down.

These kinds of experiences in life are not the exception. They're the norm. Stuff happens… and none of us are exempt. I was on a Zoom Call one day with Steve Wilson, a good friend from Rochester, Minnesota, who leads an apostolic ministry called Isaiah 9:7. As we were getting ready to pray he said something that really struck me. He said, "We are living in the season of the swirl."

Indeed! Life is swirling all around us and it can cause us to feel totally out of control. What are you dealing with today? Does your life feel like it's swirling at times? Surveys show that Baby Boomers today are most concerned about four things; health, family, finances and world events. Let's look at each of these topics and then consider how we can survive the swirl and find peace in the midst of every storm.

Health and Wellness

My mom once told me, "Enjoy life in your 60s because when you hit 70 everything starts to fall apart!" An article by Scripps.org[1] published on September 28, 2021 lists the top ten health issues for Baby Boomers as Type 2 Diabetes, Heart Disease, Cancer, Alzheimer's Disease, Depression, "Sandwich Generation" stress, Arthritis and

Joint Replacement, Osteoporosis, Flu and Pneumonia, and Covid-19 (or the next virus or variant to come along).

What a lovely list! If you're a "Boomer" it's quite likely that you're dealing with several of these health concerns right now or certainly could name others who are. Couple this with rising health care costs, exorbitant prescription drug prices and the potential insolvability of government programs like Medicare and Medicaid, and this is definitely an area of "swirl" for our generation. Most of us know that if we eat healthy, stay active and avoid tobacco and excessive alcohol we can significantly lower our risk of developing chronic health conditions like those mentioned above. Questions persist, however. Will I stay healthy enough to enjoy travel, hobbies, family and independent living? Will I lose my eyesight, hearing or memory? Will my health insurance cover my medical costs? Will I be a burden to my kids someday?

One Sunday morning a pastor decided to use a visual demonstration to add some punch to his sermon emphasis. Four worms were placed into four separate glass jars. The first worm was put into a jar containing whiskey. The second worm was put into a jar of cigarette smoke. The third worm was put into a jar of chocolate syrup and the fourth worm into a jar of rich, clean, black dirt. At the conclusion of his message the minister reported the following results. The first worm in alcohol – dead. The second worm in cigarette smoke – dead. The third worm in chocolate syrup – dead but happy. The fourth worm in black dirt – alive and thriving! The pastor turned to his congregation and said, "What can we all learn from this demonstration?" An older lady in the back quickly raised her hand and said, "Pastor, I think it means that as long as you drink, smoke and eat chocolate, you won't get worms!"

As you can see there are a variety of approaches to consider when it comes to your health and wellness! The Apostle Paul suggests this one: **"Do you not know that your bodies are temples of the Holy Spirit, who is in you, whom you have received from God? You are not your own; you were bought with a price. Therefore honor God with your bodies" (1 Corinthians 6:19-20).**

Let's be honest. Some of us treat our bodies more like garbage disposals than temples. It may be a good time to re-examine our choices. The larger point made in these verses is that God is concerned about the whole package; body, soul and spirit. Each part of us impacts the other. The Apostle John alludes to this in his third letter addressed to a church elder named Gaius. He says: **"Dear friend, I pray that you may enjoy good health and that all may go well with you, even as your soul is getting along well"** (3 John 1:2). Are you getting along well? Are your body, soul and spirit in alignment with your goals for the remaining years of your life? Paul offers this great counsel. He concludes: **"So whether you eat or drink or whatever you do, do it all for the glory of God"** (1 Corinthians 10:31). Now that's a jar into which I'm willing to drop a worm!

> God is concerned about the whole package; body, soul and spirit. Each part of us impacts the other.

Family Pressures

A second major area of "swirl" for Baby Boomers is family. Many of us are members of "The Sandwich Generation." We may have grown up on bologna and cheese but this sandwich is different. We are the ones squeezed in the middle caring for both parents and children at the same time, and often grandchildren too. Our older loved ones may need more frequent calls, texts, assistance with shopping, bill paying, rides to appointments and emotional support. Loneliness is also huge, especially among those who have lost spouses and are now doing life alone. Having to make transitions in living situations can add one more layer of stress.

At the same time, our adult children often continue to need wise counsel, encouragement, occasional financial assistance, help with projects like house renovations, and of course, taking care of grandkids. My wife, Colleen, retired from teaching three years ago after a long career. At first there was just relief… but at the same time she missed her daily interaction with colleagues who had become dear friends over the years, as well as her First Graders. Several months later she went through a period of asking, "What next, Lord? How can I serve you now?" All of this while she was spending three days a week helping care for several of our youngest grandchildren. One day it dawned on her that for now this *is* her ministry! She has been enjoying her important role as Grandma more ever since.

As "Boomers" we take these responsibilities very seriously. We love and care in all these ways willingly even though they can take a toll on our own health, finances, relationship with our spouse and personal plans. In **Ephesians 6:1-3** Paul says: **"Children, obey your parents in the Lord, for this is right. 'Honor your father and mother' – which is the first commandment with a promise – 'so that it may go well with you and that you may enjoy long life on the earth.'"**

About 10 years ago the Lord really impressed this commitment on my heart. I sensed the Spirit saying, "For the rest of your parent's lives do everything you can to honor and serve them." I had always tried to be a faithful son… but I sensed the Holy Spirit calling me to take it up another notch. My dad Gary passed away in October of 2020 at the age of 88. My mom Betty is 89 and still living independently. What a blessing for me and my siblings to help care for them… having been cared for by them for so many years. They have created a wonderful legacy of faith and family for us all!

We tend to think of the words in **1 Corinthians 13:4-8a** as applying to marriage because that's where we've heard them repeated most often. Take a few moments and try filtering this portion of scripture called "the love chapter" through the situations you're dealing with in your own family or extended family right now. I think these famous verses will speak to you with even deeper meaning.

"Love is patient, love is kind. It does not envy, it does not boast, it is not proud. It does not dishonor others, it is not self-seeking, it is not easily angered, it keeps no record of wrongs. Love does not delight in evil but rejoices with the truth. It always protects, always trusts, always hopes, always perseveres. Love never fails."

You may find yourself staring down an extraordinarily challenging situation right now related to your loved ones on either side of the sandwich. When we love with the "Jesus love" described here we have the template we need for caring for others with humility and perseverance. I met a single mom recently, for example, who is working two jobs in order to care for her aging mother as well as a younger brother with epilepsy. Her stress level is through the roof. At a time in her life when she wished she could slow down a bit, her responsibilities simply won't allow it. The financial pressure is just too great, which is the next area of "swirl" for our generation.

Financial Security

Many "Boomers" have discovered they're simply not financially prepared for their 4th quarter of life. Financial security is a great source of stress. Traditional retirement income has been based on the so-called "three-legged stool" consisting of Social Security, private pensions and personal savings. The reality is that Social Security remains in jeopardy with only small annual increases at best. Private pensions have gone from being provided by most companies to being optional. Personal savings are not only historically low but subject to emergencies that can quickly wipe them out. That's why in order to supplement their various sources of income many seniors plan to work at least part-time well into their 70s.

> Traditional retirement income has been based on the so-called "three-legged stool" consisting of Social Security, private pensions and personal savings.

Expectations have changed too. Surveys show that most Baby Boomers hope to live-out their "retirement years" with the same standard of living they have enjoyed in their "working years." Financial planners counsel that this will require 60-80 percent of "pre-retirement" income. In other words, if a couple is making $100,000 per year during their "working years," they will need to make $60,000–$80,000 per year during their "retirement years" to maintain a similar standard of living, with annual adjustments for inflation. While many seniors do experience lower taxes, housing and living expenses, financial freedom represents a tall order when considering the possibility of 25 or more years of life yet to be lived.

In 2020, during the most difficult days of the Covid pandemic, it is estimated that nearly 30 million Baby Boomers were laid off, cut back to part-time, or chose to retire. During this season it became even clearer that companies today value tech skills more than experience. While many "Boomers" will be forced to go back to work because of financial pressures, it is unlikely that their previous positions will be available.

From a positive standpoint, the pandemic also caused older adults to reflect on what is really important to them and decide to pursue it. Many who were able have given up work and are now enjoying more time with family and friends, traveling, volunteering or just relaxing. Will the future allow it? As of 2022, inflation is at a 40-year high and economists are predicting a recession in 2023. It appears that financial security will continue to be a major area of swirl for "Boomers."

World Events

The fourth area that really causes stress for Baby Boomers is world events. While the younger generations are increasingly uninformed (watch some of the "person on the street" interviews), our generation has lived on news and likes to stay on top of things. With the myriad of 24-hour cable news shows available today ranging from FOX to CNN we are bombarded with one crisis after another. Reactions can range from concern to fear to anger to resignation. I consider myself to be a news junkie. I rationalize that as a pastor I need to know what's going on in the world, and of course, am always looking for great sermon illustrations.

I consider myself to be a news junkie.

Sometimes this desire to always be informed of local, national and world events works to my detriment. It can cause me to be overwhelmed and discouraged by the negative… and lose sight of the positive. Too much news can cause us to feel hopeless rather than hopeful, forgetting that God is still in charge and that good things are happening everywhere. The fact is that they are just not reported as much.

The pressing issues as of this writing include the Russian invasion of Ukraine, increasing threats from China, soaring inflation with the highest gas and grocery prices in history, illegal immigration at our southern border exceeding 2 million people per year, drug cartels, Fentanyl deaths, sex trafficking, Covid fall-out, exploding crime, debate over critical race and gender theory, political corruption, parental rights, economic policy, environmental policy, election integrity and more. Is your head swirling now!

As you are reading this chapter how many of these issues are still on the front burner? What world events and global crises have come along since? Nothing would indicate that this "season of the swirl" is going to end anytime soon related to these four major areas of concern for Baby Boomers; Health and Wellness, Family Pressures, Financial Security and World Events. Is there hope?

The Swirl of the Spirit

I have good news! The Holy Spirit is swirling too! Think back with me to the first Holy Week. The disciples' lives had been shattered when the one they believed to be the Messiah had been beaten, whipped, tried and crucified. Their faithfulness had been tested and found wanting. Their futures seemed uncertain in spite of all that Jesus had promised. The women had found an empty tomb that first Easter morning and a "bright as lightening" angel had announced that Jesus was alive!

Peter and John had confirmed their story. Later that day two of Jesus' followers had run back 7 miles from Emmaus to Jerusalem to tell the others how they had walked and talked with Jesus on the road but were kept from recognizing Him until they had broken bread together. It all seemed unbelievable. Their heads and hearts were swirling… and then Jesus showed up!

It may have been the same room where just four days earlier He had washed His disciples' feet and shared the meal we now call "The Lord's Supper." His first words on that Easter Sunday evening? **"Peace be with you" (Luke 24:36b)**. I'm guessing they had heard Him say it a thousand times before. Even so they were startled and frightened and thought they were seeing a ghost. Jesus responded: **"Why are you troubled, and why do doubts rise in your minds? Look at my hands and my feet. It is I myself! Touch me and see; a ghost does not have flesh and bones, as you see I have" (Luke 24:38-39).**

Just to prove it He ate a piece of fish. Apparently ghosts don't like fish! He explained again the necessity of His suffering and death and opened their minds to understand the scriptures. Even so, Jesus knew they needed more. He declared: **"You are witnesses of these things. I am going to send you what my Father has promised; but stay in the city until you have been clothed with power from on high" (Luke 24:48-49).**

What had His Father promised? It was the Holy Spirit (see John 15-16). The Greek word is *"paraclete."* It means "one who comes alongside." Jesus was saying, "Stay where you are until My Spirit has come alongside to counsel, comfort and empower you for the sake of being My witnesses to the world." That's why He counseled, "Wait for it!" The truth is that we can do a lot by our own strength… but to accomplish anything that will last we need the power of God flowing through us.

They waited for fifty days after the resurrection! Imagine these followers of Jesus, grown men and women, waiting in that upper room, talking, praying, laughing, reflecting, sharing meals, coming and going and wondering what would happen next. That's a long time to just hang out. I don't know many people who are good at waiting. I'm certainly not; not at waiting in line at the grocery store or in traffic on the freeway… or for Jesus to reveal what He's got up His sleeve next. After everything these disciples had seen and experienced I'm guessing they were getting pretty restless too.

The Jewish festival of Pentecost (Shavuot) was a feast of thanksgiving for the first fruits of the wheat harvest. This year it would become evidence of the first fruits of the resurrection, the outpouring of the Holy Spirit on all believers. This is how it happened.

> I don't know many people who are good at waiting. I'm certainly not; not at waiting in line at the grocery store or in traffic on the freeway… or for Jesus to reveal what He's got up His sleeve next.

"When the day of Pentecost came, they were all together in one place. Suddenly a sound like the blowing of a violent wind came from heaven and filled the whole house where they were sitting. They saw what seemed to be tongues of fire that separated and came to rest on each of them. All of them were filled with the Holy Spirit and began to speak in other tongues as the Spirit enabled them" (Acts 2:1-4).

Thus began a positive "season of the swirl" that continues to this day. Just as the Holy Spirit blew into the lungs of those first disciples and literally "fired them up" for their Calling as ambassadors for Christ, this same Spirit is available to fill us today. How do we survive the swirls that hit us hard? We do life by the power of the Holy Spirit, not the powers of this world!

The effect was immediate. Peter, the same disciple who had denied Jesus three times the night before his crucifixion, stood in the market square of Jerusalem that day and preached what could rightly be called the first Christian sermon. His three-points? "Jesus is the Messiah! You killed Him! God raised Him from the dead!"

The response of the crowd resulted in one of my favorite quotes in the Bible. In **Acts 2:37** it says: **"When the people heard this, they were cut to the heart and said to Peter and the other disciples, 'Brothers, what shall we do?'"**

To be "cut to the heart" means that the message Peter shared really got through to them. When the Word of God is boldly proclaimed and energized by the Holy Spirit this should always be the result. Peter was a man of action. He responded to their question: **"Repent and be baptized, every one of you, in the name of Jesus Christ for the forgiveness of your sins. And you will receive the gift of the Holy Spirit. This promise is for you and your children and for all who are far off – for all whom the Lord our God will call" (Acts 2:38-39).**

Who qualifies for forgiveness and the in-filling of the Holy Spirit? This promise is good for everyone who believes… even that person you might consider to be far from the Lord… even if that person is you. God doesn't want anyone to miss out on His gifts? Something amazing happened on that first Christian version of Pentecost. Three thousand people believed and were baptized and the Christian Church was born! This same Holy Spirit is available to fill us personally and energize the Church today and every believer who is a part of it. I'm going to suggest four imperatives that we must embrace if we're going to overcome our challenges and not only survive, but thrive! First…

God doesn't want anyone to miss out on His gifts?

We Must Wake Up

Prophets of old like Isaiah challenged the Israelites with exhortations like: **"Awake, awake! Rise up, Jerusalem… (Isaiah 51:17a)** and **"Arise, shine, for your light has come, and the glory of the Lord rises upon you" (Isaiah 60:1).**

The Apostle Paul echoes these verses when he says: **"Wake up, sleeper, rise from the dead, and Christ will shine on you. Be careful, then, how you live, not as unwise but as wise, making the most of every opportunity, because the days are evil" (Ephesians 5:14-16).**

The phrase, "Be careful, then, how you live," jumps out to me as both an admonition and a word of encouragement for those of us in the Baby Boom generation. Let's be honest with ourselves. If we're going to live out the rest of our days with purpose and passion we really do need to "wake up" and allow the light of Christ to shine both on us and through us. This is a word for all who are followers of Jesus and it has no expiration date!

My Grandpa, Hiram Ford, farmed until his late 80s. He had this amazing ability to take 5 minute naps and wake up totally refreshed. To this day I will say, "I need a little Grandpa Ford snooze." The problem is I don't always wake up after 5 minutes! When it comes to our world today we can't afford to fall asleep any longer. It is only when we wake up to God's plans and purposes that we will be motivated to live the rest of our lives accordingly. Only then will we feel an urgency to make wise choices with our time and the most of every opportunity. Only then will we recognize the real challenges we're facing and apply every ounce of our talent, resources and energy to overcome them. Second…

We Must Partner Up

Life isn't meant to be lived alone. If we're going to survive "the season of the swirl" we all need partners with whom to share the journey. Elijah had Elisha. David had Jonathan. Ruth had Naomi. Paul had Silas. Mary had Martha. Jesus had Peter, James and John. Here are some other famous partnerships you may recall. The Lone Ranger had Tonto. Batman had Robin. Lucy had Ethel. Fred had Barney. Captain Kirk had Mr. Spock, Maxwell Smart had Agent 99. Fred had Ginger. Johnny had Ed. You get the idea. Teamwork wins the day! What partners come to mind for you?

We all need encouragers. We all need people in our lives who will love us unconditionally, celebrate the good times, hang-in there with us during the challenging times and hold us accountable when we get off track. These partners may include parents, siblings, spouses, friends, mentors, work associates, small group members, bosses, boards and more. Some relationships are more formal. Others more casual. Each relationship is only as meaningful and helpful as we allow it to be.

In **Ecclesiastes 4:9-12** it says: **"Two are better than one, because they have a good return for their labor. If either of them falls down, one can help the other up. But pity anyone who falls and has no one to help them up. Also, if two lie down together, they will keep warm. But how can one keep warm alone? Though one may be overpowered, two can defend themselves. A cord of three strands is not quickly broken."**

Isn't it true? We all desire a good return for our labor. We all need others to pick us up when we fall. When we experience loneliness we need the love of others to keep us warm. When we are overpowered by our enemies, real or imagined, we need a partner to help us stand up and fight. The "cord of three strands" mentioned in these verses is often related to marriage; husband, wife and God woven together in a relationship that is not easily broken. What a beautiful description these verses also provide of the power of partnership when God is at the center.

If you're in a tough place right now, don't go it alone. Share your struggle with someone else. Ask for help. Find a friend who will "talk it through" and then "walk it though" with you. Remember, two are better than one! Third…

We Must Armor Up

Our battle is about more than just earthly challenges and daily pressures. This "season of the swirl" also has to do with unseen spiritual forces that are warring against us.

In **Ephesians 6:10-13** the Apostle Paul makes this clear when he says: **"Finally, be strong in the Lord and in his mighty power. Put on the full armor of God, so that you can take your stand against the devil's schemes. For our struggle is not against flesh** and blood, but against the rulers, against the authorities, against the powers of this dark world and against the spiritual forces of evil in the heavenly realms. Therefore put on the full armor of God, so that when the day of evil comes, you may be able to stand your ground, and after you have done everything, to stand."

The devil is a schemer. Other passages in the Bible refer to him as a deceiver and the father of lies. I think that Paul wanted the first Christians to know that there is more going on in this world than what we can see with our own eyes. I think he wants us to know it too. This passage doesn't say "sit back and wait for Jesus to rescue you." It says, "put on the armor of God and take your stand!"

First, our strength is in the Lord, which highlights the importance of having a personal relationship with Jesus. Second, that strength comes from His mighty power, which is nothing less than the resurrection power we've been given as His disciples. And third, we must put on the full armor of God in order to overcome evil and win the day. Would a soldier go into battle without his helmet or gun? Would a police officer go on shift without her Kevlar vest? Why would we ever take on forces of evil without the protective equipment God has given us? Paul continues:

"Stand firm then, with the belt of truth buckled around your waist, with the breastplate of righteousness in place, and with your feet fitted with the readiness that comes from the gospel of peace. In addition to all this, take up the shield of faith, with which you can extinguish all the flaming arrows of the evil one. Take the helmet of salvation and the sword of the Spirit, which is the word of God. And pray in the Spirit on all occasions with all kinds of prayers and requests. With this in mind, be alert and always keep on praying for all the Lord's people (Ephesians 5:14-18).

> Would a soldier go into battle without his helmet or gun? Would a police officer go on shift without her Kevlar vest?

What does your spiritual armor consist of? Look again! You will see truth, righteousness, peace, faith, salvation, the Spirit, the Word of God and prayer. Not a bad requisition list for any spiritual soldier! And also note, this passage takes us back to where we began. Paul counsels, "Be alert."

Over the years I've seen the most collateral damage done to Christians when they try to live the Christian life by their own strength, unaware of spiritual warfare and unequipped to do battle for things that matter. The devil is quite content, I think, to leave us alone when this is our approach to life. We are more than capable of messing things up ourselves. On the other hand, when we get serious about living for Jesus and making a real difference in this world, we become a target. That's when we must "be strong in the Lord and in his mighty power." Have you put on the full armor of God? Your future well-being depends on it! Fourth…

We Must Step Up

One of the questions that is at the heart of this book and its challenge to Baby Boomers is, "Will we rise-up or just ride it out during this final season of our lives?" We have "stepped-up" to every challenge in the past. I believe we will do it again. First, we must wake up and see the world as it really is. Second, we must partner up and determine not to go it alone. Third, we must armor up in order to defeat both the seen and unseen forces seeking to deceive and destroy. Only then will we be equipped to step-up to every challenge, both today and in these years to come.

Many of us can think back to the day or season when God first called us to come and follow. That call isn't a once and done. Every challenge we face in life is like a fork in the road. We can choose which way we will go… or if we will go at all. Many of us are at that decision point today. Will we go forward in faith or shrink back in fear? Will we cling to our possessions or discover the joy of generosity? Will we choose the path of comfort and convenience or risk a new adventure? Will we operate by our own strength and ability or learn to walk in resurrection power?

The Apostle Peter declares: **"Dear friends, do not be surprised at the fiery ordeal that has come on you to test you, as though something strange were happening to you. But rejoice inasmuch as you participate in the sufferings of Christ, so that you may be overjoyed when his glory is revealed" (1 Peter 4:12-13).**

This is "The Season of the Swirl." Many a fiery ordeal has come to test us, but take heart! The Spirit of the Living God is swirling too! His glory is being revealed for the whole world to

Many of us can think back to the day or season when God first called us to come and follow. That call isn't a once and done.

see. Come to Him and experience your personal Pentecost. His Spirit will bring a new spark to your life and a fire in your soul that will light up the world!

Questions for Personal Reflection or Group Discussion:

1. What major area of "swirl" is stressing you out the most these days: Health and Wellness, Family Pressures, Financial Security or World Events? Other? Ask yourself why?
2. What has been your understanding or experience of the Holy Spirit?
3. Beyond your spouse, who are your partners in life? Who do you turn to for questions, support and accountability?
4. Describe an area in your life or specific situation where you sense God calling you to "step up."

Notes:

1. *"10 Top Health Concerns for Baby Boomers,"* (Scripps.org, September 28, 2021)

CHAPTER 9

Challenge the ISMs!

O ur world is deeply divided. The list of divisions is extensive and often subject to great hyperbole by those in the media. Conflict sells. I contend that as human beings we have far more in common than what divides us. Bring a dozen reasonable people into the same room for a conversation and there will be a significant number of shared values related to family, faith, work, hobbies, hopes and dreams.

Instead, we are constantly told that our society is irreparably divided into black vs. white, brown vs. yellow, male vs. female, rich vs. poor, young vs. old, gay vs. straight, owners vs. workers, conservatives vs. liberals, evangelicals vs. mainliners, privileged vs. underprivileged, democratic vs. autocratic. We become so convinced that these dichotomies are intractable that we find it difficult to even have an honest conversation about them. Could there be something even deeper at the root?

I believe that those of us willing to ask the question, "What will I do with the rest of my life?" must come to terms with what I call "The Schisms of the ISMs." If we don't we will continue to find ourselves frustrated, confused, angry and divided in this world. We must not only be aware of the "schisms" that are dividing us but the associated "isms" that have caused us to accept these divisions as reality. Only then will we be able to counter them with the truth of God's Word, cultivate greater unity in our various circles of influence and make a genuine impact in the world around us. So what is a *schism*?

A schism is a division, conflict, split, separation or alienation between people, groups, philosophies or organizations.

Think of the Berlin Wall. From 1961 to 1989 it both physically, psychologically and ideologically separated East Berlin from West Berlin, and in fact, East Germany from West Germany. Like any schism, the "Berliner Mauer" was symbolic of an unnecessary division between people who were all Germans. That's what schisms do. They falsely divide in order to confuse our minds and control our actions. They are the work of the devil.

Why are there so many schisms in our world today? To be honest about it, sinners do exactly what we would expect them to do. They sin! In **Romans 3:23** Paul says: **"For all have sinned and fall short of the glory of God."** I may try to convince my wife that I'm the perfect husband but she isn't buying it. She knows me too well! Sin is at the heart of every great division in our world. While true, I'm not willing to settle for such a general statement. For the remainder of this chapter we're going to highlight five "isms" that

> I may try to convince my wife that I'm the perfect husband but she isn't buying it. She knows me too well!

are robbing us of the peace and purpose we so desire in life. But first let's also ask, "What is an *ism*?"

An "ism" is a belief system, doctrine, philosophy or school of thought held by people, organizations and societies.

Grammatically speaking, an "ism" is a suffix attached to the end of a word. Here are some examples of "isms" that I'm sure are familiar to you: atheism, capitalism, hedonism, legalism, patriotism, pragmatism, racism, liberalism, romanticism, sexism, socialism and skepticism. Sometimes "isms" are also connected to names that represent political philosophies like Marxism or Exceptionalism. Or an "ism" might describe a certain style of art, for example, Impressionism.

Just for the fun of it, check out these "isms" and take a shot at guessing what they mean: academicism, holobaptism, experientialism, titanism, millenarianism, pansexualism, laicism, psychopannychism and adoptionism. Any ideas? I know that when I first saw them I had none. There are literally hundreds of "isms" making their way around culture today, a lot of which are totally obscure. Here are the definitions for these.

- Academicism: the doctrine that nothing can be known.
- Holobaptism: the belief in baptism by total immersion in water.
- Experientialism: the doctrine that all knowledge comes from experience.
- Titanism: a spirit of revolt or defiance against social conventions.
- Millenarianism: the belief in a thousand year age culminating in the second coming of Christ.
- Pansexualism: the theory that all thought is derived from sexual instinct.
- Laicism: the doctrine of opposition to clergy and priests.
- Psychopannychism: the belief that souls sleep from death until resurrection.
- Adoptionism: the belief that Jesus was adopted and is not the natural son of God.

The Big Five

If you go on an African safari your goal is to see the "Big Five Animals." They are the Lion, Elephant, Cape Buffalo, Leopard and Black Rhino. Any of these amazing creatures can be lethal. If you tour America today you won't have to look far to see the "Big Five Isms." They are Individualism, Humanism, Denominationalism, Materialism and Universalism. They are all lethal as well, wreaking havoc on society and threatening our well-being and legacy as Baby

Boomers. I would suggest that virtually all other "isms" are off-shoots of these five. As I shared, our strategy must be to identify them and counter them with the truth, starting in ourselves. The first is Individualism.

Individualism

Individualism is the belief that individual rights and interests are paramount and transcend the needs of a group, organization or society.

When we make ourselves king, every decision in life is evaluated from the viewpoint of "What's in it for me?" The Holy Trinity becomes "me, myself and I." Are there some positive aspects to Individualism? Certainly! As I shared in Chapter 2, "Boomers" have been raised with a "rugged individualism," the same spirit that built this great nation. We have set personal goals, worked hard to accomplish them and improved both our lives and the lives of those around us.

> When we make ourselves king, every decision in life is evaluated from the viewpoint of "What's in it for me?" The Holy Trinity becomes "me, myself and I."

Strong and courageous individuals have the ability to rise-up above the crowd and confront evil and injustice ranging from the bully on the school playground to the unethical boss at the office or construction site to the deranged dictator demanding fealty from his citizens.

Talented individuals have been on the forefront of excellence in business, science, sports and more. Many of the great inventions of our generation have come into being as a result of the creativity and hard work of talented individuals long before they became a team effort. In addition to seeking personal excellence, individuals often demonstrate, amazingly so, the strength to endure suffering and trials from facing cancer to losing a child to surviving as a prisoner of war. When the crowd says "This way!" an individual who exhibits a high level of self-confidence will say, "No! That way!" Kind of like our mothers used to preach: "Just because everybody else is jumping off the cliff doesn't mean that you have to follow!"

When Individualism goes unchecked, however, it carries some tremendous downsides. Consider these:

- Rather than "other-centered" we can become "self-centered."
- Rather than "obedient" we can become "rebellious."
- Rather than "humble" we can become "prideful."
- Rather than "integrated" we can become "compartmentalized."
- Rather than "connected" we can become "isolated."
- Rather than "peaceful" we can become "anxious."
- Rather than "serving" we can become "striving."
- Rather than "partnering with others" we can become "self-sufficient."

Back in 2002, Pastor Rick Warren from Saddleback Church in Lake Forrest, California, wrote a book that became the best-selling Christian book of all time. It was called "The Purpose Driven Life." The opening line in that book is "It's not about you!"[1] Pastor Rick goes on to explain that our personal quest for fulfillment, satisfaction and meaning in life can only be found in first understanding and then doing what God put us on Earth to do. That is to love God and love others.

Do you believe it… that your purpose in life is greater than yourself? I can tell you that if you choose to go it alone and spend most of your days "looking out for #1," you will never enjoy the depth of relationships that Jesus desires for you. We can take a cue from Jesus' personal example to us.

The night before He was hung on the cross Jesus declared: **"I no longer call you servants, because a servant does not know his**

> *Do you believe it… that your purpose in life is greater than yourself?*

master's business. Instead, I have called you friends, for everything that I have learned from my Father I have made known to you" (John 15:15).

That is one profound statement! As friends of the Savior, you and I have access to everything that Jesus has received from His Father in Heaven. It's mind-boggling! How do we receive this download of spiritual insight? We trade Individualism for trust! We learn to walk in a daily, living, authentic relationship with Jesus, not isolating but going deep. That's when all His blessings become ours! The next "ism" that is so powerfully undermining faith and civility in culture today is Humanism.

Humanism

Humanism teaches that human beings know better than God and therefore do not need Him if in fact He even exists.

Humanism purports that the Word and the ways of God are outdated and irrelevant for life today. Knowledge and personal experience are king. By extension, a committed "secular humanist" desires to remove God from every institution and place of influence in society. Examples include removing prayer from public schools and nativity scenes from city halls but this philosophy is far more insidious. "Humanist Manifesto I" was published by Raymond B. Bragg in 1933. Humanist Manifesto II was released in 1973 and Humanist Manifesto III was just made public in 2022. They are all a product of the American Humanist Association. One of the oft-quoted lines from the 1973 Manifesto is "No deity will save us; we must save ourselves."

Key tenants in all three Humanist creeds are:

- There is no God.
- There is no Creator. Humans are the result of evolutionary change.
- Knowledge of the world is derived by observation, experimentation and rational analysis. Faith has no place.
- There are no moral absolutes because there is no eternal law.

- Socialism is the best way to create a fair and just society.
- There is no life after death, only nothingness.

What a depressing worldview, and yet, it is this philosophy of Humanism that is entering every aspect of our lives today at an alarming pace. It has a strong influence in classrooms from your local public school to Harvard and Yale. The "traditional media" supports this agenda through propaganda couched as science and political correctness. The government adds its imprimatur through a misguided application of the separation of Church and State. Hundreds of organizations, corporations and foundations, from the W.H.O. to the United Nations to the A.C.L.U. to Disney to Carnegie and Rockefeller base their decisions on this philosophy. We see it even in the Church where a desire to be loving and affirming of every belief and lifestyle has led to a noticeable compromise of biblical truth.

For example, I went to a wedding recently at a supposedly Christian church where there wasn't even one mention of Jesus by name in the whole service. Instead, we were treated to a bunch of psychological jargon that essentially advised, "Give it your best effort and I hope things work out." It wasn't "… as long as you both shall live," but rather "… as long as you both shall love." That's the insipient effect of Humanism today on clergy and the congregations they serve.

To counter this "ism" we must shine the light of love and truth into every philosophy that intends to replace God with self. Remember, darkness is merely the absence of light. We cannot abdicate our children and grandchildren to the deceptions of Humanism.

> We cannot abdicate our children and grandchildren to the deceptions of Humanism.

In **1 John 4:1-3** the apostle counsels: **"Dear friends do not believe every spirit, but test the spirits to see whether they are from God, because many false prophets have gone out into the world. This is how you can recognize the Spirit of God:**

Every spirit that acknowledges that Jesus Christ has come in the flesh is from God, but every spirit that does not acknowledge Jesus is not from God. This is the spirit of the antichrist, which you have heard is coming and even now is already in the world."

Secular Humanism, in its most basic form, represents the original deception of Satan. It suggests that if we eat from the tree of "the knowledge of good and evil" represented by the philosophies of this world we can know what only God knows and become like Him. Bottom line! When we do, we won't need God anymore nor any reminder of Him in society. While in the midst of this battle for truth we must remember something very important.

In **2 Corinthians 10:4** Paul says: **"The weapons we fight with are not the weapons of the world. On the contrary, they have divine power to demolish strongholds. We demolish arguments and every pretension that sets itself up against the knowledge of God, and we take captive every thought to make it obedient to Christ."**

Dr. Ed Silvoso, the Founder and President of Transform Our World, defines a spiritual stronghold as "… a mind-set impregnated with hopelessness that causes us to accept as unchangeable, situations that we know are contrary to the will of God."[2] Strongholds lead to double-mindedness that results in spiritual and emotional instability, a place where a person can be easily deceived by Satan and by others.

If hopelessness has crept into your thought life or become your knee-jerk reaction to difficult challenges, you need to check for a spiritual stronghold. This unhealthy mind-set may be rooted in a negative childhood experience or destructive word spoken over your life that you have long forgotten… and yet it continues to grip your subconscious.

My dear friend, Bob Bagne, leads a ministry called Hope Connection that ministers primarily to those in recovery. At one evening session he asked this question around a circle of 20 people. "What was it that first triggered your use of alcohol or drugs in a way that led to addiction?" Eighteen out of the twenty people at the meeting said that it was something their father had said or done.

One said that it was their mother and one said they didn't know. Bottom line! They had received this "false word" as true and it had so wounded their hearts that alcohol or drugs became the salve for their pain.

A stronghold can develop when you latch on to anything that doesn't align with the truth that God loves the world (John 3:16) and sent His Son to seek and to save everything that was lost (Luke 19:10), including you! It is our failure to deal with strongholds that has steadily opened the door to Humanism which is filled with lies and hopelessness that war against God. Spiritual strongholds can only be broken when we acknowledge them, claim the promises of scripture and pray for release or have others pray with us. God is so faithful to set us free!

Even though this Humanist philosophy is invading every aspect of culture today, we cannot give up our calling to challenge it with the truth. We will never be able to stand firm for the truth if the truth is not in us. Under the leading and power of the Holy Spirit we can demolish every argument that sets itself up against God, and in the process, lead millions to Christ. Baby Boomers, the time is now for our generation to rise-up everywhere and restore our culture based on biblical values because the need for God has never been greater. A third "ism" that is rocking our world today is Denominationalism.

> We will never be able to stand firm for the truth if the truth is not in us.

Denominationalism

Church history is filled with division. The first major split that happened in Christianity is called "The Great Schism of 1054." It resulted in the Eastern Orthodox Church which is Greek and the Western or Roman Catholic Church which is Latin. About 500 years later, a Catholic Priest named Martin Luther, who served in Wittenberg, Germany, called for dialogue and reform around the question, "How are we saved? Is it by good works or faith or both?"

Instead of a discussion, Luther was excommunicated. The split that occurred became known as the Protestant Reformation. Hundreds of Christian denominations are the result today.

A Denomination is a grouping of Christian congregations united under a common faith, distinctive doctrine, identifiable practice and legal and administrative oversight. Examples today include Catholic, Lutheran, Methodist, Episcopalian, Baptist, Evangelical Free and Assemblies of God. A denominational affiliation can certainly provide some benefits to a local congregation. These may include a shared history, doctrine and practice that can serve as a hedge against heresy in a changing world. Denominations also have the potential to maximize the distribution of offerings by providing a united global mission response, especially through parachurch organizations and ministries like Samaritan's Purse or World Vision. Most Denominations also provide some level of spiritual oversight and accountability through various forms of administration. So what is Denominationalism then?

Denominationalism occurs when the common faith, distinctive doctrine, identifiable practice, and legal and administrative hierarchy become exclusive and cause it to separate from others in the body of Christ.

Denominationalism is so divisive because it elevates the "distinctives" of one group over the "foundational teachings" of the whole group. Our human tendency is always to make our "one thing" more important than the "whole thing." That's why far too many congregations still operate in isolation and competition rather than friendship and shared mission. One person observed, "The claim to fame becomes more important than lifting up the Name."

Early in my ministry at Christ Church I was blessed by the friendship of a retired Lutheran Missionary to Tanzania named Harald Palm. Harald had a brother who was a Baptist Pastor. At family gatherings they would often get into theological discussions, even arguments, especially

> *Denominationalism is so divisive because it elevates the "distinctives" of one group over the "foundational teachings" of the whole group.*

127

about things like Baptism. Of course, Harald would argue for "infant baptism" and his brother would argue for "believer baptism." One day Harald told me, "After years of this we decided that our debates had gone too far. We agreed that from that point forward we were going to approach the subject of Baptism like eating fish. You can either complain about the few bones you find or you can enjoy the meat! We decided that we would enjoy the meat."

How do we counter the schism of Denominationalism? We do so by making the "main thing the main thing," and that main thing is Jesus! In **Ephesians 2:12-14** paraphrased, Paul brings counsel to one of the greatest religious schisms of all time, the separation between Jews and Gentiles. He says: **"… before, you were separated from one another without any hope of reconciliation. But now Christ Jesus has brought you together… for he has destroyed the barrier, the dividing wall of hostility."**

In my humble opinion, Denominationalism is "going, going, gone!" The Holy Spirit is replacing this "ism" with something far greater. It involves "unity in the essentials" and diversity in the "non-essentials" for the sake of the mission of the Gospel of Jesus Christ to the world. And oh how sweet it is! The next "ism" that can profoundly impact the way we run the race of life is Materialism.

Materialism

Materialism is a preoccupation with money and possessions as a source of fulfillment to the exclusion of relationships and spiritual values.

At the peak of her career, Madonna, a Baby Boomer, sang, "I am a material girl living in a material world."[3] We might not like to admit it but many of us are singing the same tune yet today. Materialism is about the accumulation of money or possessions under the false assumption that an abundance of "things" will lead to happiness. If we buy-in (pun intended) we literally begin to value possessions more than people. Have we forgotten that we didn't come into this world with anything… and we certainly can't take anything with us when we leave? Have you ever seen a U-Haul being pulled behind a hearse?

The influence of Materialism is pervasive. By the time our children reach 20 years of age many will have seen more than 1 million commercials, each marketing happiness through their product. As kids growing up in the 50s or 60s, it was a big day when the Sears and Roebuck or J. C. Penney catalog showed up at the front door. Remember? We could circle everything we wanted for our birthdays or Christmas or bend over pages. Post-It Notes hadn't even been invented!

Today our grandchildren submit their wish-lists on Amazon where it's estimated that 12 million products are for sale, most of which can be delivered to our front doors free of charge in 2 days or less. A recent report estimates that advertisers in the U.S. spend more than $12 billion annually just to reach the youth market. These figures represent dramatic increases over those from previous decades.

The myth that Materialism pushes again and again is that the more we have the happier we will be. The problem with this philosophy is that it's never enough. We think, "If I just had one more _____ then I would really be happy." Fill in that blank with a bigger home, car, boat, ATV, promotion, vacation, larger bank account or whatever. Life becomes motivated by getting rather than giving. It's the agenda of the Secular Humanist revealed once again that purports that man is the owner, and if there is a God, He is viewed like a genie in a bottle. When I call, God is expected to respond as a "dispenser of things." Otherwise He ought to stay out of my business.

The rub is that Jesus taught just the opposite. In **Luke 12:15** He said: **"Watch out! Be on your guard against all kinds of greed; life does not consist in an abundance of possessions."** When we invest our lives in things rather than people we set ourselves up for great disappointment.

I'm reminded of a home builder I knew who became very wealthy. Over a period of many years his construction company built hundreds of beautiful homes. His success had allowed him to accumulate a lot of possessions, "big boy toys," including an amazing collection of classic cars. He had built a large pole barn on his property just to hold them.

One day he invited me to visit his home and see his cars. They really were beautiful, about 20 in all. I said, "Larry, do your wife and kids enjoy this hobby with you – like going to car shows and stuff?" He had two grown sons and a daughter. What he said really surprised me. With great sadness and a bit of resignation on his face he said, "My kids don't want anything to do with me right now. They say that I wasn't there for them when they were growing up. I was always gone building houses and growing my company. Now the only time they show up is when they need something. They basically look at me like a cash machine."

I said, "I'm so sorry to hear that. That must be very painful." Larry looked out over his collection of cars valued at least a million dollars and said, "You know, pastor, I would give up every one of these in a moment for the opportunity to have a loving marriage and family. That would mean everything to me." This story is repeated hundreds of thousands of times today in the lives of those who have fallen into the trap of Materialism.

> Financial planners are predicting that in the next 20-25 years we will experience the greatest transfer of wealth the world has ever seen from the richest generation the world has ever known. That's us, the "Boomers."

Financial planners are predicting that in the next 20-25 years we will experience the greatest transfer of wealth the world has ever seen from the richest generation the world has ever known. That's us, the "Boomers." Will we leave our children and grandchildren more than just our material wealth?

A Christian biblical worldview regarding money and possessions has the potential to be a blessing to the next generations rather than a curse. Foundational principles are:

- Everything belongs to God. He is the owner. We are the managers.
- There is no distinction between what is sacred and what is secular.

- We are more blessed when we give than when we receive.
- We will reap what we sow.
- God is able to provide for every need in abundance.
- We have been blessed to be a blessing.
- We must hold our possessions lightly or they will take hold of us.

In order to break the stronghold of Materialism we must get our values and priorities regarding our money and possessions aligned with these values of God. When I served a church years ago in Portland, Maine, there was a wonderful elderly woman in the congregation by the name of Rebecca Malpass. She lived into her 90s. I tried to visit her in her home every month or so for conversation, devotions and Holy Communion. I would say, "How are you doing today, Becca?" She would often respond, "Just fine, pastor. I've still got my buttons on straight." That was her way of letting me know that she still had it together. I loved it!

What happens if your top button is off? All the others are out of alignment too! The reality is that when we put our material possessions ahead of both God and people, all of life quickly gets out of alignment; marriage, family, work, hobbies etc. By contrast, when we adopt a biblical worldview regarding our money and possessions, all the other blessings in life come back into proper alignment. This is the key to turning success into significance.

Jesus says: **"Do not store up for yourselves treasures on earth, where moths and vermin destroy, and where thieves break in and steal. But store up for yourselves treasures in heaven, where moths and vermin do not destroy, and where thieves do not break in and steal. For where your treasure is, there will your heart be also" (Matthew 6:19-20).**

In this paradigm, every spending decision is a spiritual decision. Will this new purchase truly be a blessing both to me and to others, or am I merely falling prey once again to a false notion of happiness and security. Martin Luther, the leader of the Protestant Reformation in Germany in 1517, is often quoted as saying, "I have held many things in my hands and I have lost them all. But whatever I have placed in God's hands; that I still possess." Have you placed all that you are and have in the hands of Jesus? When you do, the things that are most important in life can never be taken away. At the top of my list of the "isms" that are deceiving Baby Boomers, along with every other generation, is Universalism.

Universalism

Universalism is the philosophy that everyone will be saved regardless of their belief.

Universalism teaches that there are many roads to heaven and that it doesn't matter which one you choose as long as you're sincere. The message is simple. "Find a path that works for you and run on it." While Universalism pretends to unite, it actually divides. Those who don't agree with this philosophy are deemed to be arrogant, misled or intolerant.

Universalism denies God's plan of salvation for the world as revealed in the Bible including the necessity and result of the death and resurrection of Jesus Christ. It contends that a loving God would never condemn anyone to Hell, if indeed there is a Hell. Code words like "diversity" and "inclusivity" provide cover for a loss of faith fundamentals. The authority of scripture is questioned because the sacred texts of all religions are believed to be equally valid.

> *Code words like "diversity" and "inclusivity" provide cover for a loss of faith fundamentals.*

In the philosophy of Universalism, Gospel proclamation is considered an affront to the right of each person to choose their own way. Evangelism is also a cause for offense–the notion that we should try to convince or convert someone to our way of thinking or believing. The Holy Trinity is viewed as a sexist religious construct needing revision. Our highest calling, we are told, is to social justice and the acceptance of all people.

The tenants of Universalism represent another "line in the sand" when it comes to the history of Christianity. In the 1st century the prevailing question was, "Who is Jesus?" Miracle worker? Prophet? Teacher? Fraud? Son of God? In the 16th century, as I said earlier, the question that birthed the Protestant Reformation was, "How are we saved?" Good works? Faith? A combination of the two? In this 21st century, the most common question asked today is, "Are there many roads to heaven?" The most definitive statement in the Bible in response to this question belongs to Jesus in **John 14:6**. There He says: **"I am the way and the truth and the life. No one comes to the Father except through me."**

That was a "drop the mic" moment, unless you believe like many do, that this statement is merely a fabrication by the early church to lay their claim to religious exclusivity. That might be a plausible assertion if it were not for the fact that Jesus' claim in John 14:6 is backed-up by more than 100 similar passages in scripture. Let's look at several just to give you a frame of reference.

In **1 Timothy 2:5-6** it says: **"For there is one God and one mediator between God and mankind, the man Christ Jesus, who gave himself as a ransom for all people. This has now been witnessed to at the proper time."**

Acts 4:11-12 reiterates: **"Jesus is the stone you builders rejected, which has become the cornerstone. Salvation is found in no one else, for there is no other name under heaven given to mankind by which we must be saved."**

And one more. **1 John 5:11-12** declares: **"And this is the testimony: God has given us eternal life, and this life is in his Son. Whoever has the Son has life; whoever does not have the Son of God does not have life."**

Jesus' followers literally staked their lives on these truths! C. S. Lewis, in his classic book first published in 1952 called "Mere Christianity," famously said, "You must make your choice. Either this man (Jesus) was, and is, the Son of God; or else a madman: or something worse. You can shut Him up for a fool; you can spit on Him and kill Him as a demon; or you can fall at His feet and call

Him Lord and God. But don't come to Him with any patronizing nonsense about His being a great human teacher. He hasn't left that open to you. He didn't intend to."[3]

Fellow "Boomers," has this concept of Universalism crept into your thinking today? Have you come to believe that there are many roads to heaven, many paths to run on that all end up at the same place? Or is there one particular way that we have been called to go; the way of Jesus? Your answer to this question will largely determine how you run the rest of your race of life. My heartfelt prayer and desire for you and for the sake of your legacy is that you will choose Jesus.

Challenge the ISMS

As I've shared in this chapter, the "Schisms of the Isms" must not be allowed to divide our minds and keep us separated from others. We must instead stand firm on these universal truths that are at the heart of the Christian faith:

- God is love.
- We are sinners.
- Jesus is our Savior.
- Forgiveness and heaven are a free gift for all who believe.
- The Gospel is Good News for the whole world.
- Life is to be lived for Jesus every day.

As Baby Boomers we can lovingly but convincingly challenge the false premises of Individualism, Humanism, Denominationalism, Materialism and Universalism. Our ability to live our best lives and positively influence the generations that follow us will depend on it. It's time for us to go on a safari and bag "The Big Five."

Questions for Personal Reflection or Group Discussion:

1. Do you agree with the opening line of Pastor Rick Warren's "Purpose Driven Life" book which says "It's not about you!" When can Individualism lead to self-centeredness and pride?

2. Why is it so tempting to think that we know more about what is good for us than God? Describe an example of the impact of Humanism which has resulted in removing God from many parts of society?

3. If you are a Christian, how important is a Denominational identity in your life today? Do you see it as a positive or a negative?

4. How do the false promises of Materialism influence your spending decisions? When it comes to your priorities in life, do you have your buttons on straight?

5. Why do you think that Universalism is so widely accepted today? How might Jesus' exclusive claim as the only path to God actually be liberating instead of restrictive?

Notes:

1. Rick Warren, *The Purpose Driven Life* (Grand Rapids, MI: Zondervan, 2002), p. 21.
2. Ed Silvoso, *That None Should Perish* (Ventura, CA: Regal Books, 1994), p. 155.
3. Madonna, *Like a Virgin* (New York, NY: Sire Records, 1984).
4. C. S. Lewis, *Mere Christianity* (Westwood, NJ: Barbour and Company, 1943), p. 52.

CHAPTER 10

Go Beyond Nice!

Words have power! Positive words can inspire vision, encourage achievement, teach truth, comfort those in sorrow and express the deepest kind of love. Negative words, on the other hand, have power to crush dreams, demean character, lie, distort and spew vicious hatred. Remember the phrase, "Sticks and stones may break my bones but words can never hurt me?" It's not true, is it! Words have tremendous power to build-up or tear-down. Look at this sampling of scriptures that speak about the power of the tongue:

- **Psalm 52:2-4 "You who practice deceit, your tongue plots destruction; it is like a sharpened razor. You love evil rather than good, falsehood rather than speaking truth. You love every harmful word, you deceitful tongue."**
- **Proverbs 18:21 "The tongue has the power of life and death, and those who love it will eat its fruit."**
- **Jeremiah 9:8 "The tongue is a deadly arrow; it speaks deceitfully."**
- **James 3:8 "... but no human being can tame the tongue. It is a restless evil, full of deadly poison."**

- **Proverbs 15:4 "The soothing tongue is a tree of life, but a perverse tongue crushes the spirit."**
- **Psalm 141:3 "Set a guard over my mouth, Lord; keep watch over the door of my lips."**

King David, who wrote many of the Psalms, knew the power of the tongue to speak good or evil. As a young shepherd boy he had taken courage to face the Philistine giant called Goliath. David told him: **"You come against me with sword and spear and javelin, but I come against you in the name of the Lord Almighty, the God of the armies of Israel, whom you have defiled. This day the Lord will deliver you into my hands, and I'll strike you down and cut off your head" (1 Samuel 17:45-46).**

Goliath had spoken curses against God. David spoke praise! His confidence was in the Lord and you know the rest of the story. Years later the Apostle Paul would offer this counsel: **"Do not let any unwholesome talk come out of your mouths, but only what is helpful for building others up according to their needs, that it may benefit those who listen" (Ephesians 4:29).** Each of us has the opportunity to choose words that build-up or tear down.

Minnesota Nice

In Minnesota there's a phrase used to describe the temperament of our people. It's called "Minnesota Nice." Minnesotans are known for being friendly, welcoming, kind and encouraging. We always look for the best in people and situations. Sometimes this can lead to passive-aggressive behavior or things being left unsaid that should be said. However, most of the time, "Minnesota Nice" is a very endearing quality.

As I've previously mentioned, I lead a state-wide ministry called Bless Minnesota. Our primary focus has been to activate the "body of Christ" all over the state to "adopt streets in prayer." We call it "prayer with legs" because we not only encourage people to pray for their neighbors, coworkers, classmates, city officials and more… but they are to build relationships, respond to needs and share the love of Jesus. We have hundreds of streets adopted in about 165 Minnesota cities. That's a lot of "Minnesota Nice!"

About 4 years ago Colleen and I were doing a two-week Great Lakes trip during the month of July for summer vacation. One day we were heading north with our camper on the western shore of Lake Michigan. Colleen was sleeping. I was thinking and praying about the ministry of Bless Minnesota, with my eyes open!

I was saying, "Lord, we've been at this for about 8 years now. What do you have for us next?" That's when the Holy Spirit dropped the phrase "Go Beyond Nice" into my heart. I immediately knew what it meant. "Minnesota Nice" is great and we celebrate the qualities that make our state special. However, to truly Bless Minnesota we must "Go Beyond Nice!" Christians are called to demonstrate radical love for the world and every person in it.

We made this phrase our motto and God has been teaching us more about what it means ever since. I'm convinced that for our Baby Boom generation to make a lasting impact we must also "Go Beyond Nice!" This world needs nice people, yes! Even more, it needs people who are passionate to see others come to Christ and then be used by God to help bring about the transformation of our cities, states and nation. We have so much more to give! Instead of just riding it out, our Call is to rise-up and be the difference makers God has challenged us to be!

Christians are called to demonstrate radical love for the world and every person in it.

Bless, Don't Blast

To quote my friend, Pastor Allen Cardines from Nanakuli, Oahu, Hawaii, if we are going to move beyond just being "nice people," we will have to learn to "bless instead of blast." In my experience it all begins with personal relationships. We have to make our enemies our friends! We have to move beyond our comfortable circles to reach those who don't yet know Jesus.

In Chapter 2 of his pioneering book called *Prayer Evangelism*[1], Dr. Ed Silvoso lays the foundation of a 4-step strategy taught by Jesus to His disciples as found in **Luke 10:1-9.** There we read:

"After this the Lord appointed seventy-two others and sent them two by two ahead of him to every town and place where he was asked to go. He told them, 'The harvest is plentiful, but the workers are few. Ask the Lord of the harvest, therefore, to send out workers into his harvest field. Go! I am sending you out like lambs among wolves. Do not take a purse or bag or sandals; and do not greet anyone on the road.

When you enter a house, first say, "Peace to this house." If a man of peace is there, your peace will rest on him; if not it will return to you. Stay in that house, eating and drinking whatever they give you, for the worker deserves his wages. Do not move around from house to house. When you enter a town and are welcomed, eat what is set before you. Heal the sick who are there and tell them, "The kingdom of God is near you."'"

Dr. Silvoso highlights four primary relational principles in this text, that when implemented with love and compassion and the guidance of the Holy Spirit, will not only lead people into the kingdom of God but will also help them bring the kingdom of God to this earth.

They are:

- Bless: Speak peace to people and systems in your sphere of influence (vs.5-6).
- Fellowship: Build relationships with those outside of the kingdom of God (vs.7-8).
- Minister: Respond to their felt needs in the name of Jesus expecting miracles (vs.9a).
- Proclaim: Announce that the kingdom of God has come near and is available to them through Jesus Christ (vs.9b).

The principles of Prayer Evangelism are progressive. It's only when we first Bless, Fellowship and Minister to the needs of others that we earn the right to share the Gospel. Blessing them (speaking peace to them and their homes) will open the door to their house. Fellowship (listening and sharing) will open the door to their hearts. Ministering (responding to their needs) will put them in touch with the power and presence of the Lord in a tangible way, and when that transaction takes place, Proclaiming (sharing the Good News of Jesus) becomes a natural response rather than one that is forced. Otherwise we can come across as uncaring or even manipulative. This Luke 10 teaching is intended to be a lifestyle not a program. This is the model we teach all our street adopters across the state. It is the essence of what it means to "Go Beyond Nice."

Bless Minnesota also sponsors an annual emphasis called Bless Minnesota Week. It begins on the first Thursday in May with the National Day of Prayer. People from a great variety of churches and ministries gather on the steps of our state capitol to pray for our state and nation and the various areas of culture, i.e. church, business, education, government etc. Many of the legislators break from session to come out to receive prayers of blessing and guidance for their decisions. It's a very special time of prayer and praise each year.

During the Bless Minnesota Week that follows, our purpose is to turn this "day of prayer" into a "lifestyle of prayer" in which we become the hands and feet of Jesus. People all over Minnesota are encouraged to do tangible acts of kindness in Jesus' name. The stories we hear are so encouraging! Here is one of my favorites.

Somebody in Line

A woman was praying one morning during Bless Minnesota Week just this past May asking the Holy Spirit to show her what she might do or who she might help. At one point in her prayers she sensed the Lord saying, "I want you to help somebody in line today." She wondered what that could mean. She had some errands to run which included some shopping at her area Costco. You know, that place where you can't leave without spending at least a $100 on something you didn't

"I want you to help somebody in line today."

know you needed when you walked in the door! That place!

She did her shopping and while she was in the check-out line, the person ahead of her realized that in taking care of her two little kids she had forgotten her purse and wallet in the car. She was terribly embarrassed and flustered by the situation. As she tried to determine just what to do next the woman who had prayed immediately spoke up and said, "I'd like to pay your bill for you today." This young mother said, "No. No. I couldn't possibly let you do that. It's $286!"

The older woman responded, "While I was praying this morning the Lord told me that I was to help somebody in line today and I believe you are the one. I would be so blessed if you would let me buy your groceries today." Nearly speechless and in tears the woman agreed and the two of them left the store (with the kids) praising God for this wonderful blessing; one who gave and the other who received. Now there's a pretty cool example of what it means to "Go Beyond Nice!"

It's at the Lost and Found

My Bless Minnesota week also left me with an unexpected blessing that demonstrated God's love and grace so clearly. After Easter we had gone to Florida to celebrate my mother's 88th birthday with my siblings at my brother's place in Ocala. When we arrived home I mistakenly left the bag with my Bi-Pap machine hanging on the airport wheelchair we used to help transport mom. I had forgotten to put a name tag on it and didn't realize I had left it until we got home, 45 miles away. There was nobody to call at the late hour.

I immediately filed a missing baggage report online with the airline with all the details. Within the next week I received two emails saying, "Sorry. No luck finding your missing bag." At that point I called the medical supply house where I had gotten the machine and asked how I might go about getting it replaced. She looked up my account and insurance information and said that my Bi-Pap machine was the most expensive state-of-the-art machine they make, valued at about $9,000. She also said that it was questionable whether my insurance would pay for it. I nearly fell off my chair!

She said that part of filing a claim would require that I return to the airport and inquire personally with Baggage Claim… and then also file a missing bag report with the airport police since my Bi-Pap may have been stolen. What a hassle! I did that somewhat ironically while I was on my way to a radio interview with KKMS 980 AM regarding Bless Minnesota Week. No bag. I was feeling pretty discouraged.

That night I went to bed praying, "Lord, I would really like to find my Bi-Pap machine. If it's out there, please show me where." In the middle of the night I had a very vivid dream (see Chapter 5) that seemed to go on for some time. In the dream I heard the Lord saying, "It's at the Lost and Found. It's at the Lost and Found." It was like a message flashing on a billboard, the words were so clear.

> In the dream I heard the Lord saying, "It's at the Lost and Found. It's at the Lost and Found." It was like a message flashing on a billboard, the words were so clear.

I told Colleen about my dream right away that morning. I said, "I think I know where my Bi-Pap machine is at. It's at the Lost and Found." She said, "What makes you think that?" I said, "The Lord told me in a dream last night. I will have to find out if there is such a thing." I had a very busy day but I did manage to go on the MSP airport website, and after much searching, in the smallest print down near the bottom of their Home Page, there it was! "Lost and Found." I called the phone number they gave, and wouldn't you know it, was directed to go to another website and fill-out another form. That was as far as I got that day. And oh yeah, I also told my son Matt about my dream.

The next day I called the number again to remind myself of the website I needed for the new form when somebody named John actually answered the phone. I told him my name and that I was calling about a Bi-Pap machine that I had left at Terminal 2 about 10 days ago. He said, "Is it a Phillips or a Resmed?" I said, "Neither. It's a Respironics." He said, "Let me check." He came back in about a minute and said, "I've got two of them here." My heart leaped! I said, "I've got the serial number for my machine right here." He quickly matched it up and said, "Yes! I've got your Bi-Pap." I said, "Praise God! You don't know how happy that makes me."

He said, "When do you want to come and pick it up?" I said, "Right now. I'm on my way!" Lost and Found, as it turns out, is on the lower level of Terminal 1 at MSP. Anything that is lost, left behind or confiscated by TSA at security ends up there. John said, "Don't even try to find us. Just pull up in front of Baggage Claim and I will bring your machine up to you." I called him when I got there and in about a minute he was there with my Bi-Pap. I handed him a $5.00 bill for a small tip which he refused, saying, "No thank you. This is just what we do." And then he added, "By the way, I like your license plate." My license plate says, BLESSMN. I said, "Yes, in addition to being a pastor at a church in Otsego I lead a state-wide ministry called Bless Minnesota and this is actually Bless Minnesota Week. You have been a huge blessing to me!" He said, "That's awesome! I'm a follower of Jesus too."

During that Bless Minnesota Week I had found several ways to bless others, but I was the one who got blessed the most that day. While I was driving home from the airport I said, "God, if you are willing to give me such a direct revelation like this about a Bi-Pap machine, how much more must you want to speak to me about visions and plans for my life, Christ Church and Bless Minnesota… if only I will invite you to do so?" I was encouraged more than ever to "Go Beyond Nice" knowing that God returns every blessing in ways that go beyond what we can even think or imagine.

True Humility

To "Go Beyond Nice!" we must be prepared to follow the example of Jesus. Jesus taught that the greatest among us are called to be humble and that the "least of these" will be raised-up to places of honor and blessing. This reversal of human values was ultimately demonstrated on the cross, as Jesus, the greatest man to ever live, willingly sacrificed His life for our sins. If you're looking for an example of how to live the Christian life, don't look at the person who is prideful and showy with their gifts. Look to the one who is humble. Look to the one who will set aside their own status to kneel down and wash the feet of others… whatever their need may be.

> *If you're looking for an example of how to live the Christian life, don't look at the person who is prideful and showy with their gifts. Look to the one who is humble.*

In Jesus' culture, when a traveler arrived at his destination, having walked the dusty roads of Palestine, a servant would take a basin of water and wash the person's feet as a gesture of welcome and hospitality. It wasn't something that the head of the household would ever do. No wonder the disciples were so surprised, and even resistant, when on the day we now call Holy Thursday, during what we now call The Last Supper, Jesus got down on His knees and washed His disciples' feet.

In **John 13:3-5** we read: **"Jesus knew that the Father had put all things under his power, and that he had come from God and was returning to God; so he got up from the meal, took off his outer clothing, and wrapped a towel around his waist. After that, he poured water into a basin and began to wash his disciples' feet, drying them with the towel that was wrapped around him."**

The significance of this act is extraordinary in our world today where success, status and posturing are everything. It's noteworthy that just prior to this His disciples had been arguing about who would be the greatest in heaven. Jesus not only wanted to give them a practical example of the upside-down reality of the kingdom of

God… but also the reason they could live this way too. Jesus knew who He was. He knew that He had come from God and was soon returning to God. His identity wasn't dictated by the values of this world. Friends, unless our identity is also firmly established in Christ, it's not likely that any of us will have the desire or the courage to set aside our worldly reputations and humble ourselves before others.

Peter, the same "water walking" Peter, had a problem with Jesus' approach. When it was his turn he challenged: "**'Lord, are you going to wash my feet?' Jesus replied, 'You do not realize now what I am doing, but later you will understand.' 'No,' said Peter, 'you shall never wash my feet.' Jesus answered, 'Unless I wash you, you have no part in me.' 'Then, Lord,' Simon Peter replied, 'not just my feet but my hands and my head as well'" (John 13:6-9)**!

Two things here. First, we rarely understand why Jesus is doing something in our lives when it's happening. It's the same reason the writer to the Hebrews declares: **"Now faith is confidence in what we hope for and assurance about what we do not see" (Hebrews 11:1).** Second, Jesus' example of servanthood isn't offered up as a nice option for those who are especially kind. No, if we want to "be in Him" and have "Jesus in us," this is a command. Jesus reiterated this teaching in **John 15:12-14** when He said: **"My command is this: Love each other as I have loved you. Greater love has no one than this: to lay down one's life for one's friends. You are my friends if you do what I command."**

The Spirit-filled Christian will be "mighty in the Lord" but humble in relationship to others. Just imagine the impact we Baby Boomers could have if we decided to spend the rest of our days serving rather than relaxing… and giving rather than getting. Just imagine the lives that could be transformed forever if we "Boomers" were to set aside all our worldly "claims to fame" and spend these years serving others like Jesus served us? In a world where ego is applauded and we are told to "look out for number one," it would lead to nothing short of a spiritual revolution! I am

> *The Spirit-filled Christian will be "mighty in the Lord" but humble in relationship to others.*

asking God to re-kindle this fire of love and service in our generation so that we can truly leave a lasting legacy to those who follow.

Faith Beyond Belief

To grasp the depth of this "Jesus life" we need what I call "Faith Beyond Belief." It's a close sister of "Go Beyond Nice!" Here's the equation:

Faith Beyond Belief = Belief + Trust + Obedience

Faith that goes beyond mere *belief* in God must include both *trust* and *obedience*. As Christians we are often quick to say we believe in God and trust in Jesus… but then continue right on "doing life" our way. No wonder we suffer with wounded hearts and orphaned spirits. *Trust* makes *belief* real and tangible. I love this illustration of the difference. If I placed a nice, wooden, dining room table chair in front of you right now I could say, "What is this?" You would respond, "It's a chair." I would say, "Are you sure? Do you really believe it's a chair?" You would say, "Of course it is. I can see it with my own eyes." I would say, "Do you trust that it could hold you up?" You would say, "Yes, of course! Are you implying that I'm overweight?" I would say, "No! I'd never suggest that! I was just wondering why it isn't holding you up?" You would say, "Because I'm not sitting on it." I would say, "Then why don't you sit on it to show me that you not only believe in that chair but trust it to hold you up?" You would say, "Yes, I will," and sit on it!

You *believe* the chair exists. You *trust* that it will hold you up. But you must take that step of *obedience* and actually sit on it to demonstrate your sincerity. This is an important issue when it comes to faith in our world today. Many claim to believe, few trust and even fewer are obedient. Parents, how would you feel if your kids or grandkids said they believed in you and trusted you… but never obeyed you? Not good, right? I wonder if God doesn't feel the same way about us sometimes as His children. Which of these three aspects of faith do you tend to struggle with the most; belief, trust or obedience? Why do you think that is the case?

My oldest son, Matt (and Leah) and their family lived in our home for 5 years while he was starting a business. Two of our now 10 grandchildren were born while they were with us. These were wonderful years! My grandson, Sam, who is an awesome young man today, had trouble listening as a kid. That is not unusual, I know! When he was about 4 years old I was gently scolding him one day saying, "Sam, Papa doesn't want to have to tell you three or four times to do something. When I ask you to do something I'd like you to do it right away. This is what we've been working on!" He looked at me, and very innocently stated, "Papa, I'm not working on that." He had me! All I could do was smile!

I think that Father God often gets the same response from us as His children. He says, "When I show you in my Word how to live I'd like you to do it. I don't want to have to tell you over and over again." Our response? "I believe in You… and I trust You with most of my life… but that obedience thing is really hard. "Papa, I'm not working on that."

After Moses received the Ten Commandments and shared them with the Israelites he said: "**Walk in obedience to all that the Lord your God has commanded you, so that you may live and prosper and prolong your days in the land that you will possess" (Deuteronomy 5:33).** We have to remember that anything God asks us to do is for our blessing. When we both "trust and obey" it positions us to walk in the favor of

> "Papa, I'm not working on that."

God and be a blessing to others. The Apostle James adds: **"Do not merely listen to the Word, and so deceive yourselves. Do what it says" (James 1:22).**

Our tendency is to think that any call to obedience in the Bible is just an attempt to lay guilt on us, cramp our lifestyle and wrap us up in a bunch of rules and regulations. Just the opposite! When faith and trust are combined with obedience we are set free to be all that God created us to be. That's why "Faith Beyond Belief" is a prerequisite if we are to "Go Beyond Nice." Without it, just "nice" will feel like enough.

I love how Paul puts it in **Romans 2:4** and I'm paraphrasing. He says: **"It's the kindness of God that leads to repentance."** We can't just talk somebody into believing in Jesus and following Him. They must experience His love personally. The only Bible that most people will ever read is you! Think of people in your circles of involvement and influence right now who would be deeply touched by even one heartfelt expression of kindness. Can you reach out? Will you find a tangible way to show them the love of Jesus?

Go Low to Go High

To "Go Beyond Nice" requires both humility and boldness, tenderheartedness and tenacity. Jesus taught that we must humble ourselves first and then God will raise us up. One day He called His disciples together. He said: **"You know that those who are regarded as rulers of the Gentiles lord it over them, and their high officials exercise authority over them. Not so with you. Instead, whoever wants to become great among you must be your servant, and whoever wants to be first must be slave of all. For even the Son of Man did not come to be served, but to serve, and to give his life as a ransom for many" (Mark 10:42-45).**

When we humble ourselves in this world and serve others after the example of Jesus, he will raise us up. He will bless us. He will promote us. He will give us greater wisdom and authority for every task set before us. We don't have to flash our spiritual credentials as Christians. We simply need to let others see Jesus at work in us!

As part of our Bless Minnesota ministry we have gone to the highest man-made place in Minnesota for the past 6 years to pray and declare blessings over our state. It is the I.D.S. tower in downtown Minneapolis. Every first Wednesday of May, the day before the National Day of Prayer, Colleen and I lead a team of both pulpit and marketplace leaders to the 51st floor where we gather in the beautiful conference room of the law offices of Schwebel, Goetz and Sieben. On a clear day you can see 50 miles or more. We pray together for one hour and the Lord always shows up. When we come down the elevator (at a very high speed) we are always humbled by what the Holy Spirit has revealed and more committed than ever to see Minnesota transformed by the love, presence and power of Jesus.

This past October 3, 2022, we experienced another "high" that caused us to "go low." A team of Bless Minnesota partners climbed Eagle Mountain which is about 45 minutes inland from the North Shore of Lake Superior, not that far from Canada. It is the highest natural point in Minnesota. There is both a sign and a medallion pounded into the rock that declares this fact.

When we reached the summit our team shared scripture, prayer and Holy Communion, interrupted only once by two young college girls that we were able to bless. It was as though the Lord had reserved a 45 minute time-slot for us. During the prayer time the Holy Spirit showed me a picture of the prophetic act we were to share together. One of our team members was wearing a wooden cross that had been made by her husband who had passed away two years earlier. With her permission I took that cross, set it on top of the "high point" medallion, and anointed it with oil declaring the covering of Jesus and the outpouring of the Holy Spirit over the State of Minnesota. It was a powerful moment and many prayers, prophetic words and declarations poured forth. Before we left we buried that anointed cross under a nearby rock as a reminder of our declaration that Jesus is Lord over Minnesota.

After soaking in the breathtaking view for a while longer it was time to come back down the mountain, get back home and get to work. We felt like Jesus' disciples after their experience on the mountain of transfiguration. We knew we had been in the presence of the Lord but weren't quite sure what was next. I sensed the Holy Spirit saying, "Greg, I bless you with these mountaintop experiences to encourage you so that you when you come down you will humble yourself, your gifts and ministries for the sake of my kingdom." I had asked the Lord to break my heart once again for the people of Minnesota.

The next morning I was looking at the photos I had taken at the summit. Take a closer look at the photo of the medallion, cross and anointing oil. Do you see the face behind it, the eyes, long hair and beard? I said, "Lord, is that you, our rock and redeemer?" I immediately heard Him say, "No. It's Aaron." That's when I remembered that one of the scripture readings we shared on the mountain was Psalm 133.

There it says: **"How good and pleasant it is when God's people live together in unity! It is like the precious oil poured** on the head, running down on the beard, running down on Aaron's beard, down on the collar of his robe. It is as if the dew of Hermon were falling on Zion. For there the Lord bestows his blessing, even life forevermore" (Psalm 133:1-3).

That's what we want for Minnesota. I know it's what you want for your town, city, state and nation. Friends, when we go low, Jesus raises us up. When we go high, He brings us back down with renewed purpose and passion to serve Him. Wherever we are in the process, we must be willing to lay down the things that God has given us personally for the "much more" that He wants to give us together.

Paul says it so beautifully in the 2nd chapter of Philippians, one of my favorite books of the Bible. He encourages some of the first believers:

"Do nothing out of selfish ambition or vain conceit. Rather, in humility value others above yourselves, not looking to your own interests but each of you to the interests of others" (Philippians 2:3-4).

And then he continues with these Spirit-inspired words: "In your relationships with one another, have the same mindset as Christ Jesus: Who, being in very nature God, did not consider equality with God something to be used to his own advantage; rather, he made himself nothing by taking the very nature of a servant, being made in human likeness. And being found in appearance as a man, he humbled himself by becoming obedient to death – even death on a cross! Therefore, God exalted him to the highest place and gave him the name that is above every name, that at the name of Jesus every knee should bow, in heaven and on earth and under the earth, and every tongue acknowledge that Jesus Christ is Lord, to the glory of God the Father" (Philippians 2:5-11).

In order to go high in life we must first be willing to go low. It is the way of Jesus.

> Wherever we are in the process, we must be willing to lay down the things that God has given us personally for the "much more" that He wants to give us together.

Volunteer Enthusiastically

This servant heart is the essence of volunteerism which is a significant way to "Go Beyond Nice." It may surprise you that I haven't devoted an entire chapter to this topic. Many would respond that the obvious answer to the question, "What will I do with the rest of my life?" is to volunteer! That's kind of what people think we seniors should do. I don't disagree, however, if the heart isn't there, if the motivation isn't right, just putting in a few hours for an organization won't lead to the meaning and happiness we truly desire. When we approach opportunities to volunteer as opportunities to serve others with the love of Jesus the impact goes up exponentially, both for us and those we are serving. From that perspective, every chapter in this book is an encouragement to our generation to give of ourselves generously!

When you explore this topic you will find that the list of possible benefits of volunteering is extensive. Volunteering potentially combats depression, reduces stress, makes you happy, increases self-confidence, provides a sense of purpose, leads to new friendships, keeps you active both mentally and physically, contributes to your community and impacts the lives of others. All true! Which of these benefits would be important to you if you were to volunteer for a church, non-profit or community organization?

The key, I think, is to reflect on your gifts and passion as you consider various opportunities to serve. What is an issue that especially touches your heart? Is it caring for those who are hungry or homeless? Is it working with children or youth? Is it helping older seniors? Is it building things? Is it just being a friend? What is right for one person may not be right for another.

To discover the possibilities just Google "Opportunities to Volunteer in (your community)." You may be surprised by how many worthy organizations are seeking kind, enthusiastic volunteers to help carry out their mission. In the Elk River, Minnesota area where I live these include food shelves, youth organizations, a pregnancy center, hospitals, senior centers, nursing homes, parks and recreation, the police and fire departments, local schools both public and private, community festivals, churches and so much more.

Don't be afraid to try out several volunteer opportunities and see what fits you best. Perhaps there is an area where you can serve together with a spouse or even a grandchild. What a great way to make memories while helping others. A "Boomer" from Christ Church, who is a faithful volunteer in our ministry, also finds it very important to serve in the community. For her that is delivering "Meals on Wheels." She says, "Every meal I drop off becomes an opportunity to brighten a person's day and leave a blessing." I pray that you can find a similar way to touch the lives of those around you!

Be Real

Oh how the people in our world need to see that God is real and that He is real in us. They need Him to drop a word into their heart while they're driving down the road on vacation. They need someone to "bless not blast" even when they don't deserve it. They need someone to buy their groceries in a desperate moment. They need God to reveal something in a dream that speaks of His love and grace even in the little things. They need a grandson to teach them truth. They need to discover that there is joy when the equation for faith includes belief, trust and obedience. They need someone to surprise them by bending down to serve instead of expecting to be served. They need to experience the presence of God in both the highs and the lows of life. Most of all, they need the touch of a human heart to leave a blessing.

Our God is that God! We can be those "someones!" Our generation is so full of love and compassion. Baby Boomers have always had the heart to come to the rescue of those who are lost, lonely and hurting. We were born and raised with the "kindness" gene. Now, in this critical season, we need God's help to step-up and "Go Beyond Nice!" When we do we will change this world for the better and the generations that follow will speak of us as those who truly cared!

Questions for Personal Reflection or Group Discussion:

1. Would others say that you are a nice person? On the basis of what evidence? What would it look like in your life for you to "Go Beyond Nice?"
2. Describe an unexpected blessing you have experienced? Did it motivate you to be a blessing to others?
3. If you are to live with "Faith Beyond Belief," which part of the equation must develop the most in your life; Belief, Trust or Obedience?
4. Describe a mountaintop experience you've had and reflect on how it spoke to you spiritually. What was the toughest part of coming down from the mountain?

Notes:

1. Ed Silvoso, *Prayer Evangelism* (Ventura, CA: Regal Books, 2000), Chapter 2.

CHAPTER 11

Walk Wet

Minnesota's moniker is "The Land of 10,000 Lakes." In the northern half of our state there is water everywhere. Just drive around the next bend and it's likely you will find another beautiful lake amidst oak, birch and pine forests. The mighty Mississippi River begins as a trickle flowing out of Lake Itasca in northern Minnesota. From there it gains volume from 100s of tributaries and flows 2,348 miles to the Gulf of Mexico bisecting the whole United States. On Minnesota's north eastern border is Lake Superior, the largest fresh-water lake in the world by surface area, holding 10% of the world's fresh water. In addition to their sheer beauty, these water resources in Minnesota provide millions of people, both citizens and visitors, with awesome opportunities for recreation from swimming, boating and fishing in the summer (water skiing was invented here) to ice fishing and snowmobiling in the winter. We are also learning to "walk wet." Let me explain!

The Bible begins with the Book of Genesis and the story of creation. It says: **"In the beginning God created the heavens and the earth. Now the earth was formless and empty, darkness was over the surface of the deep, and the Spirit of God was hovering over the waters" (Genesis 1:1-2).** The Bible ends with the Book of Revelation and an amazing declaration. The Apostle John says: **"Let** the one who is thirsty come; and let the one who wishes take the free gift of the water of life" (Revelation 22:17b).

Between these bookends, there are more than 700 "water references" in the Bible. Many of these scripture passages have a deeper spiritual meaning. Water often speaks of the Holy Spirit that is available to every "dry soul" in need of a "fresh drink" from above. For example, in **John 4:10,** Jesus made an intriguing comment to a woman drawing water from the historic Jacob's well. She questioned how a Jewish man could ask for a drink from a Samaritan woman. Jesus responded: **"If you knew the gift of God and who it is that asks you for a drink, you would have asked him and he would have given you living water."**

> *Water often speaks of the Holy Spirit that is available to every "dry soul" in need of a "fresh drink" from above.*

The "living water" that Jesus describes is exactly what so many of us need in the world today. In spite of all we have, our spirits often feel dried up and far away from God. Jesus' words illustrate one very simple but profound biblical truth. We cannot be transformed into new creations in Christ, or live meaningful lives that will lead to a lasting legacy, apart from the presence and power of the Holy Spirit at work within us. Only God can refresh a soul! In this chapter we're going to look at several "water stories" that speak to this truth. I encourage you to consider for yourself what it would mean for you to "walk wet," anointed and covered by the Spirit of God for all your days! The Spirit-filled life is full of adventure and surprises that will not only bless you personally but increase your passion to make a difference in the lives of others.

New Wine

I love doing weddings! I suppose that I have presided at about 300 of these special days by now, including my siblings, children, nephews and nieces. There are so many great memories and stories that could be told; the bride who tripped on her way down the aisle, the groom who said "dividing love" instead of "abiding love" and the precocious little ring bearer who told me he was the "ring burier." Every wedding is a happy occasion as family and friends gather together to celebrate with a couple as they begin their new life together. On one such occasion, Jesus, his newly called disciples, and his mother Mary were invited to a wedding in a town called Cana in Galilee. We read about it in John, Chapter 2. This was right at the beginning of Jesus' 3 years of public ministry. He would have been about 30 years old.

This wedding took place on a Tuesday. The day didn't really matter because back then the whole town was invited. No need to send in your RSVP online and indicate chicken or steak! The celebration could last for days depending on the wealth of the family. At some point during this particular wedding reception something terrible happened. The wine ran out! This may not seem like a big deal to us but in Bible times wine was the staple. No punch! No beer! No root beer! The whole reception was threatened along with the reputations of the bride and groom and their families.

Mary informed Jesus about the problem as only a mother can do… like she expected him to do something about it and do it now! His objections to her request were not received. His mother simply looked at the servants and said: **"Do whatever he tells you" (John 2:5).** Perhaps this is the first important take-a-way from our story. To be successful in life always do two things; do what your mother tells you and what Jesus tells you!

The Bible says that there were six stone jars nearby each capable of holding 20-30 gallons of water. They were normally used by the Jews for ceremonial washing, like "foot washing," to show hospitality to guests who had travelled the dusty roads of Palestine. Jesus told the servants to fill them full. Imagine how many buckets of cool, clean water they had to draw from the well in order to do that. That's between 120 and 180 gallons of water. When they finished, without any fanfare Jesus simply told them to ladle out a sample and take it to the Chief Steward. Think of him like a Banquet Coordinator today. He tasted the water that had now become wine and was amazed. He called the Bridegroom aside and basically said, "Everyone I know serves the best wine first but you have saved the best for last!"

The Wedding at Cana story concludes: **"What Jesus did here in Cana of Galilee was the first of the signs through which he revealed his glory; and his disciples believed in him" (John 2:11).**

Friends, I believe that Jesus has saved the best for last in our lives as Baby Boomers. When we invite Him to be a the center of both our celebrations and our challenges He promises to meet us right where we're at and transform us… like water into wine. Those giant clay pots went from being "religious containers" to "carriers of blessing."

> I believe that Jesus has saved the best for last in our lives as Baby Boomers.

They were "filled to the brim," a symbol of Jesus' desire to fill us up with His Spirit so that we can contribute to the celebration of life. How amazing that Jesus' first miracle took place at a wedding reception. His disciples believed and we are invited to do the same. What's the next big event in your life? How about inviting Jesus to be your guest of honor?

Water and the Spirit

Nicodemus was a curious man. As a well-respected Jewish Rabbi it wasn't right for him to be interested in a man claiming to be God… but he was. So one night under the cover of darkness he arranged a private meeting with Jesus. He began by stating what was obvious to him. He said: **"Rabbi, we know that you are a teacher who has come from God. For no one could perform the signs you are doing if God were not with him" (John 3:2).**

Jesus responded: **"Very truly I tell you, no one can see the kingdom of God unless they are born again" (John 3:3).** Born again? What? Jesus had his attention! **"'How can someone be born when they are old?' Nicodemus asked. 'Surely they cannot enter a second time into their mother's womb to be born'" (John 3:4)!**

Nicodemus couldn't comprehend that the birth Jesus was talking about was spiritual, not physical. Next Jesus said: **"Very truly I tell you, no one can enter the kingdom of God unless they are born of water and the Spirit. Flesh gives birth to flesh, but the Spirit gives birth to spirit. You should not be surprised at my saying, 'You must be born again'"** (John 3:5-7).

This late-night dialogue makes it clear. In order to become a Christian we must experience a spiritual rebirth. We don't become followers of Jesus by becoming a member of a church, gaining a certain amount of knowledge about the Bible, doing enough good things or getting all our questions answered. The only way to a relationship with God our Creator is through faith in His Son, our Savior Jesus Christ. When we put our complete trust in Him we are filled with the Holy Spirit and are changed… transformed. **2 Corinthians 5:17** puts it so beautifully: **"Therefore, if anyone is in Christ, the new creation has come: The old is gone, the new is here!"**

Have you been "born again?" Has your life been changed from the inside out? What is your story? Was there a moment in time when you heard Jesus' message of love and forgiveness and responded to it or did your faith develop over a period of time? As I shared in my testimony in Chapter One, it was really both for me. There was never a time in my life that I didn't believe in Jesus, and yet, there were several very important moments of making that commitment my own. The point is that when it happens we know that it is real because our hearts are touched at a depth we never imagined possible.

Jesus' reference to being "born of water and the Spirit" is also a reference to baptism. For centuries there had been "ritual washings" that were done to prepare people to offer their sacrifices in the temple. The symbolism was "clean yourself up on the outside before you ask God to clean you up on the inside." When Jesus was baptized in the Jordan River by His cousin, John the Baptist, those watching caught a glimpse of what was to come. The heavens opened, the Spirit of God descended upon Jesus in the form of a dove, and a voice from heaven declared: **"This is my Son, whom I love; with him I am well pleased"** (Matthew 3:17).

159

Notice that all three members of the Holy Trinity were present at this crucial moment in Jesus' life. The Father spoke from heaven. The Son presented Himself for baptism as an example to us all. The Holy Spirit anointed Jesus for the ministry that lay ahead. Following Jesus' resurrection, and the outpouring of the Holy Spirit on all believers on Pentecost, every baptism became a baptism of the Holy Spirit. To this very day, baptism is meant to be far more than a religious ceremony with a certificate to prove it. Baptism is intended to be a prophetic declaration of the love, forgiveness and grace of God… irrespective of age or accomplishment. It combines God's promises in Jesus with our response of faith and trust.

The gift of the Holy Spirit received in Baptism is intended to be a constant source of "in-filling" so that we in turn can "pour-out" God's love to others. In order for this to happen we must "walk wet" in the anointing presence of God. If you've been feeling like a dried-out sponge, turn to God right now and ask for a fresh outpouring of the Holy Spirit upon your life today! You don't have to arrange a meeting under the cover of darkness like Nicodemus. Just open your heart and declare, "I want more."

Living Water

Let's return to the "water story" I mentioned in the introduction to this chapter, the one commonly referred to as the Woman at the Well. It's found in John, Chapter 4, and has long been one of my favorites.

> *The gift of the Holy Spirit received in Baptism is intended to be a constant source of "in-filling" so that we in turn can "pour-out" God's love to others.*

In this compelling encounter Jesus teaches that life in the Spirit is like a deep well that never runs dry. It's like "living water" that quenches our deepest thirst.

Think of times in your life today when you get physically thirsty. For me, it's after mowing the lawn or doing some kind of outside work on a really hot day. Yes, even the land of the "Frozen Chosen" gets hot and muggy on occasion. It even reached 100 degrees one day in June this year. I share this to dispel the rumors that there is snow on the ground 365 days a year here in Minnesota! At any rate, Colleen is always encouraging me to drink more water and stay hydrated.

I also experience spiritual thirst. It usually comes after a challenging season of ministry when I'm exhausted and in need of refreshment. There was a Scandinavian pastor named Christer Stendahl, a former Dean of Harvard Divinity School and a bishop in Sweden, who once wryly said of the Lent and Easter season, "Christ is risen! The pastors are dead!" Sometimes we are dead in more ways than one!

My spiritual thirst also comes after seasons of growth and success when I realize that to go to the next level I need more of God, or perhaps I should say, God needs more of me! Maybe you've been there… when deep in your heart you know that what you've got left to give by your own strength just isn't enough.

The Samaritan woman at Jacob's well was blessed to have both her physical and spiritual thirst met by Jesus who told her everything she had ever done and still loved her. He'll do that for you too! And even more, as she shared her testimony, many others in her town also came to believe and receive Jesus as their Savior. A passion to lead others to Christ is one of the best evidences of the Spirit in our lives today. Let's take a closer look at this beautiful story.

Jesus was an itinerant preacher. He traveled from town to town sharing the good news of the kingdom of God. One day Jesus and His disciples had left Judea and were on their way back to Galilee, the region of His hometown of Nazareth. This took them through Samaria to a town called Sychar, near the revered location of Jacob's well. It was noon. The disciples had gone into town to buy food. Jesus was tired and thirsty Himself, one of those indications in the scripture of His humanity. He sat down by the well perhaps to rest just a bit before drawing out water.

When a Samaritan woman came to get her daily supply, Jesus said: **"Will you give me a drink" (John 4:7)?** She was very surprised by His request for two reasons. First, Jews didn't talk to Samaritans. They didn't associate with each other because Jews considered the Samaritans to be a mixed race not worthy of being adherents of the Law. Second, in this first century culture a man simply did not talk to a strange woman in public. It was considered unseemly. Even so, Jesus said: **"If you knew the gift of God and who it is that asks you for a drink, you would have asked him and he would have given you living water" (John 4:10).**

I call it "water talk." Jesus had a way of getting people's attention. Just like He had done with Nicodemus, his provocative question left this Samaritan woman wanting to know more. She said: **"Where can you get this living water" (John 4:11)?** Jesus replied: **"Everyone who drinks this water will be thirsty again, but whoever drinks the water I give them will never thirst. Indeed, the water I give them will become in them a spring of water welling up to eternal life" (John 4:13-14).**

The theme of nearly every soda commercial, or "pop" as we call it in Minnesota, has something to do with refreshment. Drink this brand and your thirst will be quenched. The beer companies really push this message. The problem is that these drinks only temporarily satisfy your thirst. The "living water" that Jesus delivers comes with the promise that we will never thirst again… and not just for a day, a week or a month… but all the way to eternal life. Can I order a whole truckload please? That's not necessary! The best part of Jesus' promise is that this "living water," which is a symbol of the Holy Spirit in us, is absolutely free!

> The "living water" that Jesus delivers comes with the promise that we will never thirst again… and not just for a day, a week or a month… but all the way to eternal life.

When the Samaritan woman asked for this water Jesus asked her to go and get her husband and come back. He knew, of course, that she didn't have a husband, and in fact, had previously had five husbands. When he pointed this out to her she quickly turned the subject to religion. She said: **"Sir, I can see that you are a prophet. Our**

ancestors worshipped on this mountain, but you Jews claim that the place where we must worship is in Jerusalem" (John 4:19-20).

Isn't that exactly what we do when Jesus gets too close? We change the subject. We talk religion. We debate theology. We fall back on tradition. We remind others of how much the Church has hurt us. Excuses! Excuses! What we don't realize is that when we hold Jesus at arm's length we are preventing Him from giving us that cup of "living water."

"'Woman,' Jesus replied, 'believe me, a time is coming when you will worship the Father neither on this mountain nor in Jerusalem. You Samaritans worship what you do not know; we worship what we know, for salvation is from the Jews. Yet a time is coming and has now come when the true worshipers will worship the Father in the Spirit and in truth, for they are the kind of worshipers the Father seeks. God is spirit, and his worshipers must worship in Spirit and in truth'" (John 4:21-24).

Do you see the words, "Yet a time is coming and has now come…" tucked in the middle of Jesus' response? Fellow Baby Boomers, we are living in a day and time when past traditions, lukewarm religion and lame excuses just won't cut it. Authentic believers are approaching the Father in Spirit and in truth. They have had their thirst quenched by "living water" and are not going back to their old parched way of life. They are "walking wet" experiencing daily infillings and outpourings of the Holy Spirit. They are discovering the "more" of life in the Spirit and will settle for nothing less.

The Samaritan woman at Jacob's well who met Jesus on that warm noon-time day had no idea that she could be loved in spite of her past. Maybe you've thought the same thing in the midst of life's terrible mistakes, the ones we think we can never live down. All of a sudden it dawned on her that she could be talking with the Messiah, the Savior of the world. She didn't even need to ask. Jesus declared: **"I, the one speaking to you – am he" (John 4:26).** She was so excited that she left her water containers, ran back to town and said to the people: **"Come, see a man who told me everything I ever did. Could this be the Messiah" (John 4:29)?**

It was her form of "water talk." Ask a question. Raise their curiosity so they would want to learn more. It worked. The townspeople came out to meet Jesus too, more conversation ensued and many became His followers. Friends, Jesus sees everything you've ever done and still loves you. Come to the well of his amazing grace and enjoy a drink of "living water" with your Savior. Jesus will quench your thirst in a way you may never have imagined possible. In the process He will teach you how share your faith story, tip conversations in His direction and tap into people's deepest desires.

Pool Party

Just as the new school year was getting started, a college student in Florida posted an invitation on Facebook announcing a pool party for a few friends at his apartment swimming pool. Over a thousand students showed up. Oh the joys of social networking! Everything went fine until the young apartment security guard tried to take charge of the situation and a few of the football players in attendance threw him into the pool!

Pools were scattered everywhere around the temple court in Jerusalem… but not the kind you swim in. They were used for everything from bathing to ritual washing by Jewish pilgrims prior to entering the temple to offer a sacrifice. One of them was called the Pool of Bethesda. It was called a "place of mercy" because for many generations the Jewish people believed that occasionally an angel of the Lord would come down from heaven and "stir the waters" as though someone had temporarily turned on the jets in a hot tub. If you were the first one to jump into the pool when this happened, you would be healed. It was like a mystical divine lottery. Just one problem. It was tough to get a jump on anybody if you couldn't walk!

Because of this reputation, the pool of Bethesda had become a gathering place for the disabled; those who were blind, lame, paralyzed and in need of a miracle from God. Enter the main character of this "water story," a poor man who the Bible says had been an invalid for

38 years. An invalid is a person who has a physical disability. The man is not named and we don't know his precise age, but the clear implication is that he couldn't walk because he was just lying there. In all likelihood, someone had been carrying him to the pool for years; a family member, a friend, placing him close to these "magical waters" every morning and picking him up every night, all the while hoping that his lucky day would come. It never did!

That is until Jesus showed up... not an angel to stir the water, but the Son of God to stir the soul. The scripture says: **"When Jesus saw him lying there and learned that he had been in this condition for a long time, he asked him, 'Do you want to get well'"** (John 5:6)? That's an interesting question, isn't it? Wouldn't Jesus have assumed that this crowd of the disabled all wanted to get well? The truth is, that just like this invalid, some of us have been sick for so long we don't know what it means to be well. We don't know life any other way. You see, healing involves more than just our bodies. It involves our souls and spirits. That could be why Jesus asked the question.

The truth is, that just like this invalid, some of us have been sick for so long we don't know what it means to be well.

I think that too many of us, and in particular "Baby Boomers," have come to "own" our sicknesses and disabilities to the point where they have become our identity. "I have anxiety. I deal with depression. I'm an alcoholic. I have trouble with anger." The list goes on. These labels often garner attention and sympathy from others. They can even provide a misguided kind of personal validation that is hard to let go. If you are seeking God for healing of any kind, a good question to ask is, "Do I really want to get well?" You must be willing to let go of your past and find your true identity in Jesus.

This man's implied answer is yes but he responded to Jesus with a "poor me" excuse. He said: **"Sir... I have no one to help me into the pool when the water is stirred. While I am trying to get in, someone else goes down ahead of me"** (John 5:7). Sounds a lot like our victim culture today, doesn't it? We will never really know Jesus' assessment of the situation but it really doesn't matter. He didn't come into this world to be a social worker or a counselor. He came to save us… to "call us out" of our old life of sin, sickness and bondage and "call us up" to a new life of forgiveness, healing and freedom. Jesus simply stated: **"Get up! Pick up your mat and walk" (John 5:8).** And he did! **"At once the man was cured; he picked up his mat and walked" (John 5:9).**

While we celebrate another Bible story of a miraculous healing, let's not miss the point. We are the helpless man in this story. Jesus is saying to us, "Do you want to get well?" Have you ever waited for God to show up in your life, to answer your prayers, to give you a miracle and wondered why He never did? Have you ever heard about amazing miracles taking place in the lives of others and wondered why you weren't invited to the pool party?

Maybe you have just assumed that something is wrong with you, that you aren't faithful enough, spiritual enough or lovable enough. Maybe you have just assumed that you aren't worth it to God? People, that's a lie of Satan. That's the "invalidation" that fills our world today and leaves so many of us wounded, orphaned, helpless and hopeless.

What miracle do you need today? Does your marriage need a spark? Does your son or daughter need rescuing? Do your finances need a bail-out? How about your grades or career or health? Could it be that you have been listening to the wrong voices, hanging out in the wrong places, waiting for the gods of this world to cut you a break and grant you life's lottery? Could it be that you are missing the very one standing in front of you, reaching out His hand, calling you to get up and walk? The world declares you "in-valid." Jesus declares you to be of immense value; worthy of love, worthy to be a son or a daughter!

The Spirit-filled life is not some mystical stirring of the waters reserved for a few lucky ones. It's an outpouring of "living water" that invites every person to be healed, take up their mat and run! Do you want to be well? Reach out and take Jesus' hand today!

Godly Tears

Did you know that tears are 98% water? The other 2% consists of oils and salts. Some of us leak a lot of water! I get it from my mom, Betty. She's always been a crier; happy, sad or nothing much at all. I tear up pretty easily too. Tears can come when I'm saying goodbye to children or grandchildren, hear a testimony of a transformed life, celebrate a wedding, grieve at a funeral, watch my favorite sports team win in overtime, sing a moving worship song or enjoy a great book or movie. Did you know that Jesus cried on two occasions that are recorded in the Bible? I'm guessing there were many others. He was a man of deep compassion. The first was upon learning that His friend Lazarus had died. The second was as He looked out over the city of Jerusalem.

Lazarus was a friend of Jesus and the sister of two women, Mary and Martha. They were from Bethany. Jesus had stayed in their home and enjoyed their company. We don't know his age but when Lazarus took sick, Mary and Martha called for Jesus to come from some distance away. By the time He arrived, Lazarus had died and been buried for four days. In their grief, Mary and Martha expressed both frustration and faith that if Jesus had been there, Lazarus would still be alive.

This is a tough one. We've all had times when we've called for Jesus to come and help us… or help a loved one or friend… and felt like He either didn't hear our prayer or make it in time. It's so hard to have faith when God's timing doesn't align with ours. Someone once told me, "God is never early or late. He's always right on time." I believe it and try to remember it when my prayers don't seem to be answered, at least not in the way or timing that I think is best. Jesus could have shown up in a moment or healed Lazarus from afar. He is omniscient, all knowing. He is

> This is a tough one. We've all had times when we've called for Jesus to come and help us… or help a loved one or friend… and felt like He either didn't hear our prayer or make it in time.

omnipresent, everywhere at once. He is omnipotent, all powerful. However, as we shall see, even in the case of His dear friend, there was a greater purpose that was about to be revealed.

Jesus told Mary and Martha: **"I am the resurrection and the life. The one who believes in me will live, even though they die; and whoever lives believing in me will never die" (John 11:25-26a).** It is one of the clearest promises of eternal life found anywhere in the Bible. When Jesus saw the tears and deep grief of these two sisters, and heard the weeping of others who had come to comfort them, He was: **"… deeply moved in spirit and troubled" (John 11:33).** What follows is the shortest and perhaps most heartfelt verse in scripture. Just two words: **"Jesus wept" (John 11:35).**

As you probably know, Lazarus was raised from the dead that very same day. As great a miracle as this was, I want to highlight the love and emotion exhibited by Jesus for Lazarus and his sisters. Sometimes we think that Jesus floated about two feet off the ground, oblivious to the pain and suffering of people here on Earth. Sometimes we also think that our best play is to be tough and not show our emotions… or just keep our needs to ourselves. That's not our Savior and it shouldn't be us.

One of the "fruits of the Spirit" described in **Galatians 5:21-22** is love. It's the chief evidence of Christ in us. Following Jesus' example, the Spirit-filled life should always manifest itself in love and compassion for those who are hurting. When it does, there will be "Godly tears." The Apostle Paul later counseled some of the first believers with these words. He said: **"Be kind and compassionate to one another, forgiving each other, just as in Christ God forgave you. Be imitators of God, therefore, as dearly loved children and live a life of love, just as Christ loved us and gave himself up as a fragrant offering and sacrifice to God" (Ephesians 4:32-5:2).**

We find the second example of Jesus' tears in the Gospel of Luke. It happened near the end of His triumphal entry into Jerusalem on the first Palm Sunday. We read: **"As he approached Jerusalem and saw the city, he wept over it and said, 'If you, even you, had only** known on this day what would bring you peace – but now it is hidden from your eyes'" (Luke 19:41-42).

A similar example is found in **Matthew 9:36.** There it says: **"When he saw the crowds, he had compassion on them, because they were harassed and helpless, like sheep without a shepherd."**

I want you to know that when you lose a friend or a loved one, Jesus weeps with you. When you struggle with issues confronting your marriage or family, Jesus has compassion on you. When you look out at the world and are grieved by the millions of people who have never heard or received the truth about Jesus… or have knowingly turned their backs on Him, Jesus' heart breaks with yours. Jesus teaches us to be "deeply moved in spirit and troubled" for those who are hurting in this world, even to the point of tears. We serve a compassionate Savior who is not afraid to cry for those He loves. Are you?

Thirst No More

I hope you have been touched by these "water stories." Even more, I pray they have moved you to long for the Spirit-filled life. "Boomers!" There are people all around you who are thirsty for the same kind of experiences enjoyed by that bride and groom at the wedding reception in Cana who witnessed Jesus' first miracle; the Pharisee Nicodemus who came at night with his questions and discovered the meaning of being "born of water and the Spirit;" the Samaritan woman at Jacob's well who received love when she least expected it and "living water" for a lifetime; the man at the pool of Bethesda who experienced Jesus' healing power; and Mary, Martha and Lazarus who became "first fruits" of Jesus' promise of resurrection from the dead and eternal life in heaven. If we are to live this season of life to the fullest we must claim these promises as our own and learn to "walk wet." We must drink deeply from the well of life and then let it overflow and bless all those around us.

Questions for Personal Reflection or Group Discussion:

1. Which one of the "water stories" in this chapter was your favorite? How did it speak to you?

2. Are you willing to entertain the possibility that Jesus has saved the best for last in your life? If this were true how would it change your outlook on these next years?

3. What does it mean to you to be "baptized in the Spirit?" Why does Jesus promise to continually fill us with His love, presence and power?

4. What is a sickness in body, soul or spirit that has kept you down for years? If Jesus came to you and asked, "Do you want to get well?" how would you answer?

5. Describe a time when you prayed to Jesus for help and didn't feel like you received it? How do you reflect upon it today? Did it result in you pushing God away or drawing closer?

CHAPTER 12

Live Generously!

During the next 25 years it is predicted that Baby Boomers will be the source of the largest transfer of wealth in American history, in the neighborhood of 68 trillion dollars. That is about 70% of the accumulated wealth in the United States. "Boomers" have been the beneficiaries of a lifetime of post-World War II economic growth even with its dips and turns. This has allowed for a great accumulation of assets including real estate, stocks, additional investments and legacy businesses. Generation X (1965-1980), Generation Y or Millennials (1981-1996) and Generation Z (1997-2012) stand to inherit big bucks.

Some financial analysts and wealth managers say "not so fast," however. Baby Boomers are living longer than ever. Nearly half have little or no retirement savings and only 1 in 4 has a pension. And interestingly, 75% of "Boomers" are less interested in leaving an inheritance and more interested in living well today. Couple this with concern that passing along large amounts of money to the next generations may not be in their best interest and many questions remain.

To that end, I want to encourage our Baby Boom generation to live generously during these remaining years of our lives, not only with our money but with our time, talents and investment in the lives of others. When we do I'm convinced we will experience the blessings of God.

You have all heard the phrase: **"The love of money is the root of all kinds of evil" (1 Timothy 6:10a).** Notice that it doesn't say that money is evil. Money is a neutral thing. It can be used for good or evil or something in between. However, when we make the desire for money and possessions the priority in our lives, at the expense of our relationship with God and others, it will destroy us. Here's the larger context:

"Godliness with contentment is great gain. For we brought nothing into the world, and we can take nothing out of it. But if

> *Money is a neutral thing. It can be used for good or evil or something in between.*

we have food and clothing, we will be content with that. Those who want to get rich fall into temptation and a trap and into many foolish and harmful desires that plunge people into ruin and destruction. For the love of money is the root of all kinds of evil. Some people, eager for money, have wandered from the faith and pierced themselves with many griefs" (1 Timothy 6:6-10).

This is a warning that applies to every generation today. It applies to those who have accumulated wealth, those who have little wealth and those who anticipate receiving inheritances during the historic transfer of wealth that is coming. Buyer beware! Perhaps the greatest danger on the horizon is that the allure of wealth will pull more and more people away from genuine faith in God. Jesus said: **"No one can serve two masters. Either you will hate the one and love the other, or you will be devoted to the one and despise the other. You cannot serve both God and money" (Luke 16:13).**

I recently conducted a funeral for a 46-year old woman who died after a year-long battle with cancer. One of the qualities that was highlighted about her life was her generosity. It was said that she would welcome people into her home, even strangers, with food, clothing and a place to stay. She was someone who would literally give others the proverbial "shirt off her back." Would you like the same thing to be said about you when you die? Do you know how to become known as a generous person? By being generous!

In this chapter I'd like to challenge you to consider **"Seven Keys to Generous Living."** Generosity is a reflection of the love of God at work in our lives. The key to generous living is generous giving. One leads to the other and the reverse is true as well. Here's the thing. Generosity isn't just an occasional act like when somebody says, "I think I feel like being generous today!" and leaves a big tip. It is way more than a mood that hits us once and awhile. It's a lifestyle that flows out of our relationship with God who is the most generous giver of all! Remember? **"For God so loved the world that He <u>gave</u> His one and only Son…" (John 3:16a).**

Generosity has to do with how we approach everything "we are" and everything "we have" including our money, possessions, family, friends, work, entertainment, time and talents. Generosity isn't something we do. It's something we are! Generous living is "grace-filled living!" When it flows from the heart it becomes a response of love, not guilt. When it comes to the question, "What will I do with the rest of my life?" our perspective on our money and possessions is critical! I hope these "keys" to generous living will challenge

> *Generosity isn't something we do. It's something we are!*

you to reflect further and consider changes in both attitude and actions as you move forward. I accept the same challenge myself. So here we go! First…

Put your Hope in God, not Stuff

Several years ago I bought a new Ford F-150 truck with all the toots and whistles. It's a beauty! It required some salesmanship, not at the dealer but with my wife. I had wanted a truck ever since my brother Mike and I owned a used Ford truck during our college years when we operated "Pagh Brothers Lawn Service." It never seemed to be the right time. It had been on my "bucket list" ever since.

173

I said, "Colleen, if I don't get that truck now I may never get it!" She said, "That would be just fine. We don't need a truck!" I said, "Honey, we don't need a truck but I want a truck! Pretty please! You can pick-out the next 10 movies!" I even rolled out a list I found online entitled, "Ten Reasons Every Man Should Own A Truck." It helped me a little. To make a long story somewhat shorter, Colleen likes to see me happy so she eventually agreed I could get my truck. I had tears the day I picked it up! The salesman said, "You know that when you get a truck you also get a lot of new friends." I said, "I have enough friends and their trucks already have scratches!"

Did my truck change who I am? No, not really, although many perceive me to be more manly now. HaHa! Does my enjoyment in driving my truck really make me happier in life? No, I'm happy already because my real happiness isn't attached to my stuff but to my Savior. This is the balance we must all find between enjoying our possessions but not being possessed by them.

A little later in Paul's letter to Timothy he says: **"Command those who are rich in this present world not to be arrogant nor to put their hope in wealth, which is so uncertain, but to put their hope in God, who richly provides us with everything for our enjoyment. Command them to do good, to be rich in good deeds, and to be generous and willing to share. In this way they will lay up treasure for themselves as a firm foundation for the coming age, so that they may take hold of the life that is truly life" (1 Timothy 6:17-19).**

You might want to read these verses a second time. They are packed with wisdom! Bottom line. If we want to take hold of the life that is "truly life" we must put our hope in God and not money or material things. A far better way to live is to be rich in good deeds and generous in giving! Second…

Re-Work Your Balance Sheet

As businesspeople know, a balance sheet is used to track assets, liabilities, and equity (or what we commonly call net worth). From an accountant's perspective, assets are things like businesses, properties, stocks, bonds and cash. Liabilities are debts that are owed against those assets. Equity is the difference between the two. By way of example, we all understand a house to be an asset and the debt against it to be a liability. If the house is worth more than you owe, the difference is what is called "equity," and in this case, positive equity.

In God's economy these three components of a balance sheet are understood very differently. In his book, "Inheritance: How God's Economy Works," author David Choe suggests that assets are those things we contribute to in life that will last forever. They are incorruptible. They are eternal. On the other hand, those things that we normally consider to be assets, as mentioned above, are actually liabilities. We don't really own them. They are simply entrusted to us for a season. Our job is to be wise stewards of God's gifts. These liabilities only become assets when we leverage them for Jesus' mission here on earth.

What is our equity, then? It's the difference between what we think we own and what we know God owns. It is the difference between earthly treasure and heavenly treasure; things like faith, love and deep relationships. No wonder that Jesus warned: **"Do not store up for yourselves treasures on earth where moths and vermin destroy, and where thieves break in and steal. But store up for yourselves treasures in heaven, where moths and vermin do not destroy, and where thieves do not break in and steal. For where your treasure is, there your heart will be also"** (Matthew 6:19-21).

In God's economy we are each lent temporary resources in the form of time, talent and treasure (a liability or debt needing to be repaid) and we're expected to produce a return in the form of what God considers eternal assets. This concept is reiterated in **Luke 12:48b** where Jesus said: **"From everyone who has been given**

much, much will be demanded; and from the one who has been entrusted with much, much more will be asked."

With what have you been entrusted? If you are intent on living a purposeful life and leaving a lasting legacy, it may be time to re-work your balance sheet on the basis of "kingdom values." The equity you accrue will not only have an impact now… but for all eternity! Third…

Seek Advancement on God's Management Team

As I just shared, the Bible is clear. God is the owner. We are the managers. **Psalm 24:1** declares: **"The earth is the Lord's and everything in it; the world, and all who live in it."** We might like to think that we own a lot of stuff. In reality it's all on loan from God. We weren't born with anything and we won't take anything with us when we die. We just get to use it for a while. A "steward" is someone who manages another person's property or possessions. One who is a good steward manages well bringing a return for the Lord! That means changed lives. That means that we are blessed to be a blessing.

It's like The Parable of the Bags of Gold in **Matthew 25:14-30**. A wealthy man was going on a long journey so he called his financial managers and entrusted his wealth to them while he was gone. To one he gave five bags of gold. To the next, two bags of gold, and to the third, one bag of gold. It was an extraordinary amount of money. When the owner returned sometime later he did a performance review.

The first man had invested wisely and turned 5 bags of gold into 10. The second man had similarly doubled his investment by turning 2 bags of gold into four. The third man, however, had failed to invest out of fear of losing the 1 bag of gold entrusted to him. He had effectively buried his treasure. The first two men were praised by the owner and given even greater wealth to manage. The third man was not only stripped of his responsibilities but his bag of gold was given to the one who had 10. The lesson? Invest wisely with the resources God has given you to manage!

Is God a capitalist expecting a significant return on His investment? Is He a socialist seeking a redistribution of wealth? Neither! God has His own economy. The world economy is based on greed, money, power and success. God's economy is measured by generosity, service and faithfulness. In God's economy our performance review is based on taking the talents and abilities He has given us, investing them wisely and giving Him the glory (translate, profit)! A good manager does their job well because they love the owner.

What bags of gold has God placed in your hands today? What are you doing with them? Settle the ownership question first and then get to work investing all that God has given you. After all, He is returning someday too! Fourth…

Seek to Excel in Giving, not just Getting

In order to encourage the young Corinthian Christians who were wealthy, the Apostle Paul used the example of the Macedonian believers who were poor. He said: **"In the midst of a very severe trial, their overflowing joy and their extreme poverty welled up in rich generosity. For I testify that they gave as much as they were able, and even beyond their ability" (2 Corinthians 8:2-3a).**

Do you know many people who overflow with joy in the midst of extreme poverty? I saw it in Africa but have seldom seen it here in America. Do you know many people who stretch to give generously, even beyond their ability? Instead, even those who have much often give only begrudgingly. Highlighting this amazing testimony Paul continued: **"But since you excel in everything – in faith, in speech, in knowledge, in complete earnestness and in the love we have kindled in you – see that you also excel in this grace of giving" (2 Corinthians 8:7).**

Most of us try to excel in our profession, families, sports, hobbies… and maybe even our faith. How many of us try to excel in the "grace of giving?" It's a worthy pursuit because the greatest blessings in life come not in what we "get" but in what we "give." In **Acts 20:35** Jesus is quoted as saying: "**It is more blessed to give than to receive.**"

We might ask why? Here are just a few of the benefits of giving that I'm sure you have experienced. Giving helps others. When you help those in need, you add to their lives – and by adding to theirs, you add to yours. Giving also inspires others to give. The generosity of the Macedonians became a testimony to the Corinthians. Furthermore, giving teaches the importance of service and sacrifice and contributes to our well-being. Numerous studies have found that those who give of their time and resources to others are just plain happier people.

> the greatest blessings in life come not in what we "get" but in what we "give."

That doesn't mean that we "give to get!" I don't preach a prosperity Gospel! "Send me a $100 and God will turn it into $1,000!" Our motives must be pure even while we take Jesus' words at face value. He said: "**Give, and it will be given to you. A good measure, pressed down, shaken together and running over, will be poured into your lap. For with the measure you use, it will be measured to you**" **(Luke 6:38).** Are you using your resources to God's glory? What would it look like if you were to make it your goal to "excel in this grace of giving?" Fifth…

Sow what You Hope to Reap

Minnesota is an agricultural state. We understand the principles of "sowing and reaping." About 46% of the total land mass in Minnesota, or about 25,000,000 acres, is devoted to either crop farming, beef cattle, dairy production or other animal related industries. 34% of Minnesota is covered in forests, another precious resource. Another

6% is covered with water including our more than 10,000 lakes, rivers and wet lands – more than any other state. This means that only 14% of Minnesota is covered with towns and cities. Would you say we have room to grow? One more fun fact. There are only 112,000 farmers in Minnesota, which is 1.9% of the 5,700,000 people living in the state. Though small in number they have a very important role to play in our economy and the stewardship of the land.

Jesus loved to teach using agricultural illustrations because they were well understood in His 1st century agrarian culture. For example, The Parable of the Sower is found in Matthew, Mark and Luke. The main point? Sow generously on good soil and you will reap a great harvest! In **2 Corinthians 9:6**, building on Jesus' teaching, Paul puts it this way: **"Remember this: Whoever sows sparingly will also reap sparingly, and whoever sows generously will also reap generously."** Perhaps this is God's way of saying, "What goes around comes around."

Ask any farmer and they will tell you that if you want a bumper crop in the Fall you need to plant good seed in good soil in the Spring. In Jesus' day they didn't plant their seeds in neat rows. They just scattered them everywhere. This doesn't make much sense to the "seed counters" of our day but it illustrates the reckless abandon of generous living that is part of God's economy.

I have a friend named Randy Dahlheimer who is an excellent crop farmer; mostly corn, soybeans and hay. His 550 acre property is adjacent to the Mississippi River in Dayton, Minnesota and has been in the family for generations. Every Spring he plants about 200 acres of corn. It takes 34,000 corn seeds, which is the equivalent of 21 lbs., to plant 1 acre of corn. With the proper amount of fertilizer and weed control that same acre will produce 180 bushels of corn in the Fall, the equivalent of 10,080 lbs. That's 480 times what was planted. I've been out with him on his corn combine and it's an amazing thing to see. We plant in faith and obedience but only God can bring the rain, the growth and such a great harvest.

This principle is true in all of life. If we sow seeds of anger and resentment, selfishness and greed… that is what we will reap. What goes around comes around! On the other hand, if we sow seeds of love and unity, honesty and integrity, faithfulness and generosity… that is what we will reap. The same is true in our relationship with Jesus. We can choose to sow "seeds" in our lives or "weeds" in our lives. What kind of a harvest are you looking for? Sixth…

Check Your Attitude at the Door

When it comes to our money and possessions, attitude is key! As Paul continues in **2 Corinthians 9:7** he says: **"Each of you should give what you have decided in your heart to give, not reluctantly or under compulsion, for God loves a cheerful giver."**

Ivan the Great was the tsar of Russia during the 15th Century. He brought together warring tribes into one vast empire. Busy waging his campaigns he never had a family and as a result there was no heir to his throne. Ivan told those in his court that he didn't have time to search for a bride… but that if they would find a suitable woman he would marry her. His counselors and advisors searched the capitols of Europe to find an appropriate wife for the great tsar… and finally, they did. She was the daughter of the King of Greece. She was young, brilliant and beautiful. Ivan the Great agreed to marry her sight unseen.

> *We can choose to sow "seeds" in our lives or "weeds" in our lives. What kind of a harvest are you looking for?*

The King of Greece was delighted! This union would align Greece in a favorable way with the emerging giant of the north. However, he gave one condition. He said, "The tsar cannot marry my daughter unless he becomes a member of the Greek Orthodox Church." Ivan's response was, "I will do it!" A Greek Orthodox Priest was immediately dispatched to Moscow to instruct him.

Several months later arrangements were concluded and Ivan the Great made his way to Athens accompanied by 500 of his crack troops – his palace guard. He was to be baptized into the Greek Orthodox

Church by immersion, as was their custom. His soldiers, ever loyal, asked to be baptized too. The Patriarch of the Church assigned 100s of priests to give the soldiers a crash course in the Christian faith. The soldiers, all 500 of them, were to be immersed in one mass baptism. Crowds gathered from all over Greece for this special occasion.

The priests wore black robes and tall black hats, the official dress of the Orthodox Church. The soldiers were attired in their battle uniforms including their ribbons of valor and medals of courage along with their shining swords at their sides. Just one problem. This regalia reminded the Patriarch that the Church had a rule. No professional soldiers were allowed to be baptized and become members of the Greek Orthodox Church because they were trained to kill, while the Church was about life and peace. With some quick diplomacy the problem was solved. As the words were spoken and the priests began to baptize, each soldier reached to his side and withdrew his sword. Lifting it over his head, every soldier was totally immersed – everything except his fighting arm and sword. It came to be known as the "unbaptized arm."

The reality today is that when most people are baptized they hold their wallet over their head, willing to trust everything to Jesus accept their money and possessions. Do you give cheerfully or reluctantly? If we are going to learn to live generously we can't hold anything back!

Next Paul reminds us: **"And God is able to bless you abundantly, so that in all things at all times, having all that you need, you will abound in every good work. Now he who supplies seed to the sower and bread for food will also supply and increase your store of seed and enlarge the harvest of your righteousness" (2 Corinthians 9:8, 10).**

Here we're encouraged to give faithfully in response to God's faithfulness to us, knowing that He is not only "able" to bless us but "desires" to bless us. Friends, when God calls us to do something to bless others or build His kingdom, He doesn't leave us hanging. As someone once said, "If God gives the vision He will also give the provision!" Generous living comes about when we begin to trust this promise and allow Him to bring it to reality in our lives.

Look at the next two verses in this wonderful text. **2 Corinthians 9:11-12** continues the thought: **"You will be enriched in every way so that you can be generous on every occasion, and through us your generosity will result in thanksgiving to God. This service that you perform is not only supplying the needs of the Lord's people but is also overflowing in many expressions of thanks to God."**

> "If God gives the vision He will also give the provision!"

When God enriches us it is for a purpose… that we might be generous at every opportunity and see this generosity result in thanksgiving to God. One time a family from Christ Church donated a used car they no longer needed to a single mom from the community who we had helped over the years. She was desperate for transportation to get to and from work, daycare, shopping etc. and her previous vehicle had died a natural death at 245,000 miles.

The day she was picking up the donated car we took it in for an oil change and filled it up with gas. We went to the Department of Motor Vehicles to sign over the title. She was just thrilled, smiling the whole time. On the way back to the church parking lot to drop me off she said, "You know, Pastor Greg, I've been thinking about this amazing gift. This is one of the kindest things anyone has ever done for me. I am so thankful!" Before she left with her new-used car we held hands and prayed God's blessings over it, her life and family. It was a pretty special moment to see how generosity rises up in thanksgiving to God.

When it comes to living generously, attitude counts! Billy Graham was quoted as saying, "If a person gets their attitude toward their money and possessions straight, it will help straighten out almost every other area in life." When we give cheerfully, not reluctantly… when we trust God to provide for every good work… when we are generous on every occasion, we not only get blessed but others are led to give thanks to God! Seventh…

Pass the Test with Flying Colors

Generous living doesn't happen without sacrifice. Two more verses from **2 Corinthians 9:13-15** bear this out. Paul concludes: **"Because of the service by which you have proved yourselves, others will praise God for the obedience that accompanies your confession of the gospel of Christ, and for your generosity in sharing with them and with everyone else. And in their prayers for you their hearts will go out to you, because of the surpassing grace God has given you. Thanks be to God for his indescribable gift!"**

Does our generosity, in fact, say something about our commitment to Jesus? Paul says that it not only proves our sincerity but is directly linked to our confession of the Good News of Jesus Christ. Generous living is more than just talk. It's action. When we "walk our talk" our giving becomes a testimony to the faithfulness of God.

There is only one time in the Bible that the Lord actually invites us to test Him! In the Old Testament, in **Malachi 3:10,** He says: **"Bring the whole tithe into the storehouse, that there may be food in my house. 'Test me in this,' says the Lord Almighty, 'and see if I will not throw open the floodgates of heaven and pour out so many blessings that there will not be room enough to store it.'"**

If our Baby Boom generation is going to commit to generous living in our later years we must be willing to put God to the test regarding these principles… and then pass this test ourselves. What would it look like for God to open the floodgates of heaven and pour out His blessings on this world today where there is such great need? How many lives would be lifted out of poverty? How many burdens would be lifted from struggling families? How many heavy hearts would be drawn to their Savior?

One of the ways God chooses to accomplish this blessing is through us. To tithe is to give 10% of our income right off the top to the Lord's work here on earth. It's called "first fruits" giving. Imagine with me for a moment. What if God came to you with this deal? He says, "I want you to take care of my stuff for a while. I want you to manage it well. As a matter of fact, I trust you so much that I'm going to let you keep 90% of what belongs to me to enjoy and be a blessing in your life. I hope you'll be generous with it. However, I want you to give 10% of my stuff back to me, both as an expression of thankfulness and to help me get the word out. You see, I want everybody to get to know me for who I really am – a God of love!"

Great deal, right! Could you live on 90% of what God has given you and give back 10% for the work of His kingdom? Could you even be cheerful about it? I'd take that deal in a New York minute! As a matter of fact, Colleen and I have personally taken that deal for a number of years now and it has been a huge blessing to us. It's called "tithing" and it's a part of God's plan for our provision and financial success. It's based on a relationship of faith, trust and thanksgiving. I've never known a tither who wanted to go back. For many it's just the starting line of generosity.

I have a friend named Myles Kawakami who for years owned a large carpet business in Maui, Hawaii. During his start-up years his business was failing and he was in deep debt. At a seminar he heard that he should give his business over to the Lord. This sounded good to him since he assumed that meant the debt too! He prayed, asking Jesus to become his CEO. From that point forward his business made a significant turn-around. He didn't forget his promise. Not only did he tithe, but every year he gave 51% of his profits to ministries on the island, particularly a huge feeding program run by his wife, Joyce. Their testimony of faith has become a huge blessing to others! It highlights the fact that giving is always a matter of obedience first. It is one test we must pass in order to really experience God's blessings!

Acquire or Invest?

Many of us spend our whole lives acquiring money and possessions so that we can live-out our 4th quarter in comfort and security. I understand the need. We all have bills to pay, pleasures we enjoy, places we want to go and things we want to see and do. Even so, once we discover the joy of giving, of living generously, it becomes one of life's greatest blessings. We discover that we truly are more blessed to give than to receive!

We've learned that generosity is more than an impulse. True generosity is a lifestyle. It flows from a growing relationship with Jesus. It comes about when we realize that everything we are and everything we have is a gift from our Creator to be celebrated, appreciated and managed wisely. The simple fact is that generous living unleashes something in us. When we learn to hold our possessions lightly we can't help but think more carefully about the use of our time, talents and additional resources.

Our priorities shift. Fewer commitments are centered on our needs and more around the needs of others. Fewer dollars are spent buying one more toy for ourselves and more dollars go to help meet the needs of others. Generous giving leads to generous living. Life itself takes on a greater purpose resulting in greater fulfillment. Isn't it time that we shifted our focus from acquiring to investing, trusting God to show us the way?

> True generosity is a lifestyle. It flows from a growing relationship with Jesus.

Jesus told two contrasting stories that illustrate the difference. One is called the Rich Young Ruler and the other the Widow's Mite. Allow me to re-tell them in my own words. One day a young man fell at Jesus' feet and asked, "Good teacher, what must I do to inherit eternal life?" Surprisingly, Jesus responded, "Why do you call Me good? No one is good but God alone!" Next came the set-up. Jesus said, "You know the commandments…" and listed several of them. The young man said, "I have kept them all since I was just a young boy."

The next line in the story is critical. It reads: **"Jesus looked at him and loved him" (Mark 10:21a).** No more playing around! He said, "There is one thing you lack. Go sell everything you have and give it to the poor. Instead of being so attached to your money you will find treasure in heaven. Then come follow Me." That was when the young man's countenance fell. The Bible says: **"He went away sad, because he had great wealth" (Mark 10:22b).**

This man's riches caused him to be one of the very few people in the Bible who personally encountered Jesus and walked away disappointed and discouraged. The truth is that we cannot trust Jesus with our whole lives unless we are willing to trust Him with our money and possessions.

Jesus was an observer of people. He was able to see into the depths of their hearts. During the first Holy Week, just a couple of days before Jesus' crucifixion, He sat down to rest in front of the temple in Jerusalem. It was a pause, a short break from the crowds, the questions, the uproar to look over the multitude of people going about their business, people for whom He would soon give His life. One elderly woman who Jesus discerned to be a widow caught His eye. It was Passover Week and people were coming to put their offerings in the temple treasury. It was like a toll booth basket on the side of the temple building. Money could be heard clinking and clanking as coins were dropped down the chute.

The rich, dressed in their finest apparel, put in large sums of silver and gold. It was obvious they hoped others would notice. The widow came in her own unpretentious way and put two small copper coins in the treasury that only amounted to one penny. Upon observing this, Jesus called His disciples and said to them: **"Truly I tell you, this poor widow has put more in the treasury than all the others. They all gave out of their wealth; but she, out of her poverty, put in everything – all that she had to live on" (Mark 12:43-44).**

Notice the contrast between the rich young man and this poor widow. One withheld while he lived in abundance. The other gave everything while she lived in poverty. One represents a lack of trust, the other a total commitment. Those two small coins may have literally represented her next meal or a small amount of oil to light her lamp. There were lots of reasons she might have chosen to hold on to those coins. She could have thought, "What difference will my small gift make? No one will even notice."

The distinguishing mark of this widow's gift wasn't merely its proportion to her means. It was what Jesus saw in her heart that lifted this gift out of routine into the realm of true sacrifice. It was her need to give, her faith to give, and her trust in God to provide that has now inspired generations to live generously. The "widow's mite" became a mighty testimony for us all! The gift which counts is the gift which costs!

Friends, life is measured not by what we give but by what we withhold. Jesus said: **"For where your treasure is, there your heart will be also" (Matthew 6:21).** He wants us to go away from every encounter with Him feeling blessed, not sad. I challenge you to live generously and experience the wealth that only God can give.

Questions for Personal Reflection or Group Discussion:

1. Do you consider yourself to be a generous person? Would others say the same? React to the phrase, "Generosity isn't something we do. It's something we are!"

2. Evaluate your balance sheet. On the basis of God's economy, reflect on your assets, liabilities and equity. What might need some re-working?

3. Where are you sowing seed in your life today? (Investing your time, talent and resources.) What harvest would you like to see?

4. Name three of your most valuable material possessions? How would it change your relationship with Jesus if you lost them?

5. Describe a time of need when God unmistakably provided for you? Describe a need you have right now where you are asking God to do the same?

CHAPTER 13

Knock Down Walls!

One of the great callings upon our generation as Baby Boomers, I believe, is to be peacemakers. It makes sense, doesn't it? We're the "Make Love–Not War" generation! That slogan emerged out of the 60s protest movement when the Vietnam War was at its peak. Approximately 2,700,000 men and women served in Vietnam in some capacity between 1955 and 1975. Most of them were "Boomers." Total casualties for the Vietnam War are listed at 58,220. It was the first war in which the United States failed to meet its objectives, leaving in defeat. It was also the first time America failed to welcome its soldiers home as heroes. Many of our generation still suffer wounds from Vietnam… both physical and psychological. There have been other wars since of course, however, Vietnam had the greatest impact on our generation.

It is sad to say but it is estimated that right now there are approximately 40 wars or significant conflicts happening in three dozen countries around the globe. How do we square this ongoing reality with the fact that Jesus came as the "Prince of Peace?" The prophet Isaiah declared: **"Of the greatness of his government and peace there will be no end"** (Isaiah 9:7a).

On the night of His birth the angels sang: **"Glory to God in the highest heaven, and on earth peace to those on whom his favor** rests" **(Luke 2:14).** During the Sermon on the Mount Jesus said: **"Blessed are the peacemakers, for they will be called children of God" (Matthew 5:9).** As He prepared for the last days of His earthly life Jesus told His disciples: **"Peace I leave with you; my peace I give you. I do not give to you as the world gives. Do not let your hearts be troubled and do not be afraid" (John 14:27).**

Given the fact that approximately 1/3 of the world's population is Christian, shouldn't peace be breaking out everywhere? Instead, the divisions seem to be growing deeper, the gaps wider. If we take Jesus' words seriously we must ask the question, "Why is the world still so divided today and is there anything we can do about it?"

In his letter to the Ephesians, the Apostle Paul reminds us that Jesus is our peace... and that He has: **"... destroyed the barrier, the dividing wall of hostility" (Ephesians 2:14b).** In this amazingly practical New Testament book, written from a jail cell in Rome, Paul describes a series of issues that represented points of division in his first century world, and not surprisingly, still do today.

> *"Why is the world still so divided today and is there anything we can do about it?"*

He highlights personal, racial, denominational, relational, marital, generational, societal and spiritual divisions. Paul begins with the premise that peace must be found in our own hearts first. Only then will we have the love, compassion and fortitude to challenge the divisions in society, from the most basic of personal conflicts to those that eventually erupt in war. Furthermore, Paul teaches that it isn't until we've developed "street cred" by seeking peace in our earthly relationships that we will truly have "spiritual cred" to challenge evil spiritual forces in heavenly places.

Ephesians reads like a "how to" manual for those truly seeking peace and unity... not just superficial agreement for the sake of appearances. In both this chapter and the next we will ask, "What could happen if today's Baby Boomers, all those who claim to believe in Jesus, passionately pursued peace? What if we used our 4th quarter to love like He loved? What if we started really treating our family members, friends, coworkers, classmates, strangers, and even enemies like Jesus treated the people He met? What if we didn't shy away from the challenging issues that are confronting society today but instead found constructive ways to address them? Would it not lead to a revolution of peace? Would the walls that divide us not come down? Would love and unity in the name of Jesus not rise up?" I believe that if we "Boomers" take the lead rather than turn away, the world as we know it will be transformed!

Individual Walls

This process must start in us. We can't give away what we don't have. When you think of dividing walls in history, what comes to mind? The Great Wall of China? The Berlin Wall? The Wailing Wall in Jerusalem? The wall at the southwestern border of the United States? The Bible tells us that the greatest wall of all time is the "wall of sin" that separates humankind from God. Sin is both a condition and an action. It means "missing the mark" of God's perfect plan for our lives. The Bible says that there is no difference between us: **"… for all have sinned and fall short of the glory of God…" (Romans 3:23).** This is the short answer to why our world is still so filled with anger, dissension and division today.

Conflicts in society are always the result of conflicts that exist deep within us… at the heart level. Because Jesus is the ultimate peacemaker, if there is little or no unity in our personal relationships with Him, there will be little or no unity in our relationships with one another. That's just how it works. Someone who is in turmoil on the inside will not be a peacemaker on the outside.

I did a funeral once for a man I didn't know. The funeral director had called and asked for my assistance and I had said, "Yes." I met with the family of the deceased and they shared stories and memories of his life and faith. I put my message together and conducted the service. Afterwards I was standing in the lobby of the funeral home. A man came up to me and said, "You know, all the nice things you said about him today… they are all a bunch of (insert expletive)! He was the biggest (insert expletive) I have ever met! Nobody could get along with him!" I told him that I didn't know the man and was just sharing what the family had shared with me. I have often wondered though, why, if the deceased was all of those terrible things, did this guy still attend his funeral?

Even for the most ornery among us, Jesus our "peacemaker" has also become our "wall-breaker!" Though we are all stuck in sin, through Jesus, a fresh start is possible. His death and resurrection are the power that breaks down individual "dividing walls of hostility." Through the gifts of forgiveness and salvation we become "new creations in Christ" and experience a new way of believing, thinking and acting that is in unity with God's love and purpose for our lives. This personal relationship also changes the way we respond to others.

How would you describe your relationship with Jesus right now?

- Non-existent
- Alive and growing
- Religious but bored
- Took the wrong turn
- Lots of questions
- Ready for a breakthrough

Here's the good news! No matter how unlikeable a person you may have been in the past, or how far away from God you are right now, there is hope for you in the future. Through Jesus we are not only redeemed, which means "bought for a price," but reconciled and reclaimed as partners in fulfilling God's plans for this world.

I've never been a puzzle guy! My wife and her mom and sisters can spend hours sitting at a card table working together on these 500 or 1,000 piece puzzles. Pretty pictures… but "boring!" And besides, what if you get to the end and there's one piece missing. How disappointing is that! I'm convinced that Jesus shares my sentiment. He doesn't want any pieces of His puzzle to be missing when He comes again. That includes you! The picture that God desires for this world won't be complete unless we all do our part to fit together.

You see, to be reconciled is to be brought back into relationship. It is to find our place in the puzzle of life. Coming into proper alignment with Jesus is key because we will never experience greater unity with others if we are living as spiritual orphans ourselves; isolated, alone or lost under the table. We must allow Jesus to both "find us" and "fit us" into His perfect picture for our lives. Only then can He "use us" to be peacemakers in the world. Welcome again to this awesome journey of discovery!

Racial Walls

When the Apostle Paul originally wrote his letter to the Church at Ephesus, the "dividing wall" he referred to was a racial one between Jews and Gentiles. A Gentile was anyone outside the Jewish faith. There actually was a wall called "the middle wall of partition" that divided the "inner court" of the Jewish temple, which was only open to Jews, from the "outer court" to which Gentile visitors were admitted. To cross the line was punishable by death.

An excavation of the temple site in 1871 unearthed the following inscription: "No man of any other race is to proceed within the partition and enclosing wall about the sanctuary; and anyone arrested there will have himself to blame for the penalty of death which will be imposed as a consequence."[1] This "middle wall of partition" reminds us of modern manifestations of racism from Jim Crow segregation laws in the United States to apartheid in South Africa.

How revolutionary it was when Paul declared: **"He (Jesus) came and preached peace to you who were far away and peace to those who were near. For through him we both have access to the Father by one Spirit. Consequently, you are no longer foreigners and aliens, but fellow citizens with God's people and members of God's household…" (Ephesians 2:17-19).**

Because everyone has equal access through Jesus as fellow citizens and members of God's household, we cannot allow earthly "walls of partition" to divide us anymore. As Christians we must "call out" racial inequities wherever we see them still existing. The following definitions are a composite of key elements I have gleaned from a number of sources and are certainly subject to debate. See what you think?

Race refers to a group of persons related by common descent or heredity. Today, race is an arbitrary classification of humans often based on a combination of physical characteristics such as skin color, facial form, eye shape, and recently, various genetic markers.

Ethnicity refers to social groups who share a common cultural heritage often including language, values, religion, customs, behavior and attitudes.

Prejudice is the result of preconceived opinions or feelings about a person or group based on superficial or unsubstantiated judgments.

Racism occurs when prejudice combines with power and leads to any attitude, action or institutional structure which subordinates a person because of race, skin color or ethnic differences.

How were you raised when it came to racial stereotypes, prejudices and judgments? My parents taught us to "love people as people" from our earliest days, however, the truth is that I grew up in small towns or affluent suburbs where there was very little ethnic diversity. It wasn't until I went to the University of Minnesota from 1971-1973 that I really experienced racial issues on a personal level. It wasn't until a couple of years later that I had my first real friend who had a different skin color than mine. Reflect on your own upbringing and how your past experiences may still inform your attitude toward race today.

Next, take a look at the community/region where you are living now. Where is racial tension the greatest? Is it being addressed in a constructive manner, simmering beneath the surface or erupting in violence? Why do you think the subject of racism has become so emotionally charged in society today? How can we as "Boomers" take the lead in breaking down these "dividing walls of hostility?"

Here is my list of "Top 10 Strategies for Knocking Down Racial Barriers."

1. Speak peace rather than curse those of another race. This approach will give you the heart of God and open your eyes to see real people.
2. Speak-up and express your feelings when someone tells an off-color ethnic joke, engages in stereotyping or makes racial slurs.
3. Build personal relationships with people of other races. Getting to know someone as a friend breaks down all kinds of barriers. Spend time in one another's homes. Eat together. Fellowship together. Share life together.
4. Learn about other races and appreciate the variety of history and gifts that exist among all of God's people in the world.
5. Worship and pray with people from other racial and ethnic groups. Learn to appreciate different musical styles and ways of expressing faith.
6. Respond to the "felt needs" of other racial and ethnic groups, meaning those needs that are most pressing in their lives today. Pray. Act. Expect miracles. In doing so, God will open both their heart and yours to see the deeper needs.
7. Take the lead in challenging institutional and social barriers where racism still exists in the church, education, business, law and government. When you see a wrong, take action with others to right it.
8. Humble yourself before others and seek forgiveness and reconciliation for wrongs both past and present.
9. Pray for one another. God will often do in the Spirit what we cannot do in the flesh.
10. Proclaim the Good News that through Jesus every person in the world is welcome in the family of God. We are sons

and daughters of the same Heavenly Father, brothers and sisters of the same Jesus.

I have a theory based on what I've shared above. If every Christian developed at least one loving friendship with someone of a different skin color, we could end racism in one generation. The "middle wall of partition" no longer exists. It's time for racial division to end!

Denominational Walls

The Christian Church today, in all its unique manifestations, is still filled with division and conflict. Among the greatest detriments to the effective spread of Christianity are the "dividing walls of hostility" that keep even Christians isolated from one another. I began a discussion of this topic in Chapter 9, "Challenge the ISMs." By one estimate there are 35,000 different denominations in the Christian Church today. Some denominations were formed to call attention to an aspect of God's Word that had been lost or neglected. Their formation was rooted in a call for reform and renewal.

> If every Christian developed at least one loving friendship with someone of a different skin color, we could end racism in one generation.

Lesser motives have often prevailed. Too many denominations, as well as individual churches, are the result of "splits" that were caused by individualism, pride, anger and personal preferences. This point of division then took root in a "claim to fame" of superiority and truth. This leads to a "tearing down" of the body of Christ rather than a "building up." Denominational divisions and in-fighting also make for a very confusing message to an unbelieving world. This is reflected in comments like, "Christians can't even get along with one another!" Or, "Why would I want to join a church when all they do is fight!"

One time a ship was lost at sea. All on board died but for one sailor who became stranded on a deserted island. Realizing that he might be there for a while he began to construct some buildings with lumber from the shipwreck, starting with a house. During the 30 years that followed he developed quite a community. "Who knows," he thought, "others may find me some day and decide to stay here."

One day his dream came true. As the rescue boat landed on shore he greeted his visitors with great joy. He said, "Let me show you this beautiful island that has become my home and the community I've built!" As they took the tour he said, "This is my house. This is the school. This is my office building. This is the police station. And, this is my church!" They said, "It's all very beautiful but what is that building over there?" He responded, "That's the church I used to go to!"

Paul had high hopes for the Church. In **Ephesians 3:14-21** we find one of the most beautiful and inspiring prayers ever written. Paul says: **"For this reason I kneel before the Father, from whom his whole family in heaven and on earth derives its name. I pray that out of his glorious riches he may strengthen you with power through his Spirit in your inner being, so that Christ may dwell in your hearts through faith. And I pray that you, being rooted and established in love, may have power, together with all the saints, to grasp how wide and long and high and deep is the love of Christ, and to know this love that surpasses knowledge – that you may be filled to the measure of all the fullness of God. Now to him who is able to do immeasurably more than all we ask or imagine, according to his power that is at work within us, to him be glory in the church and in Christ Jesus throughout all generations, for ever and ever! Amen."**

The Greek word for church is "ekklesia," which means an "assembly." In the Greek city-states representatives would gather in the town square to legislate important issues. It was said that "wherever two or three gathered in the name of Rome, Rome was there." Jesus borrowed this unifying imagery when he said: **"Again, truly I tell you that if two of you on earth agree about anything** they ask for, it will be done for them by my Father in heaven. For where two or three gather in my name, there I am with them" (Matthew 18:19-20).

This profound understanding of both unity and authority in the Greco-Roman culture is used by Jesus to describe an even greater level of unity and authority that is to exist in the Christian Church today. The term "ekklesia" reminds us that wherever two or three gather in Jesus' name, the Church is there! This lowest common denominator, in fact, represents our greatest authority.

This kind of profound unity in the Church takes work! In **Ephesians 4:3-6** Paul admonishes: **"Make every effort to keep the unity of the Spirit through the bond of peace. There is one body and one Spirit – just as you were called to one hope when you were called – one Lord, one faith, one baptism; one God and Father of all, who is over all and through all and in all."**

Scriptures like this are calling the Church back to its foundations. Paradigms are shifting! The Church is breaking-out instead of breaking-up! On Sundays the Church "gathers" for worship, study and fellowship in a variety of settings. From Monday through Saturday the Church "scatters" to serve and witness, recognizing that everyone is a minister. New ministry prototypes are being developed all over the world that remind us that the Church that was born in the Upper Room in Jerusalem was never meant to stay there. Ekklesias, unique expressions of the Christian Church, are being birthed in homes, coffee shops, board rooms and lunch rooms.

> *Paradigms are shifting! The Church is breaking-out instead of breaking-up!*

There's more! Both pulpit and marketplace ministers are treating each other as equals and forming strategic alliances to pastor the "Church of the city" made up of every believer in Christ. A renewed passion is also developing for reaching those who don't yet know Jesus or have fallen away from an active faith. Local congregations are changing their focus from "church growth" to "kingdom growth."

Cooperation is increasing. Competition is decreasing. Unbelievers are noticing! Yes, it is an exciting day for the Church of Jesus Christ!

Our city transformation leadership team in Elk River, Minnesota has spoken in more than 30 cities across the state. One time we were sharing testimony in a town of about 10,000 where the two largest churches and their pastors didn't like each other. Their competition was intense. They frequently accused each other of "sheep stealing." Derogatory words had even been spoken from the pulpit. Everyone in the community knew of their disdain for the other.

During a luncheon meeting our team shared testimony of our city-wide transformation movement and the weekly prayer meeting with pastors and marketplace leaders that took place every Tuesday at noon. It continues to this very day, now for more than 25 years. We talked about what God had done in our hearts to break down denominational walls and bring us into what we called "unity with a purpose." Knowing the situation, I challenged those two pastors by saying, "If you will become best friends your whole city will be transformed." As one of our team members prayed at the end of the meeting, one of those two pastors broke down in tears… heaving tears. The Holy Spirit was bringing conviction and repentance.

When the prayer was over, my colleague who had prayed asked the pastor if he would like to share what was happening for him. Without any hesitation he got down on his knees, turned to the other pastor, and began to confess and ask for forgiveness for his competitive, judgmental spirit and the many derogatory things he had said about the other's church. When he finished, the other pastor did the same. Before we left that day the two had hugged it out and were planning to meet for lunch. After that, the spiritual climate in the whole community began to change. Both of their ministries are thriving today.

These are all encouraging signs that denominational "dividing walls of hostility" are coming down. I believe that the impact of denominationalism will continue to diminish in the generations that are following us even as new levels of unity, like those described above, will increase. There is an urgency in our world today that demands it. Never before has there been such a need for Christians to come together and be the Church the Apostle Paul envisioned when he wrote his letter to the Ephesians.

Another extraordinarily important development happening today is that the Church is recognizing the importance and authority of the 5-fold ministry offices described by Paul in **Ephesians 4:11-13.** There he says: **"So Christ himself gave the apostles, the prophets, the evangelists, the pastors and teachers, to equip his people for works of service, so that the body of Christ may be built up until we all reach unity in the faith and in the knowledge of the Son of God and become mature, attaining to the whole measure of the fullness of Christ."**

I believe that for the Christian Church to be successful in reaching a hurting and divided world today these ministry offices must all function together in unity in the local church, in the community and the state. They represent different "callings" and "giftings" but each ministry office is equally important. The Church has always acknowledged the role of Pastors and Teachers, who are often one in the same. In the last several centuries, this same "tip of the hat" has been given to Evangelists. In more recent years the roles of Prophets and Apostles are also being rediscovered. Praise God!

When people think of a Prophet they often picture someone who predicts the future. A Christian Prophet is more likely a person who, under the leading of the Holy Spirit, declares the truth of God's Word and brings words of insight and encouragement that contribute to building up the whole body of Christ. An Apostle is a person who, by Holy Spirit inspired leadership, lays foundations in ministry and in culture that others can build upon. The Apostle Paul put it this way: **"Consequently, you are no longer foreigners and strangers, but fellow citizens with God's people and also members of his household, built on the foundation of the apostles and prophets, with Christ Jesus himself as the chief cornerstone" (Ephesians 2:19).**

These 5 ministry offices operate in many ways as concentric circles, like the ripples created when a stone is thrown into a glassy lake. Pastors and teachers most often care for a local congregation of believers, inspiring faith and discipleship. Evangelists take it a step further with boldness and creative approaches to reaching those who don't yet know Jesus and encouraging others to do the same. Prophets expand the circle again by "truth telling" and encouraging believers to see how God is moving in the world. An Apostle looks even wider to see a region, a state, a nation and beyond by casting vision and developing action steps that help build-up the whole kingdom of God.

Here is a key! No ministry office is more important than another. It isn't a hierarchy. And yet, each ministry office is vitally important in order for the whole body of Christ to function effectively. It's a partnership for the sake of equipping the whole church for greater maturity and effectiveness, just as Paul says. Reflect on this! While we are not all called to the Office of Pastor or Teacher, we are all called to minister to the needs of others and teach the truth of God's Word. While we are not all called to the Office of Evangelist, we are all called to share our faith and reach people for Christ. While we are not all called to the Office of Prophet, we are all called to declare the Word of God, discern the days and seasons of God's moving and give "words of encouragement" as the Holy Spirit leads. And similarly, while we are not all called to the Office of Apostle, we are all called to "act apostolically" by seeing the big picture and laying spiritual foundations that others can build upon. Which of these "ministry offices" most represent your spiritual giftings? How are you moving in them today to contribute to greater unity in the Church and world?

Baby Boomers! We can live-out our days doing Church as we've always done it before, stuck in old paradigms and old traditions, or we can ride the wave of the Spirit who is reviving and renewing the Church to reach the generations that are following us. It truly will take the whole Church to present the whole Gospel to the whole world. We have the passion, wisdom and experience of many years to share with others as leaders, volunteers and mentors. Whatever role we are called to play, we can be quite certain that God wants to use us to expand His kingdom unto His glory! May the children of God rise up!

Relational Walls

Troubled relationships among human beings are involved in every one of the "dividing walls of hostility" addressed by Paul in his letter to the Ephesians. Since the very beginning of time... when Adam blamed Eve and Eve blamed the serpent, people have been blaming each other. The caption found in many Bibles for the second half of Ephesians 4 is "Instructions for Christian Living." Remember that titles like this have been added by editors and were not a part of Paul's original writing, and yet, they help guide our reading.

> We can live-out our days doing Church as we've always done it before, stuck in old paradigms and old traditions, or we can ride the wave of the Spirit who is reviving and renewing the Church to reach the generations that are following us.

Paul offers one main point for our consideration in this section. He says that there ought to be a noticeable difference in the way that Christians think and act as compared with others who are not following God. He reflects: **"You were taught, with regard to your former way of life, to put off your old self, which is being corrupted by its deceitful desires; to be made new in the attitude of your minds; and to put on the new self, created to be like God in true righteousness and holiness" (Ephesians 4:22-24).**

In other words, if you are truly a Christian, people should notice the difference that Jesus makes in your life. Look at the chart below. It shows the contrast between a number of qualities that are all mentioned in Ephesians in terms of "Life Before Christ" and "Life in Christ." Which of these qualities are being reflected in your life?

Life Before Christ	**Life In Christ**
Darkness	Light
Separated from God	United with Christ
Living a lie	Living in truth
Self-centered	God-centered
Angry	Peaceful
Lazy	Hard-working
Foul mouthed	Kind and compassionate
Vengeful	Forgiving
Tearing things down	Building things up
Sexually immoral	Loving and committed
Deceptive	Transparent
Foolish	Purposeful
Drunk on wine	Filled with the Spirit
Resentful	Thankful

Rest assured, none of us is perfect. As Christians we are all on a journey of faith to become more like Jesus. Which of the qualities on the right side of the ledger would you like to see further developed in your life right now?

Paul continues with what I think is a wonderful summary statement. In **Ephesians 4:32** he declares: **"Be kind and compassionate to one another, forgiving each other, just as in Christ God forgave you."** Let's briefly consider the three qualities highlighted here, which perhaps we can all agree, are absolutely necessary to knock down relational walls of hostility. They are kindness, compassion and forgiveness.

Kindness

I did a random act of kindness once that really cost me! A Christian radio station in Minneapolis, Minnesota calls it "the drive through difference." When you're doing the drive-through window at a coffee shop or fast food joint you offer to pay for the car behind you in addition to your own bill. One day I was grabbing a cup of coffee and the person in front of me paid for me. It would have been about $5.00. In order to pass on this unexpected blessing I told the barista that I would pay for the car behind me. I forgot to look in the rearview mirror first! There were three people in the car and they ordered treats to go along with their coffee. My bill was about $26.00. All I could do was acknowledge the Lord's sense of humor as I drove away.

Kindness, as simple as it sounds, often comes with a cost and not just to our wallet or purse. I shared earlier that during Bless Minnesota Week, which is our annual emphasis that follows the National Day of Prayer in May, we encourage people all over Minnesota to do "intentional acts of kindness in Jesus' name." After all, shouldn't kindness by intentional, not random?

Titus 3:4-5a reads: **"But when the kindness and love of God our Savior appeared, he saved us, not because of righteous things we had done, but because of his mercy."** Friends, when Jesus appeared, kindness appeared! Jesus went out of his way to be kind. He was intentional about it. He was interruptible. He cared about people and He loved doing kind things for others; the paralytic lowered through the roof, the men with leprosy, the woman about to be stoned, the children who crawled up into His lap. Jesus was kind, and when we are, it becomes an important part of our witness. As a matter of fact, in **Romans 2:4** it says: **"… it's the kindness of God that leads to repentance."** Ask the Holy Spirit to reveal a specific person in your life right now with whom you can share some "Jesus kindness." It may cost you something but what a blessing you will be!

Compassion

Compassion also goes a long way toward breaking down walls that can get built up in personal relationships. Compassion means "walking a mile in the other person's moccasins," to quote that Native American proverb. Before making a judgement about someone it's important to put ourselves in their place and try to understand their life experiences and personal challenges. In other translations this word "compassion" is also rendered as "tenderhearted."

To be compassionate, to be tenderhearted is to ask, "If I were that person right now, what would I be thinking, feeling or needing?" I find that when I look at people with genuine compassion rather than judgement I am much better able to hear the voice of the Holy Spirit in terms of how I can respond to their needs. Jesus showed us all the way.

In **Matthew 9:35-36** it says: **"Jesus went through all the towns and villages, teaching in their synagogues, preaching the good news of the kingdom and healing every disease and sickness. When he saw the crowds, he had compassion on them, because they were harassed and helpless, like sheep without a shepherd."**

> *I find that when I look at people with genuine compassion rather than judgement I am much better able to hear the voice of the Holy Spirit in terms of how I can respond to their needs.*

Who do your see in your circles of influence who are "harassed and helpless?" How can you "shepherd them" to greener pastures? Notice that the word "compassion" contains within it the word "passion." Both are required in order for us to see the world as Jesus sees it and love others as Jesus loves them. Genuine compassion always leads to action.

For example, there is a wonderful non-profit organization called "Compassion International." Their calling is to positively impact the long-term development of children living in poverty primarily through child sponsorship. To sponsor a child somewhere around the globe is currently $38/month. If you were watching one of their commercials on T.V. and saw pictures of hungry, poverty stricken children and had compassion... it would mean that your heart went out to them. You might think, "How would I feel if that was my child?"

Could it be argued, however, that if you were motivated by true compassion, you would pick up your phone, call the number on your T.V. screen and sponsor a child? As I said, genuine compassion should always lead to action. I realize that we can't each personally respond to every need out there but I'm sure you get the point. To knock down "relational dividing walls of hostility" we must not only "feel for people," we must do something about it!

Forgiveness

Perhaps the most important word of our Ephesians 4:32 trio is forgiveness. Is anything more important when it comes to making peace with others? In **1 John 1:8-9** it says: **"If we claim to be without sin, we deceive ourselves and the truth is not in us. If we confess our sins, he is faithful and just and will forgive our sins and purify us from all unrighteousness."**

God is in the forgiveness business! He calls us to do the same. The writer, Oscar Wilde, is attributed with the following quote. "Always forgive your enemies; nothing annoys them so much." That may be true. The flip side is that when we withhold forgiveness we hurt no one but ourselves.

Many pastors, including me, would testify that the greatest wounds we have suffered in ministry haven't come from non-believers outside the church... but from believers within the church. When your vision or decision-making doesn't align with theirs, even well-meaning Christians can become angry and accusatory. When people are disappointed, let down or get their feelings hurt, it's human nature to lash out against the pastor or other church leaders.

In 40-plus years of ministry I've been called everything from uncaring to a false prophet! In those situations I've tried to have honest conversation, apologize when I've blown it and work toward reconciliation when possible. Sometimes people choose to stir-up more trouble, leave mad and co-opt others in the process. It's painful! I take some consolation in statements like this one shared by a very wise pastor years ago. He said, "Leading a church is like driving a bus. People will get on the bus and people will get off the bus. The most important thing is to keep driving and know where you're headed!"

In any situation, when people become angry with you, even questioning your faith and character, you have a choice to make. You can become angry right back, bitter and resentful, or by the grace of God you can forgive and move on. I've learned that by far the best choice is to release the hurt to God and forgive, as hard as it can be! Besides, then when you run into that person in the grocery store or at a grad party you can smile instead of hide!

> "Leading a church is like driving a bus. People will get on the bus and people will get off the bus. The most important thing is to keep driving and know where you're headed!"

In **Colossians 3:13-14** the Apostle Paul advises: **"Bear with each other and forgive one another if any of you has a grievance against someone. Forgive as the Lord forgave you."** This admonition reminds us of The Lord's Prayer where Jesus taught us to pray, "Forgive us our trespasses as we forgive those who trespass against us." What we have asked God to do in the "vertical" we must also be willing to live-out in the "horizontal."

Who do you need to forgive right now? Where are you feeling anger and resentment toward someone that needs to be released to God? Where are you carrying a wound that only God can heal? Forgiveness is absolutely vital in order to find peace in your heart and contribute to greater peace and unity in the world.

Martin Luther King, Jr., on numerous occasions, preached on the theme of "Loving Your Enemies." On November 17, 1957, he spoke at Dexter Avenue Baptist Church in Montgomery, Alabama. Near the end of his message he said this: "Now there is a final reason I think that Jesus says, 'Love your enemies.' It is this: that love has within it a redemptive power. And there is power there that eventually transforms individuals. That's why Jesus says, 'Love your enemies.' Because if you hate your enemies, you have no way to redeem and transform your enemies. But if you love your enemies, you will discover that at the very root of love is the power of redemption."[2]

These are such eloquent and powerful words! What is redemptive love? Paul hits it out of the park with the profound statement we have just considered: **"Be kind and compassionate to one another, forgiving each other, just as in Christ God forgave you" (Ephesians 4:32).** Real love happens when these three words; kindness, compassion and forgiveness are evident in our daily lives and relationships with others, both our friends and our enemies.

In Chapter 14 we will continue this theme as we consider marital, generational, societal and spiritual dividing walls of hostility. "Boomers!" When we confront these "gaps" that exist in our world today with the love of Jesus, even the highest walls will come tumbling down. What will we do with the rest of our lives? Certainly part of the answer to that question is found in our calling to be peacemakers!

Questions for Personal Reflection or Group Discussion:

1. What "dividing walls of hostility" are most evident where you live, work and play?
2. Do you have any good friends who have a different skin color than yours? If so, how has this relationship changed your perspective on racial issues today? Which of the "Top 10 Strategies for Knocking Down Racial Barriers" are you willing to put into action?

3. Which of the "5-fold ministry gifts" do you identify with the most? Apostle, Prophet, Evangelist, Pastor, Teacher. Think beyond titles to function.
4. Reflect on Bible stories that illustrate Jesus' kindness, compassion and forgiveness. How do they encourage you to do the same?

Notes:

1. Interpreter's Bible, Volume 10, (Nashville, TN: Parthenon Press, 1978), p. 655.
2. "Loving Your Enemies," Martin Luther King, Jr. (Excerpt from a sermon delivered at Dexter Avenue Baptist Church in Montgomery, Alabama on November 17, 1957), courtesy of the Martin Luther King, Jr. Research and Education Institute, Stanford University, Stanford, California.

CHAPTER 14

Take A Stand!

There is that old saying that goes, "Keep your friends close and your enemies closer." When it comes to human relationships we cannot help but be on the look-out. There is always someone, it seems, who wants our reputation, our money, our job and maybe even our spouse. Choosing friends and recognizing enemies is an important life skill. The fact that Jesus told us to love our enemies both proves they exist and provides us with an even greater challenge.

In this chapter we're going to pick-up where we left off in Chapter 13. The simple premise is that our world is divided, perhaps as never before. Even though we serve the Prince of Peace, we are experiencing a division among people and a rise in violence everywhere we look. Can we break the cycle? Is it possible that God could uniquely use each of us in this season of life to be difference makers?

The answer given by the Apostle Paul in his letter to the Ephesians is "Yes! Absolutely!" Writing from a jail cell, a symbol of division, Paul offers hope, encouragement and a tremendous challenge. He explains that following Jesus and embracing His values provides the roadmap to peace. He states unequivocally that through His death and resurrection Jesus destroyed: **"… the barrier, the dividing wall of hostility" (Ephesians 2:14b)**. We are redeemed, reconciled and reclaimed for God's eternal purposes. These are wonderful promises, however, God never intended that we sit back and watch the world go by. We have a role to play… and I believe, as Baby Boomers, a unique role to provide an example to the generations that come after us. In the end Paul challenges us to: **"Stand firm then…" (Ephesians 6:14a)** because our God is a God of unity and peace! This "stand" must begin in our marriages and families. When we put a hedge of protection around them we are then positioned to "stand firm" in the face of every other battle we face.

Marital Walls

That's why the next important area that Paul addresses in Ephesians is marriage. Paul's strategy for success in this all important part of our lives is simple. Husbands and wives are to submit to one another "as to the Lord." Our marriage relationships should be a mirror reflection of our relationship with Jesus. I first spoke about this in Chapter 6, "Mend and Tend."

"Submit" is a tough word in culture today. It sounds oppressive, even abusive. To "submit" is to "yield to the power, action and control of another." But isn't it true?

> *Our marriage relationships should be a mirror reflection of our relationship with Jesus.*

You can't be a Christian unless you submit, which means to yield your life to the authority of the Father, the sacrifice of the Son and the indwelling of the Holy Spirit. If you haven't entrusted your life to God in this way, you're either resisting or faking and probably not fooling anybody! The same can be said of marriage.

When the Apostle Paul says: **"Submit to one another out of reverence for Christ" (Ephesians 5:21),** he is challenging husbands and wives to love and trust one another in our marriages in the same way we have learned to love and trust Jesus. In God's math, marriage isn't a 50%/50% deal where we both give-in or give-up in order to meet somewhere in the middle. No! Christian marriage is a 100%/100% deal where both husband and wife give ourselves completely, just as Jesus gave Himself completely for us.

This is the commitment being described when the Bible says: **"… and the two shall become one flesh" (Ephesians 5:31b).** It's the difference in a marriage relationship between "self-centered *independence*" and "spouse-centered *interdependence*." Nobody is a doormat here! Instead, both partners are built-up in unity and love. Imagine how the divorce rate would fall if we all truly made our spouses #1 in our lives by loving them like: **"… Christ loved the Church and gave himself up for her…" (Ephesians 5:25b)!**

For this unity to become a reality in our marriages we have to invest. It's like making savings deposits in a bank. When tough times come you need something to draw upon. I remember doing marriage counseling one time with a couple who made it clear that they had already made up their minds they were getting a divorce. The counseling was basically about money and kids. Unfortunately, this is often the case. By the time couples come for help it's too late, barring a miracle of God. Anyhow, during the course of our conversation I asked them, "When was the last time you went away for a weekend, just the two of you?" There was dead silence. They hemmed and hawed and finally agreed that it hadn't been for at least ten years. They hadn't made any deposits in their marriage. Now, during crunch time, they had nothing to withdraw. So sad!

I thank my mom and dad for their testimony on this account. They were high school sweethearts. They got married at 19 and had me at 20. Why wait around, right! At my dad's passing they had been married 67 years. When my three siblings and I were kids we were a little hurt at times when mom and dad would go away for a couple of days, just the two of them. (We did have baby sitters!) Even though we didn't fully understand it at the time, they were modelling something extraordinarily important. Good marriages require an investment of time and loving attention.

As we got older and no longer needed a sitter we did have some adventures in their absence! One day my brother Mike and I decided we were going to make a cake. We always had cake mixes around because dad worked for Pillsbury. We got out the big mixer. We added the water, oil and egg. We got it started and decided that since it needed to mix for a while we would go out on the driveway and shoot some hoops. We didn't realize that the mixer would pick-up speed when left unattended. By the time we came in to check, our cake mix had turned into "spin art." There was batter in about a six foot circle all over the carpet and cupboards. By the grace of God we got it cleaned up before mom and dad came home and decided not to tell them that story until years later.

Another time our youngest brother, Brad, was getting ready to go to prom. Just one problem. He had broken his arm about a month earlier and had a full-sized plaster cast on it. It wouldn't fit through his suit jacket sleeve so Mike and I helped him out. We took dad's new garden shears and cut it off. As far as I remember we didn't draw any blood. His broken arm may not have been fully healed but he sure did look sharp in his prom pictures... and dad wondered why his new shears were so dull.

Married couples, in spite of the risks involved when leaving teenage children home alone, it's always a good idea to invest in your marriage relationship. Don't just settle. Don't just ride-it-out assuming that you have come as far as you can and must now suffer the rest of the way to the finish line. The hurts may be deep but our God is so faithful. The same God who blessed your marriage when you took your vows all those years ago still cares about your marriage today. When we come together in humility, not accusation, breakthroughs can happen. I've seen couples who thought their marriage was dead fall in love all over again. Don't give up. Your generational legacy is at stake!

Generational Walls

The same principles of love, humility, time and care apply to our relationships with our children and grandchildren. In

> The same God who blessed your marriage when you took your vows all those years ago still cares about your marriage today.

212

Ephesians 6:1-4 Paul says: **"Children, obey your parents in the Lord, for this is right. 'Honor your father and mother' – which is the first commandment with a promise – 'that it may go well with you and that you may enjoy long life on the earth.' Fathers, do not exasperate your children; instead, bring them up in the training and instruction of the Lord."**

It is not surprising that Paul would call upon one of the Ten Commandments to remind the youth of his day to obey and respect their parents. This was well understood. What is surprising is that he also calls upon parents to respect their children. Once again, Paul's application of Jesus' teachings are radical in their goal of knocking down even generational "dividing walls of hostility."

There was a cultural context to the counsel given here to some of the first Christian families. In the first century Roman world, women and children were treated like property and considered to be of little value. The notable exception was male sons. Any expression of a father's love for his children would have been rare, much less this strange concept of mutual honor and respect.

In terms of the expression of affection and daily involvement in our children's lives today, just the opposite is often true. Dads and moms who smother their children earn the title "helicopter parents." What exactly does Paul mean when he says, "Do not exasperate your children?" To exasperate is to frustrate to the point of being overbearing. It's when we literally drive our kids (or grandkids) crazy! Take a look at this list below and ask yourself if any of these behaviors represent your attitudes and actions when it comes to the next generations. All of them will eventually build a wall that will be hard to knock down. We exasperate:

- by being over-protective
- by showing favoritism
- by repeatedly making unreasonable demands
- by pushing achievement to the point of perfectionism
- by constantly critiquing and criticizing
- by pushing them beyond age-appropriateness

- by using love as a tool of reward or punishment
- by physical or verbal abuse
- by making them feel they are a burden or unwanted
- by "saying" but not "doing"
- by neglecting to share spiritual truth

If you recognize yourself in any of these statements you may want to repent both to God and to your kids. There have been plenty of times in my years as a father, and now grandfather, that I have had to humble myself and ask forgiveness for words and behaviors that were not Christ-like. By the grace of God, they are rare today. One such experience will stay in my memory forever. It happened when our three kids; Matt, Josh and Sarah, were still young like say from kindergarten to fourth grade. One night when we were still living in Portland, Maine they were playing on our family room floor, getting too wild, and I had asked them to settle down several times but to no avail.

In my frustration, I grabbed a wooden stirring spoon out of the kitchen drawer, walked back into the family room and shouted, "If you kids don't quiet down right now you're going to get a spanking!" Then just to show that I was serious about it I wacked the wooden spoon against the door frame. It broke in half and the big end went flying. The whole room was instantly silent and I will never forget the look I saw on my kid's faces. It was one of fear. My heart broke. I realized that I was the one who was out of control, not them. In tears I asked my kids to forgive me and determined to never let my frustration boil over like that again.

There are so many challenges confronting families today; the erosion of morals and standards, a secular educational system, the extraordinary pace of life, the mixed and often destructive messages of social media, all-consuming technological advances (i.e. we spend more time on our phones than we do talking to each other), economic pressures, spiritual warfare and the changing definitions of marriage and family.

In the face of all these challenges, Baby Boomers today have a unique calling to share faith and values with the generations that follow. Here's the truth! No matter what our age, parents never stop being parents and children never stop being children. Our job is to always demonstrate mutual love and respect within our family relationships grounded in our faith and values. For many of us, this amazing gift now extends to our grandchildren and even great-grandchildren. What a blessing and what a privilege!

In our families today, nuclear and extended, we are often operating with different agendas and different goals. Is your family on the same page? What are you working on together? Better communication? Finding quality family time? Respecting one another? Sharing faith? As families we need to learn to listen, understand and partner together. For Colleen and me, it has always been "date nights" or "weekends away." We were simply following the example that our parents had given us. Even when our kids were little, and we were broke, we still found time just for each other. This was a huge factor in helping us stay connected when life was moving fast.

> Here's the truth! No matter what our age, parents never stop being parents and children never stop being children.

When it came to our kids, while we enjoyed family time, sports, camping and church activities, we also tried to spend individual time with each one. We discovered that they would open up and share in a whole different way when it was just one-on-one. We have continued this with our grandkids today. These conversations might happen during an overnight, in the car on the road, over breakfast or lunch, shopping for school clothes, attending a sporting event, around a campfire, on Zoom or FaceTime or just hanging out. There is no substitute for time well spent if we want to knock down the generational walls that divide us.

John MacArthur, in his "New Testament Commentary on Ephesians," shared this letter of a father reflecting on this important role. He said, "My family's all grown up and the kids are gone. But if I had it to do all over again, this is what I would do. I would love my wife more in front of my children. I would laugh with my children more – at our mistakes and our joys. I would listen more, even to the littlest child. I would be more honest about my own weaknesses, never pretending perfection. I would pray differently for my family; instead of focusing on them, I'd focus on me. I would do more things together with my children. I would encourage them more and bestow more praise. I would pay attention to the little things, like deeds and words of thoughtfulness. And then, finally, if I had to do it all over again, I would share God more intimately with my family; every ordinary thing that happened in every ordinary day I would use to direct them to God."[1]

As "Boomers" we have this opportunity right now; not to do it all over again… but to do it right today… to make these years count. What would you like others to say about your marriage? What kind of a deposit would you like to leave in your children or grandchildren that will last forever?

Societal Walls

As the Apostle Paul continued to address "dividing walls" in his letter to the Ephesians, he could not avoid the topic of slavery. Slavery represents one of the most painful and striking examples of the depravity of the human soul. The thought that any human being can "own" another ought to be repulsive to any civil society or believing person. The "dividing walls of hostility" previously discussed have all contributed to the long history of slavery. Because society has allowed such strident divisions to continue to exist in our world based on race, denomination, class, gender and age, it has not been a stretch to further devalue and demonize human beings as slaves. While slavery is often more hidden in the world today, the trafficking of human beings, be it for sex, drugs or cheap labor, continues to be one of the most heart-breaking of all evils.

In Bible times, slavery was a common and accepted practice. In both Roman and Greek cultures, most slaves had no legal rights and were treated as commodities in the world of business and commerce. Slaves were bought and sold like animals or tools. When older slaves got sick, they weren't fed. A master could kill a slave for little or no reason with the only penalty being the loss of his investment. In some cases, even family members could be sold into slavery if they didn't meet with a father's approval.

In light of these common cultural practices, the Apostle Paul and the young Christian community in Ephesus were faced with some challenging choices. You see, many of the Gentiles who were coming to Christ were slave owners themselves. As they received Paul's letter they must have wondered "What counsel will he provide on this issue?" Paul's response might surprise you, as it probably did them.

In **Ephesians 6:5-9**, Paul continued to break "old paradigms" with the "new revelation" he was receiving from the Holy Spirit. He said: **"Slaves, obey your earthly masters with respect and fear, and with sincerity of heart, just as you would obey Christ. Obey them not only to win their favor when their eye is on you, but like slaves of Christ, doing the will of God from your heart. Serve wholeheartedly, as if you were serving the Lord, not men, because you know that the Lord will reward everyone for whatever good he does, whether he is slave or free. And masters, treat your slaves in the same way. Do not threaten them, since you know that he who is both their Master and yours is in heaven, and there is no favoritism with him."**

Now pause for a moment and take a look at what Paul just did here. Without ever standing up in the town square and denouncing slavery as evil, dehumanizing and contrary to God's will, he effectively cut the legs out from under it with his inspired teaching and personal recommendations. In fact, what Paul is describing here is no less than the "mutual submission" of masters and slaves in the same way that he just finished teaching this concept to husbands and wives, parents and children. Can you imagine how radical this was!

Paul's focus was never on the circumstances of the past but always on the new relationship that was possible because of Christ.

As the Church began to teach and model this new "Christian ethic," both owners and slaves began to recognize one another spiritually as "brothers and sisters in Christ." Check-out the story of Onesimus in the Book of Philemon. This put into motion a process that would eventually lead to the demise of the institution of slavery. Spirit-filled preachers like John Wesley and George Whitefield, as well as godly statesman like William Wilberforce, shared these principles of the equality of all people before God. As a result, the legal slave trade in Europe and America was eventually stopped, albeit not soon enough.

On a broader level, the fact that Paul addressed this topic in his letter to the Ephesians speaks to other walls that continue to divide society today into classes of owners and workers, rich and poor, the "haves" and the "have nots." The Babylonian economic system portrayed in the scriptures remains entrenched all around us. It is often manifested through the political and economic institutions of the world, although the institutional Church is not exempt. Its standard bearers are class envy, greed, the abuse of power, corruption and the continual desire for the accumulation of wealth at the expense of the poorest and most vulnerable among us.

Soon after His baptism and temptation in the wilderness, Jesus spoke at the synagogue in His hometown of Nazareth. He unrolled the scroll of Isaiah and declared: **"'The Spirit of the Lord is on me, because he has anointed me to preach good news to the poor. He has sent me to proclaim freedom for the prisoners and recovery of sight for the blind, to release the oppressed, to proclaim the year of the Lord's favor.' Then he rolled up the scroll, gave it back to the attendant and sat down. The eyes of everyone in the synagogue were fastened on him, and he began by saying, 'Today this scripture is fulfilled in your hearing'"** (Luke 4:18-21).

The reaction of the crowd, which was initially positive, quickly turned ugly. The people drove Jesus out of town and took Him to the edge of a cliff with the intention of throwing Him down. He miraculously walked right through the crowd and went on His way. Why were even these religious people so upset? That day, Jesus, in effect, made his claim as the Messiah, the promised one, the Savior.

He did so by taking that well-known text from Isaiah and making it personal. He didn't say, "Someday these nice things are going to happen." It was "I am the anointed one and they are going to happen right now through Me."

That is the hope of the world today. Those who are poor, in prison, blind and oppressed want to know that their lives can change for the better, not at some uncertain time in the future, but now! Jesus' message was setting the stage for the "greatest work" in all of human history. Through His death and resurrection He would touch society at its point of greatest pain.

One of the most significant walls in society today is the division between rich and poor. In his book, "Transformation," Dr. Ed Silvoso provides a definition of poverty based on a key phrase in the Lord's Prayer. The words are: **"Give us today our daily bread" (Matthew 6:11).** Poverty may therefore be defined as "lacking our daily bread," and "systemic poverty" as the "structures that perpetuate this lack of provision." On this basis, Dr. Silvoso identifies four kinds of poverty that at one time or another afflict us all. Here is an abbreviated summary shared with permission.

Spiritual Poverty afflicts those who don't know that God is their father. They are not able to pray **"Our *Father* in heaven, hallowed by your name" (Matthew 6:9).** They are spiritual orphans. They believe they are alone, that God has judged or abandoned them and that no one loves them. When trouble comes, they have no spiritual resources to draw upon.

Relational Poverty encompasses those whose focus is on themselves at the expense of the community of which they are a part. They may have great wealth but still suffer from a lack of close relationships with family, friends and associates. Or, it can be a type of relational poverty born of true loneliness in the world. They are lacking in the "us" and the "our" of **"Give *us* today *our* daily bread" (Matthew 6:11).**

Motivational Poverty is a state of hopelessness that engulfs those who have no adequate way, or means, or the confidence to tackle tomorrow's challenges. "*Daily* bread" refers to exactly that. It's an ongoing occurrence – a continuity of faithfulness. When people come under the grip of poverty, even when there is bread today, they have no hope they will be able to provide for their needs tomorrow. This leads to anxiety, fear, insecurity and sometimes greed.

Material Poverty is the most obvious manifestation of poverty because it involves lacking the resources necessary to sustain life. In this context, "Daily *bread*" may include food, water, clothing, housing and other essential resources. Material poverty always compromises people's ability to focus on their spiritual life, relationships and motivation, because when you are hungry, you can't think of anything else.

Dr. Ed Silvoso summarizes, "Systemic poverty is different from personal poverty in that it is something that most people are born into and their fate is dictated and controlled by it. Those who are not born into it are targets to be brought into it. That is why it must be eliminated – because it reflects a scheme that is diabolical in design and evil in its implementation. It deprives masses of people of their daily bread by stealing the fruit of their labor and keeping them in social misery."[2]

Could it be that so many of the programs meant to solve the issue of poverty have failed because they don't address all four aspects of poverty; spiritual, relational, motivational and physical? Trillions of dollars have been wasted because this important insight has been overlooked. Today, ministries like Transform Our World are having success because they are addressing the whole person. As we work in our own communities to overcome this "glaring social gap," God may use us to bring this broader perspective. Remember, Jesus promised "Good News" for the poor!

Spiritual Walls

The Christian Church today is suffering from a "power outage." The power that is needed to bridge the societal gaps we have considered in these two chapters is not the kind produced by nuclear or hydroelectric plants, clean-coal technology, wind turbines or solar panels. No, the power that is needed to knock down every "dividing wall of hostility" is the power of the Holy Spirit. It can only be produced by "trash to energy" technology. We must allow God to meet us where we're at, with all our sin and weakness, and transform us from the inside-out.

When the Spirit breaks through we will experience a "power surge" that will revitalize our generation to be part of the solution, not the problem. This kind of spiritual electricity can't be stored. It must be used or it will quickly dissipate. The good news is that when we stay connected to God, He continues to replenish our lives with renewed energy for every task ahead. We will never experience a shut-down!

Why do we need this Holy Spirit power? It is because we are in a battle. The spiritual battle is fought in both the heavens and in our hearts and daily lives here on Earth. It manifests itself every day in thousands of practical decisions both great and small. You see, there is another power source that is soliciting us as customers and offering cheaper rates. Its CEO is Satan himself.

The Greek word for Satan is "o'diabolos" which means the obstructer, the devil. It's the same root word that translates as diabolical. He obstructs through various diabolical evil strategies intended to keep us divided against each other rather than united with God. Satan loves confusion and turmoil. Other names for Satan found in the Bible are "tempter, accuser, enemy, thief, prince of demons, roaring lion, god of this age, ruler of this world, father of lies, serpent and deceiver."

No wonder that in the final chapter of Ephesians Paul declares: **"Finally, be strong in the Lord and in his mighty power. Put on the full armor of God so that you can take your stand against the devil's schemes. For our struggle is not against flesh and blood, but against the rulers, against the authorities, against the powers of this dark world and against the spiritual forces of evil in the heavenly realms. Therefore, put on the full armor of God, so that**

when the day of evil comes, you may be able to stand your ground, and after you have done everything, to stand" (Ephesians 6:10-13).

We looked at these verses in Chapter 7. Let's dig a little deeper. Like the coach of a championship football team, Paul offers both a "defensive" and an "offensive" strategy. He begins: **"Finally, be strong in the Lord and in his mighty power" (vs.10).** To be "strong in the Lord" most likely refers to what already belongs to us through the cross of Christ. This is our strength, the fact that we have been redeemed, reconciled and reclaimed by Jesus… the fact that "in the Lord" there is already complete unity. We could paraphrase Paul's words, "Act upon the truths I've just taught you and you will be strong!"

The word "stand" is used three times in this brief section and again in verse 14. The Ephesians, much like us today, had been sinking… imitating the world instead of following the Word of God… continuing to live in darkness rather than choosing the light. Paul says, "… take your stand," "… stand your ground," "… stand." He is both a pastor and an apostle exhorting his young congregation to remain true to the Gospel message. That's the "defensive" strategy. To be "strong in the Lord" is to secure the base camp. What are the situations in your personal life, family and community where you are being called to "take your stand" right now?

There is also an "offensive" strategy! Paul says: **"Finally be strong in the Lord <u>and</u> in his mighty power" (vs.10).** To move in "his mighty power" is to march forward and seek the transformation of our cities and nations, starting right where we are. It is to take hold of our authority in Christ to knock down every "dividing wall of hostility" that has kept us divided, weak and ineffective. It is the "Go" of the Great Commission in Matthew 28:16-20. Where is God calling you to go in His strength in this important season of your life?

> *What are the situations in your personal life, family and community where you are being called to "take your stand" right now?*

Maybe, like my wife Colleen, it is to help care for grandchildren right now, nurturing their growth and passing along faith and values.

Maybe it is bringing the light of Jesus more effectively into your workplace, running for your local schoolboard or volunteering for an organization that is really making a difference in your community. Your gifts might lend themselves to mentoring young marriages and families or you may be called to address issues like racism or poverty. In terms of the Church, every congregation needs committed leaders and volunteers to carry the true message of Jesus Christ to the world.

In this important process of using our gifts to build God's kingdom, Paul instructs us to "… put on the full armor of God" so that we can take on the "spiritual forces of evil in the heavenly realms." To put on armor is to prepare for battle! Paul continues: **"Stand firm then, with the belt of truth buckled around your waist, with the breastplate of righteousness in place, and with your feet fitted with the readiness that comes from the gospel of peace. In addition to all this, take up the shield of faith, with which you can extinguish all the flaming arrows of the evil one. Take the helmet of salvation and the sword of the Spirit, which is the word of God" (Ephesians 6:14-17).**

Every piece of armor described here represents a gift from God to both protect us and assure our victory. We are fully equipped with truth, righteousness, peace, faith, salvation and the Spirit. If you are lacking in any… go ahead and ask God to re-issue your battle armor right now!

In this spiritual war it is important to remember that Satan is not a power or force opposite or equal to God. Satan is a rebel who was kicked out of heaven. Satan is a spiritual being who remains in active rebellion against God and has leadership over other lesser spiritual beings the Bible calls demons. Jesus believed in Satan. He was tempted by him. He frequently cast-out demons and challenged evil as personified by the devil. The Bible doesn't dwell on Satan but he is acknowledged throughout. We should as well.

It's so important to remember that through Jesus we already operate from a position of victory. Jesus says: **"The thief comes only to steal and kill and destroy; I have come that they may have life, and have it to the full" (John 10:10).** In the third verse of the magnificent hymn, "A Mighty Fortress Is Our God," Martin Luther declares, "And though this world, with devils filled, should threaten to undo us, we will not fear, for God has willed his truth to triumph through us. The prince of darkness grim, we tremble not for him; his rage we can endure, for lo, his doom is sure; one little word shall fell him" (Martin Luther, 1529). Friends, that little word is "JESUS," the name that is above every name!

Paul leaves the Ephesians with one last word of encouragement. He says: **"And pray in the Spirit on all occasions with all kinds of prayers and requests. With this in mind, be alert and always keep on praying for all the saints. Pray also for me, that whenever I open my mouth, words may be given me so that I will fearlessly make known the mystery of the gospel, for which I am an ambassador in chains. Pray that I may declare fearlessly, as I should" (Ephesians 6:18-20).**

Spirit-filled prayer involves more than just our human words. It invites the Holy Spirit to give us the words and speak through our prayers. It is prayer that is "in tune" with the love, holiness and compassion of God our Father and His Son, Jesus. It is prayer that allows the Holy Spirit to intercede on our behalf when our words cannot express what is in our hearts. Paul encourages us to prayer on all occasions, with all kinds of prayers, with alertness and patience. And then he says, "Pray also for me…" that words may be given, that fear may be overcome, that the Gospel message will be clear and that there will be strength for the trials. Prayer in the Spirit is another strong weapon in our arsenal of faith.

> *Spirit-filled prayer involves more than just our human words. It invites the Holy Spirit to give us the words and speak through our prayers.*

Throughout his letter to the Ephesians the Apostle Paul calls us all to higher levels of relationship and commitment for the sake of the world. He acknowledges the gaps, the deep divisions that exist in so many aspects of society that keep both people and groups apart. In these two chapters we have considered the "dividing walls of hostility" that can exist in our relationship with God, between differing racial and ethnic groups, between Christian denominations, in personal relationships, in marriages and families, between the powerful and the weak, the rich and the poor.

We have also become keenly aware that behind it all there is a spiritual battle taking place for the hearts and souls of people and the control of this world. As we put on the "full armor of God" we are able to stand "on our feet" in the physical and "on our knees" in the spiritual, confident that the victory has already been won in Christ. Our generation, the Baby Boom generation, is uniquely positioned to lead the charge toward that day when the "Prince of Peace" will truly bring peace to this world. What could be more energizing or meaningful than that!

Questions for Personal Reflection or Group Discussion:

1. If you are married, how many years have you shared life together? What have you done and what are you still doing to invest in your relationship and continue growing as a couple?

2. Reflect on a time you had to ask for forgiveness from your spouse or children. What was their response? What's the difference between saying "I'm sorry" and "Will you forgive me?"

3. What kind of poverty is most evident in the community where you live; Spiritual, Relational, Motivational or Material? Consider some practical ways that you can help.

4. Where in life are you being called to "stand firm?" What difference might it make if you were to put on the "full armor of God" every day?

Notes:

1. John MacArthur, *New Testament Commentary on Ephesians* (Chicago, IL: Moody Publishers, 1986), p. 319.
2. Ed Silvoso, *Transformation* (Ventura, CA: Regal Books, 2007), p. 116.

CHAPTER 15

Walk Through Open Doors!

Doors! We walk through dozens of them every day. Doors can represent the welcome of a good home, the promise of a new workday, the challenge of a problem to be solved or the invitation to use our gifts to help someone in need. Doors are everywhere beckoning us to step through them and embrace the opportunities that await us on the other side. A friend recently stated, "I'm very happy with what I'm doing right now, my job I mean, but I know I won't be doing it forever. That's why I am really asking God to open and close the right doors when it comes to my future."

I hear the same thing from so many of my "Boomer" friends, neighbors and colleagues. They want to make the 4th quarter of their lives count! They are open to new opportunities to strengthen relationships, try something new for work, volunteer their time and talents to bless others and spend meaningful time enjoying hobbies and travel. What doors are opening and closing for you right now and just how will you discern which ones to walk through?

Doors are very symbolic in the Bible. The scriptures are clear that one of the ways God guides us is through "open doors" and "closed doors." Open doors are meant to lead us to a place of greater satisfaction, effectiveness and impact. Closed doors are meant to steer us clear of temptation, trouble and diversions from God's best

WHAT WILL I DO WITH THE REST OF MY LIFE?

for our lives. If you've been living under the misconception that God no longer cares to help direct your path in this way, I would suggest you reconsider!

I declare to you in faith, and on the basis of God's Word, that Jesus is still placing before you open doors to endless opportunities to love and serve Him and make a difference in this world. If you have the faith and courage needed to walk through them, you will experience blessings untold. God is not finished with you yet!

Let's consider some of the open and closed doors described in the scriptures and the counsel and encouragement they provide for our lives today. In the Book of Revelation we discover that the Apostle John, one of Jesus' original 12 disciples, had been exiled to the Island of Patmos for declaring the Gospel. In his own words he describes how one Sunday the Holy Spirit spoke to him with a voice as loud as a trumpet and said: **"Write on a scroll what you see and send it to the seven churches" (Revelation 1:11a).**

These were the churches John had personally cared for in the Province of Asia. Next, John turned and saw an amazing vision of the resurrected Christ who said to him: **"Do not be afraid. I am the First and the Last. I am the Living One: I was dead, and behold I am alive for ever and ever! And I hold the keys of death and Hades. Write, therefore, what you have seen, what is now and what will take place later" (Revelation 1:17b-19).**

John was obedient and wrote down the "revelation" the Holy Spirit gave him. Sometime later he was released from Patmos and was able to share this message with the congregations and fellow believers he loved. As John addressed the Church in ancient Philadelphia, inspired by the Holy Spirit, he declared these words of Jesus: **"These are the words of him who is holy and true, who holds the key of David. What he opens no one can shut and what he shuts no one can open. I know your deeds. See, I have placed before you an open door that no one**

> *Jesus is still placing before you open doors to endless opportunities to love and serve Him and make a difference in this world.*

can shut. I know that you have little strength, yet you have kept my word and have not denied my name" (Revelation 3:7b-8).

From this passage we see that when Jesus opens a door in our lives, no one can shut it. Similarly, when He shuts a door, no one can open it. Does this not suggest then that we should pay close attention in our lives to which doors Jesus is opening and closing?

In C.S. Lewis' classic series called "The Chronicles of Narnia," the first of his seven fantasy novels is "The Lion, the Witch and the Wardrobe." In this story a magical door becomes the children's portal to a world where good battles evil, and in order to survive, they must learn to put their trust in someone greater than themselves. The majestic lion, Aslan, is the figure of Christ. The same is true for us today. Jesus provides open doors for us to walk through that we might also experience life's adventures and overcome evil by learning to trust Him more each day.

Open doors are usually characterized by a series of events or opportunities that present themselves in our lives often unexpectedly. When considered in combination with our prayers and the nudge of the Holy Spirit, they become like a "green light" to move forward; seize an opportunity, dream a dream, pursue a course of action or advance a cause. By contrast, closed doors are like a "red light" meant to deter us from making a bad decision. Closed doors are also intended to cause us to evaluate our attitude and actions and prayerfully consider what God may be trying to teach us. Alexander Graham Bell, the inventor of the telephone, observed, "When one door closes, another one opens, but we often look so long and so regretfully upon the closed door that we do not see the one that has opened for us."

> *Open doors are usually characterized by a series of events or opportunities that present themselves in our lives often unexpectedly.*

Closed doors can be the result of our own sin, the sins of others or the work of the devil. As we continue to: **"… hear what the Spirit says" (Revelation 2:7)** we will learn to discern the difference. When our own sin results in God closing a door and withholding

His blessing, we must ask why and confess it. When the sins of others become roadblocks that impact us personally, we must remain persistent trusting that when God opens a door, no one can shut it. When we clearly recognize that Satan is throwing up the obstacle, we must: **"test the spirits" (1 John 4:1)** and stand on God's promise that: **"the one who is in you is greater than the one who is in the world" (1 John 4:4b).** Learning to discern the difference between open and closed doors requires that we walk in close relationship with Jesus.

Sometimes a closed door becomes an opportunity for God to test our faith and build our character. I was in my mid-20s and in my second year of seminary. Along with a group of fellow "pastors in training" I was assigned to a local hospital as an Assistant Chaplain. I had a badge and a Bible but absolutely no experience in making hospital calls. One day we were each given a list of names and room numbers and then thrown to the lions… I mean instructed to make our rounds.

I arrived at the first hospital room I had been assigned with fear and trepidation at what awaited me on the other side of the door. I noted that it was slightly ajar. Ever the optimist, I knocked, stuck my head about half-way inside, and cheerfully announced, "This is Assistant Chaplain Pagh. May I come in and say hello?" A very gruff and obviously frustrated female voice from the other side shot back, "Go away! I don't want any visitors today!"

I felt like running away… but quite honestly I didn't want to have to tell my supervisor that I chickened out on my very first hospital visit! I opened the door, slowly walked in and continued, "It sounds like you're having a tough day. Why don't you tell me about it?" This poor elderly woman immediately began to tear up and describe too many surgeries, too many needles, too many days away from home, and of course, added that the hospital food was terrible. I pulled up a chair, we began to talk, and 30 minutes later I was holding her hand offering a prayer for comfort and healing. By the time I left the room there was a smile, a thank you and a total change in her countenance.

I've made hundreds and hundreds of hospital visits since that first one and never again have I experienced that same initial reaction. I knew that God had temporarily closed the door that day to teach me that when I trust in Him He will always open the door to an opportunity to share His love. And when He opens it, no one can shut it!

The Open Door to Personal Relationships

When approaching a door, be it the door to your neighbor's house, your coworker's office or a teen's bedroom, the polite thing to do is knock. A knock is usually followed by an announcement or request. At Christ Church, for example, I might knock on my Associate Pastor's office door and say, "Hi Sean! Do you have a couple of minutes to talk about next week's schedule?" Pastor Sean would reply something like, "Well of course, Reverend Doctor Pagh. I'm honored to welcome you into my humble but neatly kept office!"

Jesus is also a gentleman. In His word to the Church at Laodicea in **Revelation 3:20** He says: **"Here I am! I stand at the door and knock. If anyone hears my voice and opens the door, I will come in and eat with him, and he with me."** These words speak of the open door to a personal relationship with Jesus who desires to be our Savior and friend. Did you notice the reversal that takes place in this verse? Jesus knocks and we are the ones who must open the door and invite Him to walk through it!

English artist William Holman Hunt captured Revelation 3:20 in a now famous painting called "The Light of the World" (1853-1854). The figure of Jesus is knocking on an overgrown and long-unopened door. Upon closer observation, we notice that there is no handle on the outside. As Jesus stands at the door of our lives and knocks, He begins with an announcement. He says, "Here I am!"

First He declares His identity and then His intentions. He doesn't push His way in. He lets us know that He loves us and desires to be a part of our lives but the choice is ours. We must open the door and welcome Him in! **"He came to that which was his own, but his own did not receive him. Yet to all who received him, to those who believed in his name, he gave the right to become children of God" (John 1:11-12).** When did you first hear Jesus knocking at the door of your heart? How old were you? Did you open the door? How did this decision change your life?

If you have never made this personal decision to trust Jesus, He is still knocking. His offer is still good. Regardless of your past, Jesus wants to come into your life today and fellowship with you. That means way more than just a little religion. Jesus wants a relationship. He described it in terms of eating together. Just think of how often during His life a meal became an opportunity to share His love, see Him perform miracles and witness lives changed forever:

- At the wedding at Cana.
- At the feeding of the 5,000.
- At the home of His friends, Mary, Martha and Lazarus.
- At the home of a Pharisee who was trying to trap Him.
- At the home of Zacchaeus, the crooked businessman.
- At the Last Supper with His disciples.
- With two men after walking with them on the road to Emmaus.
- At a fish fry on the beach with Peter and His disciples.

Here's the beautiful thing! This daily fellowship that we are invited to share with Jesus is meant to carry over into our relationships with other people. The "open door" to a personal relationship with Jesus is meant to become a "revolving door" of friendship, fellowship and ministry to others in Jesus' name!

The truth is that Jesus stands at the door of our hearts, lives, homes, schools, workplaces, communities and nations… and knocks. He first declares His identity and then

> The "open door" to a personal relationship with Jesus is meant to become a "revolving door" of friendship, fellowship and ministry to others in Jesus' name!

makes us an offer that is hard to refuse. When we invite Jesus to come in He promises to live with us forever. It is this "open door to a personal relationship" with our Savior that then begins to impact every other relationship we have in life, starting with our families and friends. Then, by God's grace, this door swings open even wider as we reach-out and touch the world around us.

The Open Door to Effective Work

Millions of "Boomers" are retiring every year in America and asking, "What's will I do with the rest of my life?" Millions more are continuing to work, sometimes out of necessity and sometimes out of boredom. During your working years did you enjoy your job and feel that you were doing what God had called you to do? How many of you would have preferred a different job or thought that perhaps you could serve the Lord more effectively in a different setting? Unfortunately, many have succumbed to a false separation between what is sacred and what is secular. We are all ministers, whether in the marketplace or the pulpit. All work can be done unto the glory of God!

Today your work may be around the house or the yard rather than at the office or construction site. Your work may no longer be for a paycheck but be just as valuable as you continue to share your God-given skills with others. I was blessed to know a man named Paul Hansen who had Multiple Sclerosis. Because of this debilitating condition in his life he couldn't work a regular paying job any longer but he loved wood-working. For many years he enjoyed making wooden crosses to be carried in a pocket, hung from a rear view mirror or set on a nightstand. He called them "crosses for Christ." He made thousands and sent them all over the world. Each cross was personally prayed for before it left his shop.

When Paul could no longer do the work himself he taught others. He called them "cross-making parties" as he welcomed men and women into his workshop. What an impact! Everyone at his "celebration of life" service received one of Paul's crosses as a gift and a second one to give away as a reminder of his faith and testimony. This ministry of cross-making continues today through others. When we ask for His guidance the Lord will lead us into effective work no matter what our season of life or individual circumstances.

The Apostle Paul was a dual career person working both as a tentmaker and an evangelist. You might think that Paul did the one job only to provide for the other. Hardly! Look at how God's power manifested itself through even the sweat of his labor. In **Acts 19:11-12** it says: **"God did extraordinary miracles through Paul, so that even the handkerchiefs and aprons that had touched him were taken to the sick, and their illnesses were cured and the evil spirits left them."**

This work with his hands also allowed him to preach the Gospel freely, owing nothing to anyone. It also led him to make this statement to one of the congregations he served: **"Whatever you do, work at it with all your heart, as working for the Lord, not for men, since you know that you will receive an inheritance from the Lord as a reward. It is the Lord Christ you are serving"** **(Colossians 3:23-24).**

Paul counted on "open and closed doors" to guide him in all his ministries. One of the churches he started was in a thriving center of commerce called Corinth. At the end of his first letter to the Corinthians we find him discussing another visit he hoped to make after travelling through the region called Macedonia. First he says: **"For I do not want to see you now and make only a passing visit; I hope to spend some time with you, if the Lord permits"** **(1 Corinthians 16:7).** Then we read these two very telling verses that follow. He says: **"But I will stay at Ephesus until Pentecost, because a great door for effective work has opened to me, and there are many who oppose me" (1 Corinthians 16:8-9).**

This passage makes it very clear that one of the ways Paul understood the direction of the Holy Spirit was through open and closed doors. What was happening in Ephesus? What was this "great door for effective work" that God had opened for him there? As we read his letter to the Ephesians we see that the "dividing wall of hostility" that had long existed between Jews and Gentiles was coming down. The Church was growing. Even so, Paul had experienced opposition. Read about some earlier experiences recorded in **Acts 16:6-10** that eventually led to the "kingdom successes" in Ephesus.

"Paul and his companions travelled throughout the region of Phrygia and Galatia, having been kept by the Holy Spirit from preaching the word in the province of Asia. (closed door) **When they came to the border of Mysia, they tried to enter Bithynia, but the Spirit of Jesus would not allow them to.** (closed door) **So they passed by Mysia and went down to Troas. During the night Paul had a vision of a man of Macedonia standing and begging him, 'Come over to Macedonia and help us.'** (open door) **After Paul had seen the vision, we got ready at once to leave for Macedonia, concluding that God had called us to preach the gospel to them."**

There were two closed doors during this part of Paul's journey but they led to an open door that is known as "the Macedonian Call." Had Paul gone to Asia earlier he wouldn't have experienced the same fruit because the anointing of the Holy Spirit wouldn't have been upon his trip. It wouldn't have been God's timing. However, because he waited for the "open door to effective work" in Ephesus, God gave tremendous results.

What is effective work? To your boss it may be meeting your sales quota, serving your customers well, completing a construction project on time or turning in your quarterly reports with a positive bottom line. Effective work may be measured by a raise or a promotion or at least a "job well done." The Bible says that one day we will all stand before the Lord and give an accounting of our work on Earth. In God's economy, effective work is measured by ROI – return on investment. Regardless of the type of work we are called to do, if we have invested wisely, He will say: **"Well done, good and faithful servant! You have been faithful with a few things; I will put you in charge of many things. Come and share your master's happiness"** **(Matthew 25:21)!**

What season of work life are you in today? What doors is Jesus opening for you that will lead to effective work? Effective work is not measured by temporary success but eternal impact. The Bible says that we must seize the opportunities God gives us to work while it is day… because soon the night is coming when no one will work. And whatever we do, we must work at it with all our heart, as working for the Lord and not for people. If this is your goal, continue to look for God's open and closed doors. His desire is to guide you to exactly where you should be to have the greatest impact for His kingdom.

> *Effective work is not measured by temporary success but eternal impact.*

The Open Door to Extraordinary Miracles

The Bible is a book of miracles from the beginning of the creation of the world to the open door of heaven's glory. In the New International Version of the scriptures there are about 125 references in the Old Testament and 100 references in the New Testament to "miracles, signs and wonders." In the Gospels alone there are about 35 separate miracles of Jesus recorded, although we have good reason to suspect this to be just a small fraction of the total. How do we know? The Gospel of John concludes with this summary statement: **"Jesus performed many other signs in the presence of his disciples, which are not recorded in this book. But these are written that you may believe that Jesus is the Messiah, the Son of God, and that by believing you may have life in his name" (John 20:30-31).**

These verses also provide us with the purpose for Jesus' miracles. Miracles validated his identity and authority as the Son of God and were meant to not only help people believe but experience life in His name. They also demonstrated Jesus' love and compassion for all people. Of course the greatest miracle of all is the resurrection of Jesus from the dead!

After three years of public ministry including countless miracles, Jesus challenged His disciples with this amazing promise: **"Very truly I tell you, whoever believes in me will do the works I have been doing, and they will do even greater things than these, because**

I am going to the Father. And I will do whatever you ask in my name, so that the Father may be glorified in the Son. You may ask me for anything in my name, and I will do it" (John 14:12-14).

This statement declares an "open door to extraordinary miracles" in the life of every believer. Peter and the other disciples took Jesus' words seriously and went on to perform countless miracles recorded in the New Testament in the life of the early Church. Just imagine what would change in our lives today if we too were to believe Jesus for "greater things?"

In Acts 12 we read how several believers were arrested by King Herod for declaring the truth about Jesus. James, the brother of John, was killed. The Apostle Peter was seized and thrown into prison where he was guarded by four squads of four soldiers each. I guess that Herod considered Peter to be a "high value target." In **Acts 12:5** it says: **"The church was earnestly praying to God for him."**

The night before Peter was going to be put on trial an angel appeared to him in the prison. Peter thought he was having a dream as he watched the chains fall off his wrists. He followed the angel as they walked right past the prison guards who it seems were temporarily blinded. As they approached the front gate that led to the city, even this "door" miraculously opened. Peter praised the Lord for this miracle and immediately went to the house of Mary, the mother of Mark, where many people had gathered and were praying for him. This is where this story takes a humorous twist! It says: **"Peter knocked at the outer entrance and a servant named Rhoda came to answer the door. When she recognized Peter's voice, she was so overjoyed she ran back without opening it and exclaimed, 'Peter is at the door'" (Acts 12:12-13)!**

Her fellow believers told her that she must be out her mind and that it was probably just an angel! Ha! How ironic that these believers could readily entertain the possibility that an angel was at their front door, but not Peter, when the focus of their prayer meeting was that God would set him free. And then we read: **"But Peter kept on knocking, and when they opened the door and saw him, they were astonished" (Acts 12:16).**

This story provides us with several insights that are necessary if we're going to walk through the "open door to extraordinary miracles." *First, we must embrace the fact that we are a miracle.* Peter knew it and couldn't wait to tell it. When we begin to celebrate the miracle of our transformed lives, God will increase our faith to believe for more.

Second, we must keep on knocking even if others don't believe. In other words, we must keep on demonstrating that faith is real, alive and growing and that the power of God is at work within us. Peter knew he had a testimony to share so he kept on knocking until they let him in and he could tell the amazing story of what God had done.

Third, if we have been praying for a miracle, when it shows up we must open the door and receive it. Sometimes we pray and pray but don't really believe that God will answer. Peter was standing right outside their door but they had to open it themselves to see and believe!

Fourth, we must be astonished at what God can do. The word "astonished" means to be filled with the emotional impact of an overwhelming surprise or shock. We shouldn't be surprised that our prayers have been answered but certainly astonishment in the power of God is a good thing. For extraordinary miracles to become an ordinary part of our Christian experience we must reclaim the power and promises in God's Word, and by faith, walk through the open door that Jesus has placed before us. We must recapture a sense of awe in a God who is in the miracle-working business and desires to perform miracles still today through us!

The Open Door to New Opportunities

Friends, part of considering the question, "What will I do with the rest of my life?" is to be open to new opportunities. But which ones? How will we know the direction that God wants us to go? We can ask God to show us by opening and closing doors in our lives. It's not the only way God guides us but it is an important way. Here are some guidelines to remember.

If a door appears to have been opened to you by God, let's say for a new job opportunity, your communication with Him will always be enhanced. You will receive additional confirmation as you take the next steps forward. If Satan is messing with you, communication will be thwarted and those affirmations will not come.

Next, God will not open a door that doesn't line up with His Word. God will never place an opportunity before you that would require that you compromise your faith or values in order to accept it. The same is true when it comes to relationships.

> God will never place an opportunity before you that would require that you compromise your faith or values in order to accept it.

Next, an open door will always be confirmed in prayer and by the peace that comes with it. You may still be nervous about stepping into this new opportunity but the Lord will give you the strength and peace to do it.

Next, an open door will be confirmed by wise counselors. These are trusted Christian friends who will also pray through what appears to be an open door with you and seek the confirmation of the Holy Spirit. Often we need the insight of others who can look at a situation objectively to keep us from bending a decision to our own will while claiming that it is the will of God.

Finally, an open door that is from God will always lead to blessing because, in fact, Jesus is the door! In **John 10:9** Jesus says: **"I am the door. If anyone enters by me, he will be saved and will go in and out and find pasture." (ESV)** If we heed these guidelines we will mature in our ability to read open and closed doors and discern which ones are really from God.

The Open Door to Heaven's Glory

Let's end this chapter where we began. After the Apostle John's amazing revelation, he says: **"After this I looked, and there before me was a door standing open in heaven" (Revelation 4:1).** The open door to heaven's glory begins now for all who believe. You see, the promise of heaven is about more than our future home. It's about the home that God has given us today. Remember, Jesus taught us to pray: **"Thy kingdom come, thy will be done, on earth as it is in heaven" (Matthew 6:10).** Perhaps that's why the last two chapters of the Book of Revelation describe "heaven coming down" far more than "us going up." If you are a sincere follower of Jesus, heaven is your promise! The door is wide open… and when your time comes Jesus will be waiting there with open arms. When each of us realizes that we don't have to worry about whether we are "in or out" we are freed up to live every day with purpose and meaning.

That's why as we live-out our final season of life as Baby Boomers it is so important that we continue to seek God's guidance for every potential path that lays before us. It is often through "open doors" and "closed doors" that we are able to see the way forward. Closed doors are always for our protection. Open doors are always for our blessing. Jesus is the one who opens doors that no one can shut and shuts doors that no one can open. Let's trust Him as never before to do that for us and then be ready to walk through them!

Questions for Personal Reflection or Group Discussion:

1. What are three important doors you walk through almost every day? What do they represent?
2. Is there a door to a new opportunity in your life right now that God seems to be opening? Is there a door that He seems to be closing? How are you discerning the difference?
3. Jesus continues to stand at the door of your life and knock. Are you opening this door to deeper fellowship or locking him out? In what ways?
4. What is an "extraordinary miracle" you need today? Are you ready to walk through the door when God opens it?

CHAPTER 16

Pray and Listen!

I read an interview that was done with Mike Krzyzewski several years ago, the long-time Head Coach of the Duke University Basketball team. Aside from their moniker, the "Blue Devils," I've always liked watching them because of "Coach K's" commitment to excellence. He's an older Boomer, born in 1947, and has the record for the most head-coaching victories in Division 1 college basketball history with 1,202. In addition to five NCAA national titles he has also helped lead the United States to three Olympic gold medals. He retired from coaching at the end of the 2021/2022 basketball season after reaching the "Final Four" one last time.

One nugget I found very interesting in this interview is that in all his years of coaching he never used a coach's whistle during practices. When asked why he said, "I want my players to listen for the sound of my voice." He went on to describe how during games, when he can't use a whistle, it's so important for his players to learn to hear his voice above the noise of thousands of screaming fans. Jesus wants us to hear His voice as well over all the other voices in this world shouting for our attention. We learn to hear His voice as we pray and listen.

Two-Way Street

Prayer is simply "communicating with God." It involves both speaking and listening. Sometimes our words are spoken out loud. Other times silently. Jesus prayed often to His Father in heaven. Although He was pressed by great crowds throughout His public ministry, Jesus always found time to be alone to pray; on a hillside, in a boat, in a garden. Jesus always found time to step away to connect, receive counsel and pour-out His heart to His Heavenly Father. If the Son of God found prayer to be that important, how much more should we if we want God's guidance in these days of our lives?

The disciples noticed Jesus' commitment to prayer and recognized something more personal about His prayers than the Jewish prayers they had recited since childhood. They said: **"Lord, teach us to pray…" (Luke 11:1a)**. Jesus taught them what we now call The Lord's Prayer. It serves as a model prayer yet today. It isn't meant to be said mindlessly by rote. The Lord's Prayer teaches us the elements of prayer that are important if we are going to pray effectively; worship, honor, petition, confession and thanksgiving.

Prayer is about relationship and it's a two-way street. Suppose I claim to have a wonderful relationship with my wife, Colleen, but only talk to her when I need dinner made or clothes washed. Not only would I be rightly accused of being a chauvinist but that wouldn't represent much of a relationship, would it? The same is true of our relationship with God; Father, Son and Holy Spirit. If the only time we communicate is when we have a personal need or an emergency, our relationship won't go very deep nor will our prayers be very effective.

> *Prayer is about relationship and it's a two-way street.*

Is Anybody Else Up There?

One time a skilled mountain climber was scaling a vertical face with no ropes. As he neared the top a small ledge gave way under his foot and he began to slip. At the last minute he was able to grab a piece of petrified wood protruding from the side of the mountain. Desperate, he looked up and called out, "Is anybody there? I need help!" No one answered. He called out again and again. Finally a booming voice said, "This is God. I heard you calling. How can I help?" The man said, "I've slipped on the side of this mountain and am holding on for dear life. I need you to rescue me. If you do I'll serve you for the rest of my life!" God said, "It's a deal! Let go of the branch and I'll have my angels catch you." The man shouted, "Is anybody else up there?"

There are many kinds of prayer. There are individual and group prayers. There are private and public prayers. There are prayers of thanksgiving and prayers of request. There are prayers for our own needs and prayers for the needs of others. And then there are emergency prayers like the one this man shouted from the side of that mountain.

If there is one thing that seems to be lacking in the lives of millions of people today, both Christians and non-Christians alike, it is that we pray without really expecting answers. Influenced by a "faith-challenged" secular culture, prayer is often perceived as nothing more than a "feel good" psychological exercise designed to provide comfort and support. To say "I will pray for you" might just as well be translated, "I will keep you in my thoughts and hope for the best." For those of us sincerely asking, "What will I do with the rest of my life?" we must learn to both pray and listen with faith in God even though we may not always receive the answers we want to hear. We need to learn how to "let go" and "let God."

An Invitation to Pray

One thing we know for certain is that God loves it when we talk to Him. In **Jeremiah 33:3** He says: **"Call to me and I will answer you and tell you great and unsearchable things you do not know."** In **Philippians 4:6**, Paul says: **"Do not be anxious about anything,**

but in every situation, by prayer and petition, with thanksgiving, present your requests to God." And then in **1 Thessalonians 5:16-17** he adds: **"Rejoice always, pray continually, give thanks in all circumstances; for this is God's will for you in Christ Jesus."**

To "pray continually" doesn't mean with eyes closed and hands folded. It is an attitude of the heart. It's a God consciousness that goes with us wherever we are and whatever we're doing. There is no "on-off" switch. To "pray continually" means that we are always tuned-in to our relationship with God and seeking His wisdom and direction.

> To "pray continually" doesn't mean with eyes closed and hands folded. It is an attitude of the heart.

Have you ever felt inadequate to pray? I don't mean searching for the right words but searching for the faith to trust God to answer? Have you ever wondered if God loves you enough to hear and respond to your needs… your urgent requests? Here's a verse that has the potential to trip us up. In **James 5:16** the Apostle says: **"The prayer of a righteous person is powerful and effective."** We think, "Oh, a righteous person! That leaves me out!" This is when we have to remember that righteousness is not the sum of our "good works" but rather the "work of Christ" on the cross. **Romans 3:22a** declares: **"This righteousness is given through faith in Jesus Christ to all who believe."** Do you believe? Then you can be "powerful and effective" in your prayer life. This isn't true because you are such a great "pray-er" but rather because Jesus is such a wonderful Savior!

Check-out the amazing invitation Jesus gives to us in this passage from **Matthew 7:7-8.** Jesus says: **"Ask and it will be given to you; seek and you will find; knock and the door will be opened to you. For everyone who asks receives; he who seeks finds; and to him who knocks, the door will be opened."** Let's take a closer look at these words that many of us have heard but few of us really believe. First…

Prayer is *"asking and receiving."*

When God has already revealed His will through the Word regarding a particular need; whether that need be physical, emotional or spiritual, and we pray according to His will, we can ask and expect to receive with full confidence. In **1 John 5:14-15** it says: **"This is the confidence we have in approaching God: that if we ask anything according to his will, he hears us. And if we know that he hears us – whatever we ask – we know that we have what we asked of him."**

What are you asking God for right now? Is it a new job that will provide greater financial stability? Is it a prayer for healing from a sickness or disease? Are you asking God for more love in your marriage and family? Are you seeking direction for a particular decision that is pending? According to this verse you can have confidence in approaching Him about anything. God hears you! More than that, He loves you and wants only the best for your life. Guilt free asking! I like it! Second…

Prayer is *"seeking and finding."*

When we don't know the will of God for a situation, we are to seek God's truth and wisdom for that situation until we find it. This is a very different approach than just operating by conventional wisdom or whatever may be popular or politically correct today. Our human nature is to take the easy road and rely on our own knowledge, life experience and know-how rather than continuing to seek God for true wisdom. God has given us a brain

> God hears you! More than that, He loves you and wants only the best for your life.

with which to think, yes, but no matter how bright we are (or think we are), our "go to" move must always be to seek God!

Corrie Ten Boom once asked, "Is prayer your steering wheel or your spare tire?" **Matthew 6:33** promises: **"But seek first his kingdom and his righteousness, and all these things will be given to you as**

well." When we truly seek Him with all our heart we will always find that we serve a "good, good, God" who answers our prayers! Third…

Prayer is *"knocking and opening."*

When we knock with faithful prayers, Jesus promises to provide us with answers. And if we know the will of God and are experiencing roadblocks, we are to knock and keep knocking until either God opens the door or guides us in another direction. This is faithful, tenacious, persistent, mountain-moving prayer!

The Parable of the Persistent Widow illustrates the power of what we might call "knocking prayer." Jesus told this parable to His disciples, the Bible says, so that: **"… they should always pray and not give up" (Luke 18:1b).** This particular widow needed legal protection and justice from someone who is described as her "adversary." An unbelieving judge refused to hear her case. She kept knocking on his door making her plea until he finally relented, even if it was just to get her to stop knocking and go away. Jesus concludes: **"Listen to what the unjust judge says. And will not God bring about justice for his chosen ones, who cry out to him day and night? I tell you, he will see that they get justice and quickly. However, when the Son of Man comes, will he find faith on the earth" (Luke 18:6-8)?**

This story challenges us to ask whether we have the faith of this persistent widow to keep knocking on the door of heaven even when God (our righteous judge) doesn't seem to be answering our prayers. It's not about harassing God until we get the answer we want. It's about continuing to knock until we get the answer God wants to give! Yes, Jesus says that prayer is about *asking and receiving, seeking and finding, knocking and opening.* We have been invited to talk with God every moment of every day and make our requests known to Him in the context of faith and thanksgiving. He promises to hear our prayers and answer them according to His love, wisdom, perfect timing and awesome plan for our lives. Whatever your need today, God hears you! Keep on praying!

Closet Prayer

In the 2015 movie "War Room," the marriage of Tony and Elizabeth Jordan is falling apart. He is a successful pharmaceutical salesman. She is a real estate agent. When Elizabeth meets an elderly woman who is interested in selling her house named Miss Clara, she discovers something fascinating. As Miss Clara gives Elizabeth a tour of her home she highlights her "second favorite room" which contains a "Wall of Remembrance." On this wall is a list of answered prayers. Miss Clara's favorite room is her "War Room" which is a small closet where the walls are covered with prayer requests. This is where she goes to spend her personal time with God and fervently seek Him in prayer… and man can she pray!

> *It's not about harassing God until we get the answer we want. It's about continuing to knock until we get the answer God wants to give!*

Just before Jesus taught His disciples the Lord's Prayer, He said this: **"And when you pray, do not be like the hypocrites, for they love to pray standing in the synagogues and on the street corners to be seen by others. Truly I tell you, they have received their reward in full. But when you pray, go into your room, close the door and pray to your Father, who is unseen. Then your Father, who sees what is done in secret, will reward you" (Matthew 6:5-6).**

Jesus is making two points here. First, prayer isn't about showing off. No fancy words are required, just a sincere heart. Second, for all the different kinds of prayer I mentioned earlier, none is more important than that personal conversation between you and your Father in heaven. Many Christians find that there is a special place where that intimate communication seems to flow the best. It is often referred to as a "prayer closet." I like the term "war room" even better!

It can be anywhere that will provide you with some peace and quiet to really come into the presence of the Lord. Your "prayer closet" might be your favorite chair in the family room, a swing in your backyard, a path in the woods, a bench down by the lake, a drive in your car, your cubicle at work or your bed in the middle of the night. Can you identify your "prayer closet" right now? Even though prayer is for anyplace and anytime, there are often special places and special times where we sense the presence of the Holy Spirit and can quietly sing, "It is well, it is well, with my soul." I encourage you to find that place and seek it out regularly. It is out of that heart of personal prayer that we can then intercede for others.

Standing in the Gap

Who is on your prayer list? You may not have one written down but I'm sure you can quickly identify 5 or 10 people, or groups of people, for whom you regularly pray. For us "Boomers" this prayer list always begins with our children and grandchildren. Next we include extended family, friends, fellow church members, coworkers, neighbors and even total strangers when a special need has been made known to us. Being a "list pray-er" can be a very good way to intentionally and regularly lift up the needs of others. These are called "intercessory prayers" because we are interceding, or standing in the gap, for someone else.

That person or group of people may love the Lord already and just need us to pray with them and agree in faith. At other times we will find ourselves interceding for someone who doesn't know Jesus or have the faith to pray for themselves. One time I asked a man I was visiting in the hospital if he believed in the power of prayer. He said he wasn't sure. I said, "Well I do and with your permission I'd like to pray for you right now!" I was standing in the gap. He had tears as we held hands and prayed. Only the most hardened of heart ever refuse prayer because even if they don't have the faith to believe… they are glad you do!

Sometimes I like to pray as I watch the news. It reminds me to seek God's solutions for the problems of our world rather than just being frustrated or angry about them. He didn't have satellite T.V. but the Apostle Paul said: **"I urge, then, first of all, that petitions, prayers, intercessions and thanksgiving be made for all people**

– for kings and all those in authority, that we may live peaceful and quiet lives in all godliness and holiness. This is good, and it pleases God our Savior, who wants all people to be saved and to come to a knowledge of the truth" (1 Timothy 2:1-4). As I've shared before, this means that we are even called to pray for that "other" political party and those with whom we vehemently disagree.

Here is one of my favorite stories about intercessory prayer. I can't quote it… but I'd love to share it to the best of my memory. Dwight L. Moody became a famous evangelist in the second half of the 1800's because he believed in the power of prayer to transform lives. One time he took a sabbatical to England, his home country, to get refreshed and hear from God. He wasn't planning to preach until a pastor near the place he was staying recognized him and prevailed upon him to come and speak at his church one Sunday morning.

That Sunday afternoon Moody wrote in his journal that they were the deadest crowd he had ever seen and that the only thing worse than preaching to them was that for some unknown reason he had promised to go back the next night and preach again. When he went back on Monday night, about half-way through his message, something shifted in the Spirit.

This seemingly unmovable congregation began to come to life, and near the end of his message, Moody felt compelled to ask if anyone there would like to become a Christian. A lot of people stood up. He was so surprised, that rather than extend a normal altar call, he said, "Maybe you don't understand what I'm asking. Pray about this decision some more and if you are really serious about committing your life to Jesus, come to this little room off the side of the sanctuary and meet me after the service."

When the service was over, Moody went to that room and it was packed. He said to the pastor, "Have you ever seen anything like this before?" The pastor said, "No, but I think you need to preach again tomorrow night!" So much for his sabbatical! Moody preached ten straight days and more than 400 people in this little church gave their lives to Christ. Revival had broken out and in the months ahead it lit a fire all across England.

Moody couldn't understand. These people were spiritually dead but something had changed. He later came to find out that an 80 year-old widow named Mary Ann Adelard had read one of his sermons from an American newspaper, had developed a heart for revival in her church, city and nation, and had prayed every day for months that Dwight L. Moody would come and preach at her congregation in England. This is the power of intercessory prayer! You and I are called to "stand in the gap" for others and trust the Holy Spirit to touch hearts and change lives!

Unified Prayer

More than 25 years ago we made a decision in Elk River, Minnesota, to meet together to pray every Tuesday at noon. This began a process of spiritual transformation that not only touched our lives but blessed our city. It didn't happen as a result of some fancy new program recommended by a high-priced church consultant. It came about when pastors and leaders in our community read a book by Dr. Ed Silvoso called "That None Shall Perish."[1]

This book tells the story of transformation in a city in Argentina called Resistencia which means "resistance" or "opposition." The year was 1990. At the encouragement of Ed and Ruth Silvoso, Dave and Sue Thompson along with other members of their team began meeting with pastors from very different denominational backgrounds to discuss and pray about how to "reach a city for Christ." In the process they received a word from the Lord. They came to recognize that they were not only called to pastor their local congregations but partner together to pastor their city. This led to the establishment of hundreds of "houses of prayer," in essence, "Ekklesias" doing Prayer Evangelism all over the city, as we discussed earlier in Chapter 10.

> *They came to recognize that they were not only called to pastor their local congregations but partner together to pastor their city.*

250

Simultaneously, 50 city-wide evangelistic crusades took place along with "prayer fairs" that culminated in a large, united, open-air crusade in a park, where in spite of the interference of witches and warlocks, thousands of people came to Christ, including some of the interlopers. The Church literally "filled up the city" with the Good News that Jesus had come to town (see Acts 5:28)! The immediate result was that the "church of the city" doubled in size. Where there were 70 congregations in 1990, there are over 500 today, and the province has become the most evangelical province in the nation.

The pastors in the Elk River, Minnesota area already had a close fellowship, however, upon hearing this testimony we realized that God was calling us to something brand new. We began the Tuesday Noon Prayer Meeting, which to this day includes both pulpit and marketplace ministers, and began to earnestly seek a move of God in our city and region. Instead of just focusing on our own local churches we made it our goal to build God's kingdom, intentionally setting aside "secondary" denominational differences in favor of seeking greater unity in the whole body of Christ.

In a book by Rick Heeren called "The Elk River Story,"[2] I describe how my attitude and actions changed in relation to other churches in the community from what I call "drive-by cursing" to "drive-by blessing." Instead of viewing other congregations with criticism and suspicion, I came to recognize them as partners in the cause of the Gospel. I began to pray for both their pastors and people. I encouraged my congregation to do the same.

At Christ Church we committed ourselves to be a Transformation Church where every member is a minister and our greater Call is to look beyond the "four walls" to serve the needs of our surrounding communities in partnership with others. When Christ Church came up with a good idea, one of our first questions became "How can we do this with others?" This move of the Spirit in our community and surrounding region became a testimony to so many.

A couple of key scriptures in this journey included Jesus' "high priestly prayer" in **John 17** where He prays that His disciples: **"… will become one so that the world may know."** (check-out John

251

17:20-23) and **Psalm 133** which begins: **"How good and pleasant it is when God's people live together in unity,"** and ends: **"For there the Lord bestows his blessing, even life forevermore."**

There are so many wonderful memories of what God has done over the years. In the early days we prayed in unity and saw God cut off an alarming suicide rate at our high school that led to a period of many years with no teenage suicides. We continue to intercede for our youth today. One Tuesday we prayed with our Sherburne County Sheriff and asked him for any specific prayer requests. He shared that his officers knew there was a major methamphetamine lab operating someone in our region but his detectives couldn't locate it. We prayed… and less than one week later they found it! That discovery led to one of the largest drug busts in the history of the State of Minnesota.

Another time we prayed with the Superintendent of Schools who was facing an up-hill battle regarding a bond issue that needed to pass in order to build new schools and improve others in our district. We shared what God had shown us in the Spirit; that what He wanted to do in the physical was indicative of what He wanted to do in the spiritual. This Superintendent gave our team permission to "prayer walk" the halls of Elk River High School after hours, anoint every locker with oil and intercede for the students they represented. Soon thereafter the bond issue passed.

We saw a major U.S. retailer locate their national computer center in Elk River, because in their words, "there was something that felt so positive about our city." We knew that God was changing the spiritual climate. We have seen a car dealership, a motorcycle dealership, an insurance agency, a law office, a counseling center, a bank, an oil company and many other local businesses become "Ekklesias," tangible expressions of the Church, by dedicating their businesses to God and intentionally ministering to the felt needs of the people and communities around them. There is great power in unified prayer that is focused on building the kingdom of God rather than our own personal kingdoms.

This move of God continues to this day! Just recently "the Church of the city" held a worship service at the Sherburne County Fairgrounds. The offering that was received totaling about $7,000 was presented to the Mayor of Elk River to bless the city. With his permission we also "layed hands" on him and his wife and prayed for them. In a personal thank you note, he shared that he had never felt so loved and supported. I encourage you to ask how you can partner with others to see your communities impacted.

As my good friend Dave Thompson says, "Start with prayer and then follow the trail." Find a prayer group that has a similar heart. Take your prayer life up another notch by moving beyond your needs to intercede for the needs of others; your community churches, businesses, schools, governmental leaders and public servants. When you are out and about, on a walk or a drive, make that shift from "drive-by cursing" to "drive-by blessing." Friends, this kind of focused prayer will energize you personally and change your whole outlook on your community or region.

Jesus Prays for You

While Jesus has invited us to pray and intercede for others, what a blessing it is to know that He also intercedes for us. In **Romans 8:31**, Paul says: **"What, then, shall we say in response to these things? If God is for us, who can be against us."** He continues: **"Who will bring any charge against those whom God has chosen? It is God who justifies. Who then is the one who condemns? No one. Christ Jesus who died – more than that, who was raised to life – is at the right hand of God and is also interceding for us"** (Romans 8:31-34).

I picture it this way. When we pray, Jesus is there at the right hand of the Father hearing every prayer and interceding for us. Because He loves us so much, He makes our case and then delivers the results through the Holy Spirit. The Holy Spirit speaks only what

He hears from the Father and Son, guiding us into truth. Here's why I have come to this conclusion.

In **John 16:12** Jesus says: **"I have much more to say to you, more than you can now bear. But when he, the Spirit of truth comes, he will guide you into all truth. He will not speak on his own; he will speak only what he hears, and he will tell you what is yet to come."** These verses provide wonderful insights into how the Holy Trinity functions together. Jesus not only invites us to pray but intercedes for us. What great confidence this gives us to listen for His voice.

One year I was attending the Transform Our World International Conference in Honolulu, Hawaii. I know, tough duty! My spiritual father, Ed Silvoso, invited me to sit at a table over lunch with an Argentine pastor named Omar Cabrera Jr. I knew very little about him at the time. He was very kind and asked me about my congregation. I told him about our transformation vision and city-wide partnership. I asked him what church he served. He very humbly said, "Well, my congregation is Iglesia Vision de Futuro and we actually have 230 locations serving several hundred thousand members." It turns out that his father, Omar Cabrera Sr., was a key leader in what came to be known as the Argentine Revival.

It was then that I remembered hearing about his ministry. I said, "I understand that you have been experiencing great miracles of healing in your churches. Has that always been the case or is it a more recent phenomena?" He said, "It's more recent, actually. Something had to shift in our prayers that has now released the power of God to do these miracles, even the raising of the dead." I said, "I want to learn more!" Pastor Cabrera explained, "When people used to come forward for prayer I would be attentive to whatever need they expressed and then enthusiastically begin to pray and declare the power of God to meet their need. What I learned over time was to listen first to God and pray second."

He continued, "I still ask people to share their 'felt need,' the one that is most obvious, but then before a word comes out of my mouth I ask the Holy Spirit to reveal the deeper need. I ask the Spirit to not only show me what to pray for… but give me the words to do it. Sometimes I literally open my mouth not knowing what will come out. When I made this shift to total dependence on the Holy Spirit rather than just my own faith and experience, that's when we really began seeing miracles happen."

That unexpected encounter came as a tremendous encouragement to me and changed the way I pray for people too. We can all become loving, caring, expert "pray-ers," however, if we're not first "listeners," if we're not first asking the Holy Spirit to show us what to pray for and how to pray, our prayers won't be as effective as we would like them to be. Now I will ask the person, "What do you need prayer for today?" and then, instead of diving right in, wait and listen. It may only be for a few seconds but my prayer is "Lord, show me how you would have me pray." If you adopt this approach you will find that it not only takes the pressure off of you… but opens the door to the extraordinary miracles of God.

> We can all become loving, caring, expert "pray-ers," however, if we're not first "listeners," if we're not first asking the Holy Spirit to show us what to pray for and how to pray, our prayers won't be as effective as we would like them to be.

From Personal to Powerful

Prayer represents an amazing invitation to communicate with the One who made us, loves us, saves us and desires to have a personal relationship with us today. Prayer is a "two-way street." We must learn to share our deepest thoughts, hopes and dreams, challenges and struggles. God is listening. The question is, "Are we?" An effective prayer life starts with personal prayer, "prayer closet prayer." As we grow we will come to recognize the privilege and opportunity we have to intercede for the needs of others and the world around us. To do so in unity with fellow believers is an even greater blessing. As we learn to both pray and listen for the voice of the Holy Spirit we will find our prayers becoming more personal and powerful.

As we consider our Call as Baby Boomers, some of our most effective and meaningful ministry during these years can come about as the result of prayer. There may be many things we can't do… but no matter what our age or situation in life, we can always pray! We need "War Room" prayer today for marriages and families, cities and nations. Please intercede for the generations that are following us. They need our prayers more than we know! No whistle required!

Questions for Personal Reflection or Group Discussion:

1. Reflect on the status and quality of your prayer life. Does God need a coach's whistle to get your attention or have you learned to hear His voice above the crowd?

2. Where is your "prayer closet," that place where you can really tune-in to God? When you pray, what do you find yourself doing more of… talking or listening?

3. Who is on your prayer list today? Who is that person in your life right now who really needs you to "stand in the gap" for them?

4. As you reflect on the generations that are following after us as "Boomers," what do you discern to be their greatest needs? Will you commit to pray for them and "follow the trail?"

Notes:

1. Ed Silvoso, *That None Should Perish* (Ventura, CA: Regal Books, 1994).

2. Rick Heeren, *The Elk River Story* (San Jose, CA: Transformational Publications, 2004), Ch. 7.

CHAPTER 17

Share Your Faith!

Imagine yourself on a cruise ship. I'm sure that many of you have been there. You're relaxing on the sun deck, sitting back in your lounge chair, when someone shouts that a child has just fallen overboard. The urgency of the situation would demand an immediate reaction from everyone. There would be no time to debate the various methods that might be considered to rescue the child. Any and all means would be utilized to save the child's life. Those on board would recognize the need to pull together and work as a team. No egos, no competition, just a tremendous sense of urgency to rescue the child from certain death in the ocean waters.

I am convinced that each of us must rediscover this same sense of urgency when it comes to the lost and vulnerable in our world today. Jesus Himself declares: **"For the Son of Man came to seek and to save the lost" (Luke 19:10).** As Baby Boomers we cannot afford to relax on deck for the rest of our lives while the children of this world are falling overboard by the millions. Nor can the Christian Church. It's time we claim our higher calling as the people of God and pull together to get the job done.

> *As Baby Boomers we cannot afford to relax on deck for the rest of our lives while the children of this world are falling overboard by the millions.*

No more egos. No more competition. No more complacency. The Church of the 21st century and every member of it desperately needs to recover a first-century passion for rescuing the lost and providing hope for the future. If you confess Jesus as your Savior and Lord you are a part of that Church and your testimony is desperately needed. That's why in this chapter I want to encourage you to share your faith with greater intention and confidence, starting with your own family and friends. It is one of the most important and urgent things we are called to do with the rest of our lives.

God's Story – Your Story

One thing that is unique about Christianity is that it is evangelistic. We have a message of life in Christ that is such great news that we are compelled to share it with others. The Greek word "evangel," which is the root word of "evangelism," means "bearer of Good News." Christians have been called to be witnesses to their faith in Jesus since the very beginning. Read **1 John 1:1-3** and then I've got some questions for you. The Apostle John testifies:

"That which was from the beginning, which we have heard, which we have seen with our eyes, which we have looked at–and our hands have touched – this we proclaim concerning the Word of Life. The life appeared, we have seen it and testify to it, and proclaim to you the eternal life, which was with the Father and has appeared to us. We proclaim to you what we have seen and heard, so that you also may have fellowship with us. And our fellowship is with the Father and with his Son, Jesus Christ."

What is it that you have heard and seen and touched with your own ears, eyes and hands that has made Jesus real to you? How does God's story intersect with your story in a way that can bring encouragement to others? Was there a time when you were alone and Jesus comforted you? Was there an occasion when you were afraid and Jesus brought you peace? Was there a moment when you faced a significant temptation and Jesus gave you an escape route? Was there a time when you had to make a difficult decision and Jesus guided you? Was there a season when you were sick and Jesus healed you? Was there a time that you recognized yourself to be a sinner and Jesus saved you?

If your answer is "yes" to any of these questions, you have a story to tell! These tangible encounters with the person and power of Jesus become our testimony. When our lives have truly been changed, we can't keep it to ourselves! God's story intersects with our story and a love connection is made. When both connect with the story of someone else, even someone seemingly far away from God, empowered by the Holy Spirit they become the avenue to that person's personal transformation.

What is Your "Value Add?"

Their names were Mark and Masey. I met this young couple in Florida. They were from New York and were combining business with some vacation time. We met, of all places, at a hotel putting green. After chit-chatting for a few minutes I asked them what they did for work. They owned a craft beer brewing facility and were on the verge of a significant distribution deal. They had come to Florida to celebrate and sign the new contract. They weren't married but I could tell they were way more than just business partners. When they responded in-kind and discovered I was a pastor, they began to ask some surprisingly insightful questions.

"Tell us about your church? What is the most important thing you want to communicate to your people? How does your church relate to your community? Where do you stand on issues like gay marriage? Why would someone who is very busy and doing quite well in life choose to attend there?" They were sincere but frank.

We conversed for about a half hour and I tried to share some responses that weren't preachy but would also get them to think. At one point I said, "What would it take for you to consider following Jesus and becoming a member of a local church? What would be most important to you?" They looked at each other and pondered my question. Mark responded, "Our lives are already full of family, friends, work and hobbies. There isn't a minute to spare. If we were to consider becoming Christians and joining a church we would have to see a definite 'value add.'"

Typical millennials? Maybe. However, I wonder if people of any age who were being totally honest wouldn't answer in the same way. It's true of most things in life. Why not Christianity? If we're going to commit our time, talents and our resources to anything these days, don't we expect there to be a "value add?" In the same way, it is totally reasonable that people would want to experience a real personal benefit from following Christ. This conversation gave me a whole new perspective on sharing my faith.

> If we're going to commit our time, talents and our resources to anything these days, don't we expect there to be a "value add?"

If you are already a Christian, what are the "value adds" you have experienced that have confirmed your commitment to follow Jesus? If not, what would it take? An experience of unconditional love? The revelation of truth? Forgiveness from your past? Hope for the future? Genuine friendships? Meaningful work? Real purpose in life? The promise of heaven? Good news in a world of bad news? The truth is that Jesus provides all of these benefits to those who commit their lives to Him, however, we don't get to negotiate up front. Remember, in **Matthew 6:33** Jesus says: **"But seek first his kingdom and his righteousness, and all these things will be given to you as well."**

To experience these "value adds" we must first come by faith. Only the power of God can change a human heart, and yet, my unexpected conversation with Mark and Masey reminds us to meet every person right where they're at. Before giving someone our answers we need to listen to their heartfelt questions. As we trust in the Spirit to give us love and wisdom in our responses we will be able to share our faith and plant the seeds that one day God will harvest.

Good News

A man waited anxiously at the Doctor's Office for the results of his tests. The doctor finally came in to the exam room looking very somber. He said, "I'm sorry but I have some bad news to share with you today and then some really bad news. Which do you want first?" The man said, "I guess the bad news." The doctor said, "I'm sorry to tell you that you only have two days to live." The man said, "Oh no! How could there be any worse news than that?" The doctor said, "I meant to call you yesterday."

The message we have to deliver is Good News on top of Good News! The same message that changed lives 2,000 years ago still does today. Some of our methods for sharing our faith have changed, like the internet, but the fundamentals of the Gospel never change. Why? Because: **"Jesus Christ is the same yesterday and today and forever" (Hebrews 13:8).** What is our message? It's really pretty straight forward.

God loves you. Jesus His Son died for you. When you ask Him to forgive your sins, and receive Him by faith as your Savior and Lord, He changes you from the inside-out! The Bible calls it being "born again." You become a child of God and part of His family. Your sins are forgiven. You inherit eternal life. The Holy Spirit indwells you and begins to counsel, comfort and empower you for Christian living. Life is never the same again!

This is the message of faith we are called to share with others. We may adapt these words or phrases based on the context but our testimony will always connect God's story, our story and that of the person we are trying to reach for Jesus.

When we think of a witness, we often think of a person who has "seen something" and is called to testify before a judge or jury. We've had some pretty high profile cases in Minnesota recently where dozens of witnesses have been called to "tell the truth, the whole truth and nothing but the truth, so help me God."

What are you prepared to testify when it comes to Jesus? Many accuse him yet today of being an imposter... a false prophet who was no more than a man. What do you say about him? Or flip it around. If you were put on trial for being a Christian, would there be enough evidence to convict you? Yes, we are all witnesses. It's just a question of what kind of witness we choose to be. One person said, "A witness is someone who shares on the outside what God has done on the inside."

In **2 Corinthians 5:17-20** our calling is clearly spelled out. Paul says: **"Therefore, if anyone is in Christ, the new creation has come: The old is gone, the new is here! All this is from God, who reconciled us to himself through Christ and gave us the ministry of reconciliation: that God was reconciling the world to himself through Christ, not counting people's sins against them. And he has committed to us this message of reconciliation. We are therefore Christ's ambassadors, as though God were making his appeal through us. We implore you on Christ's behalf: Be reconciled to God."**

> *"A witness is someone who shares on the outside what God has done on the inside."*

If someone serves as an ambassador for the United States to another country they don't go there on the basis of their own authority or reputation. They go with the authority of the President to represent the views of our nation. When there is a misunderstanding they stand in the gap and seek reconciliation. We are to be ambassadors for Christ. God is making His appeal to the world through the message we share and the relationships we foster. The key is to know that God goes with us. We are never alone. It is His authority that gives us access even to the highest places!

They're With Me

I've mentioned previously that my (our) seminary internship year was at Lord of Life Lutheran Fellowship in Fairfax, Virginia. Colleen and I had only been married a little over a year. The congregation was about 50% military families with many stationed at the Pentagon in Washington, D.C. One of our church members was Bill Tuttle, a four-star general in the Army. A couple of his kids were in our youth group. One night Colleen and I had just crawled into bed when the phone rang. The voice said, "This is General Tuttle. Are you sleeping yet?" I said, "No sir!" He said, "I'll be there in 5 minutes to pick you up. Be ready!" We got ready in a hurry alright having no idea the amazing experience that was in store for us that night.

It was the Fall of 1978. General Tuttle took us in the dark to Andrew's Air Base where President Jimmy Carter was about to land on Air Force One having just negotiated the Middle East Peace Accords with Israeli Prime Minister Menachem Begin and Egyptian President Anwar Sadat. Perhaps you remember. The "Who's Who" of Washington, D.C. were there on the tarmac as the Marine Band struck up "Hail to the Chief" and President Carter gave a short speech to rousing cheers. Everywhere we went soldiers assigned to the security detail saluted General Tuttle. All he said was "these two are with me" and we were allowed to pass. We never showed any form of ID during the whole evening. How things have changed since 911!

It gets even better! Sometime later these two world leaders came to Washington, D.C. for the signing of the agreement formally titled, "Framework for Peace in the Middle East." It was to take place on the White House lawn. General Tuttle called again and asked if we would like to attend with him. We arrived at the White House. There was no ID required of us once again. We were with General Tuttle.

He showed us around a bit and then said, "Would you like to see the Oval Office?" We thought, "You've got to be kidding!" He led us down a hall to the West Wing. We arrived at the door to the Oval Office. Two Marine guards came to attention, saluting General Tuttle. He said, "Would it be alright if I showed my guests the Oval Office?" One of the young marines almost apologetically said, "I'm not able to allow you to go in right now, sir. President Carter is meeting with Prime Minister Begin and President Sadat before they go outside for the signing."

Here we are, Colleen and I, young kids in our 20s, standing on one side of the Oval Office door with President Carter and these two world leaders on the other side about to make history. Our only credential was that we were with General Tuttle. What a memory! What a reminder that our credibility as witnesses for Christ resides not in ourselves but in the One who goes with us. Jesus declares, "They're with me" and opens doors to opportunities for us to be witnesses to others in ways we never imagined possible.

Living Witnesses

The Bible is the foundation for the message of hope we share. We won't be effective witnesses unless we are growing in God's Word ourselves, and as a result, in our relationship with Jesus. You can't give away what you don't have!

The whole Bible, is in fact, one big "book of witness." It unashamedly testifies to the love of God as demonstrated through His Son, Jesus. Why were 40 different authors compelled by the Holy Spirit to write the 66 books of the Bible over a period of 1,500 years? More than anything else it was to give a witness to what they had personally "heard and seen and touched," to quote that phrase again from 1 John.

The Patriarchs and Prophets of the Old Testament were "historical witnesses." They documented the mighty works of God and pointed the way to a Savior. The Gospel writers and Apostles of the New Testament were "eye witnesses." They captured the key events in the life of Jesus based on their personal experiences and first-hand accounts. As members of the family of God today we are "living witnesses." The message we have to share about Jesus is the outcome of a personal encounter, sometimes called His manifest presence, and is meant for the whole world.

> The message we have to share about Jesus is the outcome of a personal encounter, sometimes called His manifest presence, and is meant for the whole world.

Why Should I Share My Faith?

Many of us have wrongly assumed that evangelism is meant for professionals. As a result, while our faith may be very personal and important to us, we often fail to make it public to others, even our own loved ones and friends. Some in our "Boomer" generation have even proudly parroted what we often heard from our parent's generation. "I don't wear my faith on my shirtsleeve."

As Jesus was coming down the mountain where he was "transfigured" and his true identity was revealed to Peter, James and John, He says: **"Don't tell anyone what you have seen, until the Son of Man has been raised from the dead"** (Matthew 17:9b). Unfortunately, too many of us have only claimed the first part of that verse, the "don't tell anyone" part. Why is it so important that we learn to lovingly share what we have seen, heard and experienced in our relationship with Jesus? Please consider the following:

We share our faith because we have been sent to the world.

Following His resurrection, as Jesus was about to ascend to heaven, His parting words to His followers were: **"Go and make disciples of all nations."** This command is part of what is called the Great Commission from **Matthew 28:16-20**. I prefer to think of it as the Great Partnership because Jesus promised to go with us until the end of time.

That promise became reality 10 days later on the Day of Pentecost as a mighty wind and tongues of fire took the disciples out of the Upper Room and into the streets. Peter was the first one to stand in the public square and tell the amazing story of Jesus' life, death and resurrection. The crowds: **"… were cut to the heart and said to Peter and the other apostles, 'Brothers, what shall we do?' Peter replied, 'Repent and be baptized, every one of you, in the name of Jesus Christ for the forgiveness of your sins and you will receive the gift of the Holy Spirit'"** (Acts 2:37-38).

Three thousand people put their faith in Jesus that day and the Christian Church was born! To see the same results today we too must play "show and tell." We must tell people the truth about

Jesus and show it with our lives. When we do, the Holy Spirit takes our humble witness and uses it to change hearts and draw people to Christ. Next…

We share our faith because there is no other name than Jesus by which people can be saved.

Quite frankly, this is why others religions aren't passionate about being witnesses. If your belief system is primarily about "good works," there is no Good News to share… only a life of trying to keep all the rules. If your assumption is that your religion is just one of many paths to God, what's the point. Let each person find their own way. No wonder that many people consider it pushy and insensitive when they encounter someone who is passionate about their beliefs. It is this very fact that causes so many Christians to hold back. But what does that say about us if we're more concerned about what others will think than we are about sharing the life-changing message of Jesus?

The first generation of Christians didn't let that stop them. Even the word "witness" is translated in the Bible from an interesting Greek word. It's "marturia," which is also the root of the word martyr. Many of the first believers were imprisoned, beaten and even thrown to the lions in the Roman Coliseum for declaring their faith in Christ? Why were they willing to die rather than deny?

In the Book of Acts, Chapter 3, Peter and John were going to the temple one day for afternoon prayers. There at the gate was a man who had been lame from birth. As they passed by he called out to them for money. He was a beggar. They stopped and Peter looked him right in the eye and declared: **"Silver or gold I do not have, but what I do have I give to you. In the name of Jesus Christ of Nazareth, rise up and walk" (Acts 3:6).**

Taking him by his right hand Peter helped the man to his feet and immediately his legs became strong. He went with them into the temple courts walking and jumping and praising God. Imagine the amazement of the people who witnessed this miraculous healing and just how quickly the news must have spread?

Physical healing is always a sign of spiritual healing so later that day Peter testified to the astonished crowd about what they had seen and heard. In **Acts 3:16** he said: **"By faith in the name of Jesus, this man whom you see and know was made strong. It is Jesus' name and the faith that comes through him that has completely healed him, as you can all see."**

That was a testimony, wasn't it? To fast forward… some of the religious leaders were standing among the crowd listening to what Peter said. They were greatly disturbed because Peter was effectively declaring that Jesus was the Messiah, the long-awaited Savior of the world. As a result, Peter and John were arrested and thrown into jail. The next day they were brought out for questioning. Watch closely. The religious leaders asked: **"By what power or name did you do this"** (Acts 4:7b)?

Peter, filled with the Holy Spirit, replied to them: **"If we are being called to account today for an act of kindness shown to a man who was lame and are being asked how he was healed, then know this, you and all the people of Israel: It is by the name of Jesus Christ of Nazareth, whom you crucified but whom God raised from the dead, that this man stands before you healed. Salvation is found in no one else, for there is no other name under heaven given to mankind by which we must be saved"** (Acts 4:8b-10, 12).

Was Peter just a company guy sticking to the sales script? Hardly! He had walked with Jesus himself. Everything he had seen and heard and experienced had convinced him of this fact. Jesus Himself had declared: **"I am the way and the truth and the life. No one comes to the Father except through me"** (John 14:6).

I share this story because I personally believe that these claims are absolutely critical to our witness for Christ today. If we don't believe that Jesus is the only name by which people can be saved… if we don't believe that He is the only way to the Father, we will never be passionate about sharing Him with others. Could it be that this is why so many Christians are reluctant to share their faith today, even with their family and closest friends? Next…

We share our faith to show people how to escape the bondage of sin and evil.

Look at the evil we're witnessing in our world right now. The news is full of terrible atrocities being committed every day to the point where our senses are dulled or we just turn away in horror or disgust. At the root of this evil is sin and rebellion against God, but how do we escape it? Years ago I came across a parable written to describe our condition and Jesus' response. I put my own twist on it and called it "The Pit." See if it speaks to you.

"Picture a man down in a pit. The pit represents humanity's condition of sin and struggle to reach God. No matter how hard the man tries, he cannot seem to climb out of the pit on his own. Leaders of various world religions symbolically come and stand around the edge of the pit, peering down at the man, shouting advice.

The Jewish Rabbi tells him to pray harder and keep the law. Only by obedience will he be saved. The Muslim prophet tells him to submit with greater devotion to Allah and the pillars of Islam. The Hindu holy man tells him he is reaping the reward of bad karma and that his only hope is in the next life. The Buddhist Dalai Lama tells him he must empty his mind of this desire to get out of the pit and seek enlightenment. The man tries harder and harder, devoting himself sincerely to all of these religious exercises, but still finds himself stuck in the pit.

Several New Age psychics show up and tell him to stop seeking God 'out there' and discover the 'god within.' They offer to serve as a channel to his deceased loved ones who might have a word of encouragement or wisdom. An elder from the Mormon Church describes a host of rules that might result in eternal exaltation. A Jehovah Witness tells the man he's too late. They already have 144,000 anointed followers of their religion. His only hope is to try to live a perfect life and pray for God's mercy.

A Unitarian Universalist also shows up. She says, 'Concentrate on taking care of the pit and stop worrying about heaven. We're all going there some day.' An Atheist also comes to visit and declares that the pit itself is nothing but an illusion. To experience release will require mind over matter because he isn't really suffering at all. Even a witch from the Wiccan religion stops by. Sensing the man's vulnerability she says, 'Follow me and I will teach you a more powerful way to live your life.' The man in the pit finds himself sinking deeper and deeper into despair.

What a curious sight for Jesus, who also hears the agonizing cries of the man in the pit. From a distance He has observed every other religious leader urging the man on to greater works or different gods. When He arrives at the pit, he amazes all who watch. Not a word is spoken. Jesus *is* the Word. Without a moment's hesitation He jumps down into the pit. He puts His arm around the man and speaks personal words of love and compassion. And then He does the most remarkable thing. He says to the man, 'Here. Stand on my shoulders. Trust me and I will raise you up and out of the pit.' And sure enough, that man found his freedom through Christ."

Psalm 103:1-5 declares: **"Praise the Lord, my soul; all my inmost being, praise his holy name. Praise the Lord, my soul, and forget not all his benefits – who forgives all your sins and heals all your diseases, who redeems your life from the pit and crowns you with love and compassion, who satisfies your desires with good things so that your youth is renewed like the eagle's."**

The experience of so many in our world is that life is the pits! We have the opportunity to declare the Good News of a Savior who comes down to our level and invites us to stand on his shoulders. Next...

We share our faith in order to demonstrate a changed life.

This is the practical, personal side of our Christian witness. If we just come at people with a critical, judgmental posture or by quoting a bunch of scriptures... we won't get too far. As a matter of fact, the only thing we'll succeed in doing is turning them off. One time a very well-intentioned Christian couple were on a cruise. One evening they were seated with another couple for dinner and decided they would try to share their faith. The husband began by talking about the difference between a person's body and soul and shared several scriptures to that effect. He then asked if they knew where their souls were going when they died. He saw that he was not connecting but pressed on hoping to lead the other couple to Christ. Suddenly the other man pushed back from the table, stood up, stomped his foot on the floor and shouted, "The only soul I've got is on the bottom of this shoe!" He turned to his wife and added, "Dinner is over! Let's go!!"

Have you ever tried to share your faith and been met with a negative response? Not a lot of fun, right? In John 15 it says that Jesus is the vine and we are the branches and that if we remain in him we will bear good fruit. In this case that "good fruit" would have been a more positive outcome. And what are the fruit of the Spirit? In **Galatians 5:22-23** it says: **"But the fruit of the Spirit is love, joy, peace, patience, forbearance, kindness, goodness, faithfulness, gentleness and self-control."**

These fruits represent qualities we see in the life of Jesus. When people experience them in our lives they become evidence that Jesus is real and others will be much more open to listen to our testimony. In the case of this cruise ship dinner conversation it might have been better to find loving ways to get to know this other couple, listen to their story and respond with kindness and encouragement. Who knows what doors the Holy Spirit may have opened for deeper conversation!

Cultivating these fruits of the Spirit is a life-long process. Which of these qualities are evident in your life right now and which need the most work in order for you to become a more effective witness? Francis of Assisi was credited with the phrase, "Preach the Gospel at all times. When necessary, use words." Scholars actually find no record of this saying in his writings. Here is something they believe he did say that encourages us to develop the "fruits of the Spirit." He said, "It is no use walking anywhere to preach unless our walking is our preaching." Next…

We share our faith because Jesus wants everyone to be saved.

It's true! Jesus wasn't just looking for a "few good men," (and women) like the Marines. He wasn't just after the good people, the right people, those with the proper social standing. Jesus wanted everyone to know and experience the amazing love of God! In **2 Peter 3:9** it says: **"The Lord is not slow in keeping his promise, as some understand slowness. Instead he is patient with you, not wanting anyone to perish, but everyone to come to repentance."**

Repentance is a stepping stone to salvation. When we confess our sins and come to Christ, He is so ready to forgive us and welcome us into His heavenly family. Friends, we are the "whoevers" of John 3:16. Our neighbors, coworkers, classmates, friends and even enemies are all the "whoevers." Jesus died for the whole world and everyone in it. He didn't come to condemn us but to save us. We cannot rest as the children of God until everyone has heard this Good News of Jesus Christ and had the opportunity to receive Him as their Savior. This is the mission that has propelled the Christian Church forward for 2,000 years. This is why we are compelled to share our faith today. But how? You may be thinking, "I'm convinced… but that's just not me. I've never been very good at it." I understand. Sometimes I feel the same way. Let's consider some practical steps toward being more effective in our Christian witness.

How Should I Share My Faith?

If you desire to be a more effective witness, the first thing I recommend is that you dedicate or re-dedicate your life to Jesus. He must have your heart before you will ever have a heart to share your faith with others. Maybe your relationship with Him has taken a backseat to other challenges and priorities, especially during these past few years. Have a little talk with God right now and ask Him to give you a brand new beginning that includes a passion for reaching those who don't yet know Jesus.

The next thing I'd encourage you to do is pray for people that you want to lead to Jesus. Talk to God about your family, friends and neighbors before you talk to them about God. Be intentional about it. Make a list of people that the Holy Spirit has put on your heart. Make it a priority to pray for each one… and then ask God to give you both opportunities and wisdom for how you can reach-out to them. Who in your circles of influence do you want to make sure will join you in heaven some day?

Remember, you don't need a seminary degree to be an effective witness. You don't need to be a Bible scholar to share Jesus with your children and grandchildren, extended family, friends, neighbors or coworkers. Look at the Samaritan woman who met Jesus at Jacob's well one afternoon. When Jesus met her troubled life with the promise of "living water" she was changed. She went back to town and enthusiastically told the people: **"He told me everything I ever did" (John 4:39b)**, the subtext being, "… and still loved and forgave me." Jesus qualifies the unqualified when our lives are transformed by Him.

Which leads me to the next suggestion. Speak about what you have personally experienced in Jesus.

- I was stuck in sin and Jesus set me free.
- I couldn't let go of my past but Jesus released me.
- I was in desperate need of healing when Jesus brought me through.
- Our marriage was a mess but Jesus helped us find a new love.
- Our finances were in shambles but Jesus provided for our every need.

You see, as I shared earlier, a witness is someone who shares on the outside what God has done on the inside. In African American churches, the pastor might shout, "Can I have a witness?" Someone will stand-up and say, "Amen, pastor. I've been there!" Don't compare your testimony to that of anyone else. Be sincere. People want to hear your story. They want to know that you not only believe in Jesus but have seen Him work in your life.

Being an effective witness also takes practice. We couldn't expect to play a guitar well or excel at our favorite sport unless we practiced. Why would we think any differently about sharing our faith? The more we reflect upon and share our own testimony, in addition to giving God the glory for everyday blessings, the more we will be ready to respond when the Lord puts people and opportunities in our path. The Bible says: **"… always be prepared to give an answer to everyone who asks you to give the reason for the hope that you have" (1 Peter 3:15b).**

What if someone asked you, "What do you believe about Jesus?" What would you say? Or what if they asked, "What difference has He made in your life?" How would you respond? We all need a long version and a short version of our personal testimony… and we need to be able to adapt it to different people who are at different points of need or understanding. For example, when I prepare to meet someone over coffee or even for a round of golf, I try to think, "Where might this person be at today and how could I be a positive witness to them by bringing love, encouragement and wise counsel as opportunities arise?" And they will!

And most important, learn to depend on the Holy Spirit. In the Old Testament, Moses was reluctant to go and tell the Pharaoh of Egypt to "set the captives free." God said: **"Now go; I will help you speak and will teach you what to say" (Exodus 4:12).** The paraphrase would be "Don't sweat it. I've got you!" The same promise remains true for us. To be effective witnesses we need to be convinced, committed and prepared… but then we must walk by faith every day and follow the leading of the Holy Spirit.

Catch and Release

Fishing is huge in Minnesota. The Walleye is our state fish and considered the best tasting. Other coveted species include Northern Pike (Northern), Muskellunge (Muskie), Large and Smallmouth Bass, Crappies, Sunfish and several varieties of Trout in smaller streams and rivers. I like to say that I'm better at fishing than catching. There's nothing like casting a line on a placid lake during the summer… but my lures usually come back empty. On several occasions I've had the opportunity to go out with a professional guide. That's when things get fun!

That's probably how Jesus' disciples felt when Simon Peter, a professional fisherman, announced that he was heading out to fish for the night. This was sometime after Jesus' resurrection and before His ascension. The response from his buddies was immediate. "We'll go with you!" Their hopes were high but they fished all night and caught nothing. It's called "getting skunked." I know from personal experience! What's surprising is that most of those on the boat had fished the "big lake" their whole lives and knew it like the back of their hand.

The sun came up. The disciples began to row back to the shore. That's when they saw Him. There was a man standing there who called out: **"'Friends, haven't you any fish?' 'No,' they answered"** **(John 21:5).** They may have been a bit perturbed by the very question. It's like asking a local fisherman, "How are they biting?" when you don't see any fish on his stringer. They still didn't recognize Jesus. He shouted back to them: **"Throw your net on the right side of the boat and you will find some" (John 21:6).** They must have thought, "Yeah, like that's going to make any difference! Boats drift you know! The left side one minute is the right side the next!" There was no rational reason it should work.

For some reason they did it, though, and in a matter of minutes their nets were so full they couldn't even lift them into the boat. When they counted later there were 153 fish. That's like a career total for me and an unbelievable day for them! All of a sudden John turned to Peter and said: **"It is the Lord" (John 21:7)!** Peter got so excited that he jumped into the water and began swimming to shore. The others followed, dragging the net full of fish behind them. Jesus invited them to breakfast. As they conversed, He gave Peter his mission assignment. The analogy shifted from fish to sheep but the message was clear. Peter and the rest of the disciples were to pick-up where Jesus left off.

Sometimes Jesus' instructions to us don't make any sense. We're the professionals after all! We think that if we keep doing what we know, and what we've always done, somehow we will get a better result. Perseverance is important but so is obedience. Like the disciples, we need to learn that we can have the right boat, gear, experience and work ethic… and still not catch fish. Even these pros came up empty until they heard the voice of Jesus and obeyed His directions.

> **Perseverance is important but so is obedience.**

When Jesus first called His disciples He said: **"Don't be afraid; from now on you will fish for people" (Luke 5:10b).** The strategy Jesus taught is what fisherman today call "catch and release." It means to keep only what you plan to eat and release the rest back into the lake to grow bigger for somebody else to catch.

The disciples' job was to catch people, gather them in, train them up and send them out. Catch and release! When it comes to people, who are you trying to catch? Is there a parent or child who is yet to receive Jesus? How about that coworker, or neighbor or friend? When it comes to fishing for fish we may have every reason to be discouraged. When it comes to fishing for people we should never give up. So right now… identify a fish you would like to catch for Jesus. Pray for them. Speak peace over them. Ask the Holy Spirit to show you how to serve them and be a witness to them. Then go fishing and get ready for a haul!

Greater Conviction

Why do we share our faith? We share because the world is desperate for Good News and we have it in our back pocket. How do we share our faith? We take eternal truth and make it personal through our own testimony. Our children, grandchildren and the generations that follow are counting on us to share our faith and values. They may not always show it but what could be more important to their future happiness and well-being than having someone they love share the truth about Jesus? Fellow Baby Boomers, God has gifted you to do exactly that! Many of us would be willing to die for Jesus. The question we must ask ourselves today is are we also willing to live for Jesus? If so, in this important season of our lives, may we each find greater conviction and encouragement to be faithful witnesses for Christ so that others may know His love and be saved!

Questions for Personal Reflection or Group Discussion:

1. When it comes to knowing Jesus as your Savior and friend, what has been the "value add?" How might this become a part of your testimony?

2. When your life has been in "the pits," how has Jesus raised you up? What could you tell others about your experience?

3. If the pastor shouted, "Can I have a witness?" what would yours be? Reflect on the 2-minute version and the "over a cup of coffee" version.

4. Who are three fish you would like to "catch and release" to a new life of love, joy and peace in Jesus? What might be your next steps to share your faith with them?

CHAPTER 18

Engage the Culture!

Culture is a broad term that represents the combined social institutions, achievements, arts, ideas, religion and customs of a particular nation, people or social group. A subculture is a group of people within a culture that differentiates itself from the parent culture, maintaining most of its core values. A counterculture is one whose values and norms of behavior differ substantially from mainstream society and are often diametrically opposed to it.

Baby Boomers have run the whole gamut in our lifetimes. The "Hippie" movement that peaked during the 60s and early 70s is the most commonly recognized subculture of our generation because it occurred when most "Boomers" were teens. Hippies rebelled against existing authority and long-standing institutions in society, particularly the government and the military. As a subculture they embraced a different set of social norms regarding music, war, drugs, sexuality, race and religion.

Here are some other examples of subculture and counterculture groups that we have seen during our lifetimes; hipsters, surfers, ski bums, jocks, nerds, goths, punks, grunge, skinheads, hip hop, skaters, cosplayers, gamers and hackers. I'm sure you can think of more! Have you identified in the past with any of these subcultures? Do you still? What was it that attracted you?

You see, from birth until death humans are socialized into various established cultural norms and expectations for language, beliefs, behavior, dress and customs. Cultures, subcultures and countercultures develop over time, sometimes over thousands of years, sometimes within just a few years. Culture is subject to changes by forces within and without. In the past half-century exposure to cross cultural experiences have increased exponentially for our Baby Boom generation as a result of global travel, commerce, sports and new ways of communicating. Multiculturalism, a newer term in our vocabulary, refers to the importance of various cultures respecting each other's unique perspectives on life and cooperating together to form a healthy society.

Traditional American values have included:

- *Individual freedom* balanced with the willingness to respect others and follow the law.
- *Equal opportunity* coupled with competition within a set of personal and business ethics.
- *Self-determination* and *personal achievement* as the result of hard work.

All of these values combine to represent what we have called "The American Dream" which includes the assumed opportunity for a better life and a higher standard of living. These core values go back to the foundation of our nation, were undergirded by religious fundamentals and have provided a point of agreement for America to serve as the "melting pot" of the world.

Racial demographics represent one particular aspect of culture where "Boomers" have experienced great changes during our lifetimes. In our growing-up years the United States was much more racially homogenous than it is today. Census statistics bear this out. In 1960, near the end of our "Boom," the population of the United States was 179.3 million with the racial breakdown being as follows: White (88.6%), Black (10.5%), Other (.9%). Jump ahead 60 years and our nation looks very different. According to the 2020 Census the population of the United States was 329.5 million with the racial breakdown being: White (59.7%), Hispanic/Latino (18.6%), Black (12.6%), Asian (5.9%), Other (3.2%).

This increasing diversity, which is accompanied by a wonderful variety of unique cultural expressions, is challenging us all to reflect on how to engage with culture in ways that are up-building. I believe that our generation is called to play a vital role in passing along important histories, beliefs, values and traditions while at the same time embracing new ones that will benefit society. Let's first consider a biblical foundation for engaging with culture rather than standing in judgement of it.

Jesus and Culture

Jesus was born into a first-century, middle-eastern, Jewish culture. He lived in the community of Nazareth in what is now modern day Israel. He would have attended Jewish school and learned Jewish history from His parents, teachers and community leaders. He would have participated in community events with family and friends and enjoyed Jewish festivals like Passover, Yom Kippur and Hanukkah. As He became a young man He would have developed a trade. We know that Jesus learned carpentry from His father Joseph. We can imagine that Jesus was very familiar with the politics of His day living under Roman occupation. The point is that even though He was the Son of God, Jesus was born into the real world and was fully engaged with His culture. It undoubtedly helped shape who He was.

> The point is that even though He was the Son of God, Jesus was born into the real world and was fully engaged with His culture. It undoubtedly helped shape who He was.

The fact that God initiated His plan of salvation for the world in this very earthy, tangible way provides us with insight into how God views culture today. When the Gospel writer John penned: **"For God so loved the world..."** **(John 3:16a)**, he wasn't describing a God who despised the world but rather One who sent His very best to redeem it. We can be certain of this because, as we've previously highlighted, **John 3:17** says: **"For God did not send his Son into the world to condemn the world, but to save the world through him."** The takeaway? God loves the world even when we don't!

Jesus was both fully God and fully man but He didn't walk this Earth floating two feet above the ground. Just like you and me He needed sleep, got hungry, exhibited a full range of emotions, and the Bible says: **"… was tempted in every way, just as we are – yet did not sin" (Hebrews 4:15b).** The reality is that while Jesus lived in the culture of His day He also came to transform it. We are called to do the same!

Christianity and Culture

Theologian H. Richard Niebuhr, in his classic book called "Christ and Culture"[1] describes five views of the relationship between Jesus and culture. I would summarize them this way:

1. *Christ against culture:* The world is irreparably corrupted by sin. Christians must remove themselves from it as much as possible.
2. *Christ of culture:* All culture is a creation of God and is to be celebrated as good. Christians should accommodate to the changing culture.
3. *Christ above culture:* Culture is often an expression of the uniqueness and diversity of God's creation but Jesus stands in authority above every culture. All cultures are to be perfected by the Word of God and the work of the Church.
4. *Christ and culture in paradox:* Human culture is good, however, it has been tainted by sin which leads to a tension between the Creation and the Creator. Thus the saying, "We are to be in the world but not of the world."

5. *Christ the transformer of culture:* Since Jesus came to redeem the world, Christians are called to do the same, working as partners to transform the culture to the glory of God.

While all five views regarding the relationship between Jesus and culture (and therefore Christians and culture) are thought provoking, I find the first two views to be unacceptable. The first leads to separation, the second to accommodation. The first leads to "nothing goes." The second to "anything goes." There is a middle ground. There are some aspects of the third and fourth views that are intriguing. Yes, Jesus stands above every culture, and yes, we are called to live with the tension that exists between the kingdom of God and the kingdoms of this world.

However, my personal theology aligns most closely with view number five; "Christ the transformer of culture." In **Romans 12:2** Paul says: **"Do not conform to the pattern of this world, but be transformed by the renewing of your mind. Then you will be able to test and approve what God's will is – his good, pleasing and perfect will."** When our lives are personally transformed by the Gospel of Jesus Christ we are given a platform from which to declare transformation to the whole world. Jesus' goal isn't to make us all look and act the same but rather that every culture, in its uniqueness, would come to represent the character and values of God the Father and give Him the glory.

We see the tension of this calling in Jesus' prayer for His disciples in **John 17:13-18**. Reflect carefully and you will see Him expressing the dynamic of being "in the world but not of it." Jesus prayed to His Father in heaven: **"I am coming to you now, but I say these things while I am still in the world, so that they may have the full measure of my joy within them. I have given them your word and the world has hated them, for they are not of the world any more than I am of the world. My prayer is not that you take them out of the world but that you protect them from the evil one. They are not of the world, even as I am not of it. Sanctify them by the**

truth; your word is truth. As you sent me into the world, I have sent them into the world."

Do you hear the tension? Jesus could lift us out of this messy world anytime but He chooses instead to send us right into the middle of it with His light and life.

Sacred or Secular

If we are to engage with the culture in a positive way we first have to overcome our false understanding of what is "sacred" and what is "secular." In the heart and mind of God there is no distinction. **Psalm 24:1** says: **"The earth is the Lord's, and everything in it, the world, and all who live in it."** That means the good, the bad and the ugly. It is all sacred, not in a religious sense, but in a theological one. You see, as humans we like to look at other people, situations and material things and put them into categories; religious, non-religious; holy, unholy; good, bad; worthy, unworthy; touchable, untouchable. A closer examination of the Bible reveals that God only sees people and places who need His love. No labels attached.

If we approach other cultures, subcultures and countercultures by making quick judgments we will have already given ourselves an excuse to write-off about half the population. Just the opposite is required. People whose cultural expression and values are different than ours are those with whom we are most challenged to engage. You can't change the world if you hate a good portion of it. On a personal level, you can't change someone if you don't love them first… or at least come to know and understand them as fellow human beings.

> *If we approach other cultures, subcultures and countercultures by making quick judgments we will have already given ourselves an excuse to write-off about half the population.*

Look at these wonderful words to the third verse of the hymn, "This Is My Father's World," written by Maltbie Babcock in 1901. "This is my Father's world. O let me ne'er forget, that though the wrong seems oft so strong, God is the ruler yet. This is my Father's world. Why should my heart be sad? The Lord is king; let the heaven's ring! God reigns; let the earth be glad." We acknowledge that there is a lot wrong in our world. Creation is broken but God hasn't stopped loving the world and neither should we. That's why we are called to stay engaged with culture and speak words of life and truth in Jesus' name.

Cultural Ethics

This mandate, practically speaking, becomes very challenging in our daily lives. Whether at the construction site, the office, the bank, the daycare center or the local hospital, the morals and ethics that guide individuals and families in their decisions today feel more complicated than ever before.

A family of four siblings gathered around their mom's bed in the hospital's ICU and faced a very difficult decision. She had been laying there for a week now paralyzed from a stroke and unable to communicate. The doctors indicated that there was a significant likelihood of brain damage from which she would never recover.

Their dad had died several years earlier. The lead doctor in their mom's case had scheduled this meeting to ask the children whether they wanted to continue medical intervention or remove life support. If they did, the doctor said he believed that their mom would likely pass away within 24 hours.

The older brother and sister were in favor of letting mom go. They said, "She wouldn't want to live like this. She told us that so many times." Their younger sister said, "It's only been a week. What if she were to come out of this and recover to the point where she could still enjoy life?" The younger brother just looked shocked. He said, "Is it our job to play God? I don't know what we should do."

This situation has repeated itself "hundreds of thousands of times" for families around the globe from every culture imaginable. It is just one example of the difficult moral decisions that often confront us today. What would you do? What sense of ethics would guide you in making a decision like this, especially for a dear family member? Different cultures bring different perspectives regarding life and death which influence their decisions.

A Buddhist or Hindu who believes in reincarnation may approach this situation differently than an atheist who believes that when you die you simply cease to exist. A North Korean adherent to Juche who believes that when you die you go to be with your former dictator may approach this decision differently than a Christian who believes that when you die you go to heaven to be with Jesus. How does your faith speak to issues of life and death and impact how you engage with others in our culture who may hold very different values?

Morality in a Pluralistic Culture

One of the potential negative impacts of multiculturalism is the loss of a unified moral compass. Can any culture survive without finding significant common ground? Many suggest that the United States is right now in the midst of a crisis of morality that threatens to destroy us. Could we be witnessing what the Apostle Paul warned of in **Ephesians 4:14** when he described people who are: **"… tossed back and forth by the waves, and blown here and there by every wind of teaching and by the cunning and craftiness of people in their deceitful scheming?"**

In this increasingly secular culture it seems that moral decisions today are unfortunately being made primarily on the basis of one of the following four considerations:

- First, an absence of any foundational belief system. "I don't know what I believe."
- Second, a determination of what is deemed acceptable in society at any given time. "I will go along to get along."
- Third, a desire to make independent moral and ethical decisions without regard to what others think. "I'll do my own thing."

- Fourth, a utilitarian approach that takes the path of least resistance. "I just don't want any hassles!"

Can the American culture, or any culture for that matter, survive with these as the predominant norms impacting our decision making? As Christians, most would agree that we have both a calling and an obligation to strive to live a moral life. This includes representing Jesus to the world through defensible, moral, ethical and biblical principles that truly honor Him. This part of our calling as Baby Boomers is more important today than ever.

The problem is that even Christians frequently disagree on what constitutes ethics or morality in areas like wealth and poverty, business practices, the use of drugs and alcohol, gambling, pornography, marriage, sexuality, war, abortion, racial justice, immigration, the environment and more. What seems "right" to one seems "wrong" to another.

This has been especially true since the 1960s when more and more people began to see Christian morality as a stumbling block to personal fulfillment. It was during those years that many in our generation began imagining life without a "bothersome God" standing watch over their personal decisions. John Lennon captured this feeling perfectly when he sang, "Imagine there's no heaven, it's easy if you try, no hell below us, above us only sky. Imagine all the people living for today."[2]

And that is exactly what we're seeing… people living for today with no moral compass. How do we determine true north? What is the basis for moral decisions in this multicultural world? I propose that we reclaim a biblical ethic that is the result of pursuing the character of God the Father, the teaching and example of Jesus the Son, and the leading of the Holy Spirit.

Wisdom to make good moral decisions requires that we press-in to all three of these areas because faith is about so much more than just "what we believe." It is also about "how we live." In Chuck Colson's amazing cultural treatise called "How Now Shall We Live?" he says, "We are either contributing to the broken condition of the world or participating with God in transforming the world to reflect His righteousness."[3] Let's consider each of these areas as we seek a firm foundation from which to engage with culture in this very diverse world.

1. Good moral decisions are the result of pursuing the character of God the Father.

A simple definition for "character" is "what you care about." You see, unless we know what God cares about, we won't know what we should care about either. What is the character of God the Father? God is described throughout the Bible as having four immutable, unchanging qualities:

- God is omniscient (all-knowing)
- God is omnipotent (all-powerful)
- God is omnipresent (exists everywhere at once)
- God is omnibenevolent (supremely good.)

We see the character and qualities of God revealed both in creation and in God's Word, the Bible. God the Father is described as "holy, good, faithful, patient, just, merciful" and so much more. However, the quality that describes the character of God more than any other is "loving." **1 John 4:8** says simply: **"God is love."** Every moral decision must first be considered on the basis of this standard. Do our actions ultimately demonstrate in practical ways the love of God? Yes, God's love is where we should start… but it is not where we should stop. We must consider the fullness of God's character if we

> *Every moral decision must first be considered on the basis of this standard. Do our actions ultimately demonstrate in practical ways the love of God?*

are to discern and do His will as we make moral decisions in life. God is both loving and merciful but He is also righteous and just. It is His complete nature, not our opinions, that are the real standard of morality.

In **1 John 1:5-7** the Apostle John says: **"This is the message we have heard from him and declare to you: God is light; in him there is no darkness at all. If we claim to have fellowship with him and yet walk in the darkness, we lie and do not live out the truth. But if we walk in the light, as he is in the light, we have fellowship with one another, and the blood of Jesus, his Son, purifies us from all sin."**

Moral decisions come about when we "make it our heart's desire" to walk in the light, not the darkness. Can we agree that everything that is in alignment with the character of God the Father is good and right… and everything that is not in alignment is bad and wrong? The trick is to discern the difference!

One way we can discern right from wrong is by looking at both God's words and actions as recorded in the Bible. What does God bless? What does God curse or despise? One of my faith values is that I want to "bless what God blesses," and I would say, not curse, but stand in spiritual authority against the things I see in this world that are clearly against God's will. In the process, of course, we must maintain love and humility. None of us has perfect insight into God's will.

For example, from what I see in scripture, God is always on the side of life, not death. The core message of the Christian faith is that God sent His Son into this world to give His life so that we could have life both now and for all eternity. On the basis of this character trait of God I don't understand how any fellow Christian can support the practice of abortion, which I believe is the taking of human life? Surprisingly, there are many "pro-choice Christians" who do support abortion, rationalizing that an unborn child is not yet fully human and is therefore of no intrinsic value. In their view, abortion is a healthcare decision not a moral decision. Is this an example in society, as I mention above, of simply choosing the path of least resistance or personal convenience rather than carefully weighing our moral responsibilities? Should we not be willing to at least ask the question, "When it comes to abortion, who is dying?"

Two related topics that have been so divisive in society today are that of marriage and sexual identity. When the United States Supreme Court struck down all state bans on same-sex marriage on June 26, 2015, the definition of marriage changed from "between one man and one woman" to "between two people." One must ask, is this a decision that God blesses? Some would say, "Yes," based on the evaluation that if two people love each other that's all that really matters. If this is true, shouldn't we also ask, "Where are there examples in the Bible of God blessing same-sex marriage?" The fact is… there are none.

When it comes to the topic of sexual identity, the Bible says: **"God created mankind in his own image, in the image of God he created them; male and female he created them" (Genesis 1:27).** These two sexes, not 20 or 50 or 100 different sexual orientations, became the basis of marriage and family and the building blocks of every successful society. Is our sex determined by biology or by how we feel about being a man or a woman or someone else on any given day? Our children and grand-children today are being counseled to question their God-given sexual identity and it is leading to great confusion, not freedom, as many suggest. These decisions have wide-ranging consequences for our culture and the generations that follow us.

You see, a lot of people today are being encouraged to mistrust the authority of the Bible in the same way they're being encouraged to mistrust our U.S. Constitution. They're being told that the Constitution is an outdated document reflecting the values of deeply flawed people who couldn't possibly anticipate how the world has evolved today. Based on this assessment, many suggest that our Constitution must either be significantly changed or ignored. Our "woke" culture is encouraging people to look at the Bible in the same way as outdated, misinformed and irrelevant to the important issues of our time.

This view is often described as Relativism, as I shared in Chapter 9. Relativism purports that knowledge, truth and morality exist only in relation to culture and are not absolute. What this leads to, practically speaking, is the contemporary belief that "what is right" is determined by "what feels right" for you. Instead of basing moral decisions on the character and values of God, which are true for all time and place, moral decisions are to be made simply on the basis of what any person believes is "their truth" at any given moment. If a person believes that abortion or gay marriage is wrong, then it is wrong for them… but not for others who may believe differently. Moral relativism is, in fact, the operating philosophy in society today, even among many who claim to be Christians. The second part of our definition is this:

2. Good moral decisions are the result of learning from the teaching and example of Jesus the Son.

The foundational building blocks of Jesus' teaching can be seen in the Great Commandment and the Golden rule. The Great Commandment is found in **Matthew 22:37, 39**. I've quoted it before: **"Jesus replied, 'Love the Lord your God with all your heart and with all your soul and with all your mind… and love your neighbor as yourself.'"** And do you remember the Golden Rule? It's actually imbedded in **Matthew 7:12**. Jesus said: **"So in everything you do, do to others what you would have them do to you, for this sums up the Law and the Prophets."**

On the basis of these verses alone doesn't it follow that when it comes to having a standard for ethics and moral decision-making, Jesus is our benchmark? He is the one who will show us how to love God, love ourselves and love others? When the character of the Father and the teaching and example of Jesus are our starting line, the way forward with so many decisions in life becomes much clearer. I call it "cultural spiritual integration." This approach stands in stark contrast to the philosophy of the day which says, "Forget about God and just do what feels right to you."

Jesus' teaching is no flimsy thing! He came to both love us and hold us accountable in our thoughts and actions. **John 1:14** reminds us of this fact: **"The word became flesh and made his dwelling**

among us. We have seen his glory, the glory of the one and only Son, who came from the Father, full of grace and truth." We need both! Grace without truth, according to theologians like Dietrich Bonhoeffer, becomes "cheap grace," and undermines the real gift of the Gospel.

Jesus always led with grace. His understanding of morality wasn't narrowly focused on keeping the law but on ministering to the needs of others. Jesus spoke to the Samaritan woman at the well. He touched the blind, the lame and those with diseases like leprosy. He declared that the Sabbath was made for man and not man for the Sabbath. He threw the money-changers out of the temple when prayer had been replaced with profit. Jesus' morality was about other people, how we look at them and treat them. It was about His desire that everyone should come to know the Father and receive the forgiveness of their sins and the promise of heaven. It was in this context that He also spoke the truth. He called people out of sin into a new life of freedom and purpose. If we are to minister to the culture in which we live today we too must come to terms with this two-edged sword. This leads us to our third point.

3. Good moral decisions are the result of following the leading of the Holy Spirit.

One of the roles of the Holy Spirit, the presence and power of God in us, is to "illuminate God's Word," the Bible. Sometimes we can read the scriptures but struggle to understand their meaning and application for our lives. When we ask the Holy Spirit to help us, it's like He "shines a light" on words or phrases and provides divine downloads of the wisdom and understanding we need. For Christians, the work of the Holy Spirit is also intimately connected with what we think of as our conscience. If we're about to make an important decision, and in our gut we know that it's not the right one, it is more than likely the Holy Spirit speaking to us.

Discerning truth from falsehood is key in making good moral and ethical decisions… regardless of how simple or difficult they may be. When we pray… when we seek… the Holy Spirit speaks. Remember these verses? **"But when he, the Spirit of truth, comes, he will guide you into all the truth. He will not speak on his own; he will speak only what he hears, and he will tell you what is to come. He will glorify me because it is from me that he will receive what he will make known to you"** (John 16:13-14).

Did you realize that? Jesus' teaching, Jesus' truth is now made known to us through the Word and through the Holy Spirit. As I shared in a previous chapter, the Holy Spirit receives from Jesus what He has first received from the Father, and then, amazingly, shares it with us. When we learn to walk in the Spirit and listen to His voice, He reveals the truth we need to make good moral decisions. That's why we need to learn to "walk wet" in the daily anointing of the Holy Spirit. When we run dry our perspective on life usually runs off course! In the midst of pursuing the character of the Father, the teaching and example of Jesus and the counsel of the Holy Spirit, let's also remember this very important point:

4. Making good biblically-based moral decisions should not lead us to a position of moral superiority but a greater willingness to engage with those with whom we differ.

The outcome of a sincere moral life should never be judgment. We should leave the judgment to God. If we're going to engage in helpful "faith-building" and "faith-clarifying" conversations with others, however, we do need to be clear about what we believe and why we believe it. **1 Peter 3:15-16** really captures it: **"But in your hearts revere Christ as Lord. Always be prepared to give an answer to everyone who asks you to give the reason for the hope that you have. But do this with gentleness and respect, keeping a clear conscience, so that those who speak maliciously against your good behavior in Christ may be ashamed of their slander."**

For us to engage with the culture and lead people to Christ in this world of conflicting moral values, we have to approach them with gentleness and respect… not judgment. We have to know our testimony and be willing to share it. We have to be able to confidently say, "As a Christian, I follow the teachings of the Bible. This is what I have come to understand the Bible says…" about marriage, sexuality, honesty, financial integrity, medical decisions, war or whatever the topic may be… and then ask others, "What guides you in making moral and ethical decisions like this?"

> For us to engage with the culture and lead people to Christ in this world of conflicting moral values, we have to approach them with gentleness and respect… not judgment.

In 2 Corinthians the Apostle Paul talks about how Christ's love compels us to be witnesses to others, followed by this key to making it happen. He says: **"So from now on we regard no one from a worldly point of view" (2 Corinthians 5:16a).** This is so important if our faith and values are going to influence the culture around us. We must approach people from a "heavenly point of view," not an "earthly one." We must learn to see people as God sees them, sinners like all of us, yes, but also like sheep without a shepherd.

We must engage with others by both our testimony and example in order to effectively introduce them to Jesus or call them back to a vital and relevant faith. Our job is to present God; Father, Son and Holy Spirit as the source of life and the foundation of every good and moral decision in our personal lives, families and society. This is how we can impact culture today from one that seems to be running from God to one that runs to God!

The Power to Change

One day I was thinking about the fact that every message I've ever shared has been about change. I never come into a Sunday morning thinking, "Lord, I really hope you just help us all maintain the status quo today. Please help me not to push people out of their comfort zones or expect that you might really change something in their hearts." Can you imagine a pastor having that approach? I hope not! Then why would we approach the world around us and not expect that God will use us to bring about change? Our God is in the "change business!"

Change is never easy though. It isn't easy for individuals, families, churches, organizations, institutions or communities. We value what we know as normal so much that even when we see the positive benefits of change, and even desire that change, we still resist and cling to our "safe space." In this world that is changing at an extraordinary pace, I want to encourage you with two facts about change that are absolutely foundational when it comes to staying in the fight.

> *Our God is in the "change business!"*

First, we can take comfort in the fact that God never changes. In **Malachi 3:6** it says: **"I the Lord do not change."** In **James 1:17** we read: **"Every good and perfect gift is from above, coming down from the Father of the heavenly lights, who does not change like shifting shadows."** And then in **Hebrews 13:8** it says so simply: **"Jesus Christ is the same yesterday and today and forever."**

Why are verses like this so important? In a world where there is constant change they remind us that God is our rock, our firm foundation for all of life. Traditional values are being challenged on every front. It feels like "up is down" and "down is up." How good it is to know that while the values of culture will continue to change, the character and values of God never do. This foundation paves the way for the second necessity regarding our engagement with culture today. We must change! When a child doesn't grow physically or mentally we view it as a tragedy. Jesus is looking for growth and maturity in our lives as well, the kind that leads to greater moral clarity and effective witness to the world.

Look at the Apostle Paul's reflection on this in **Ephesians 4:11-16**. He writes: **"So Christ himself gave the apostles, the prophets,**

293

the evangelists, the pastors and teachers, to equip his people for works of service, so that the body of Christ may be built up until we all reach unity in the faith and in the knowledge of the Son of God and become mature, attaining to the whole measure of the fullness of Christ. Then we will no longer be infants, tossed back and forth by the waves, and blown here and there by every wind of teaching and by the cunning of craftiness of people in their deceitful scheming.

Instead, speaking the truth in love, we will grow to become in every respect the mature body of him who is the head; that is Christ. From him the whole body, joined and held together by every supporting ligament, grows and builds itself up in love, as each part does its work."

Real change, real transformation that grows to maturity must first begin in us. But how? As I've stated so often, we must go "all in!" Sergei Bubka, born on December 4, 1963, is the greatest pole vaulter of our generation. Representing the former Soviet Union and then Ukraine he won 6 World Pole Vault championships, one Olympic Gold Medal, held the pole vault indoor World Record for 21 years and broke the World Record on 35 different occasions. When asked how he achieved such excellence he said, "I throw my whole heart over the bar and the rest of me follows." When we do the same for Jesus, we will become world-changers who can lead others forward in moral and ethical clarity that is the result of both grace and truth. The fact is that people are starving for this kind of leadership!

Vote Your Values

A long-held view by many Americans is that there are two things that polite people don't discuss with others; religion and politics. The potential for conflict is just too great. I couldn't disagree more! I view these two topics as intimately related. Renowned 20th century German theologian Karl Barth is often given credit for saying, "Take your Bible and take your newspaper, and read them both. But interpret newspapers from your Bible." Today we might say, "Have both a news app and a Bible app on your cell phone side-by-side and read them often.

One time a friend said, "Do you know the definition of politics?" I totally fell for it. He said, "… 'poly' means many and 'ticks' are tiny blood-sucking creatures." People ask me if I'm a Democrat or a Republican. I like to say, "Neither. I'm a Christocrat. To the best of my ability to discern the issues of our day, I vote my biblical values." Why is this form of cultural engagement so important? Politics is the arena where culture gets codified. If we consider the political arena to be so dirty that we stay clear we will miss out on a tremendous opportunity to shape culture in a way that honors God.

When it comes to our responsibility to honor and pray for those in government the Bible is very clear. **Romans 13:1** says: **"Let everyone be subject to the governing authorities, for there is no authority except that which God has established. The authorities that exist have been established by God."** And in **1 Timothy 2:1-3** we read: **"I urge, then, first of all, that petitions, prayers, intercession and thanksgiving be made for all people – for kings and all those in authority, that we may live peaceful and quiet lives in all godliness and holiness. This is good, and pleases God our Savior who wants all people to be saved and to come to a knowledge of the truth."**

A common reaction to these verses is often, "I may pray for the candidates I voted for… but for that other guy? Are you kidding me!" Let me remind you that we are called to "bless" not "blast." Let's remember again that praying for someone doesn't mean we endorse their political positions or behavior. And yes, if our leaders pass laws that are clearly contrary to the Word of God we are morally obligated to refuse to follow them even if it means paying a severe price. This is the story of many faithful martyrs throughout the

> *If we truly desire to "live peaceful and quiet lives in all godliness and holiness" we need to pray for all our leaders, even those with whom we vehemently disagree!*

history of Christianity. However, the intent of Paul's teaching stands. If we truly desire to "live peaceful and quiet lives in all godliness and holiness" we need to pray for all our leaders, even those with whom we vehemently disagree!

From where I sit the two major political party system in the United States needs to be re-examined. I personally talk to too many voters who are either entirely uniformed on the issues or continue to vote for the party of their parents or grand-parents because "Our family has always been Democrat or Republican." I think this can especially be said of our Baby Boom generation. I find this approach to be totally unacceptable today. The issues regarding the future direction of our nation are too important to just vote a "party line" out of history or habit. Instead, we need to get informed and vote for the candidates who are most aligned with our faith and core values, from local races for School Board and Mayor all the way up to the Presidency.

Statistics vary, however it is very clear that many Christians aren't registered and don't vote because of the belief that all of politics is dirty and should be avoided. By refusing to bring insight and perspective into this important area of culture we are abdicating our influence to those who often support decisions that are completely contrary to the will of God. "Boomers" can provide an important example to younger generations regarding civic responsibility that moves beyond "talking points" and "media bias" to really examine the issues of our day and vote accordingly.

The Way Forward

To engage the culture in a meaningful way today will require that we approach others with sincere interest in their lives and clear conviction regarding our own beliefs. There is so much to learn and experience from people who have a different cultural perspective than our own. To engage effectively we must embrace the whole world and its people as sacred and loved by God. We must develop a working ethic and morality that flows out of the character of God, the teaching and example of Jesus and the leading of the Holy Spirit. We must be willing to change, grow and mature ourselves even as we continue to serve an unchangeable God. And yes, we must engage politically, understanding that our vote counts and that there is no area of conversation, especially that of "religion and politics," that is out of bounds for those seeking to follow God and transform the world! We must learn to be "in the world but not of it" knowing that ultimately our home is in heaven. Baby Boomers are uniquely positioned to bring this important cultural perspective to the generations that will follow us. I pray we never give up on that calling!

Questions for Personal Reflection or Group Discussion

1. With what culture, subculture or counterculture groups do you most identify? Has this part of your identity evolved over the years?
2. Describe the process you most often use to make moral or ethical decisions in your life.
3. What does the term "culture wars" mean to you? Share some examples.
4. What are some ways you could more effectively engage the culture of today with the goal of reaching people for Christ and influencing society?

Notes:

1. H. Richard Niebuhr, *Christ and Culture* (New York, NY: Harper and Row, 1951).
2. John Lennon, *Imagine* (London, England: Apple Records, 1971).
3. Chuck Colson, *How Now Shall We Live?* (Wheaton, IL: Tyndale House, 1999), p. 13.

CHAPTER 19

Live Your Best Life!

I arrived at church about 8:15 A.M. one Sunday morning to find a Suburban Taxi sitting all by itself near the light pole on the office end of our parking lot. I wondered, "Is someone getting a ride to the airport later?" It's quite unusual to see a taxi in our community because we are well outside the Twin Cities Metropolitan area. I parked my car in the overflow lot as usual. As I got out and began walking toward the building, the taxi driver, a black man who looked to be about 40 years old, got out of the taxi and began walking toward me. He called out, "Are you the pastor of the church?" Shouting back enough to be heard I said, "Yes I am. How can I help you?" It turned out he was there to help me.

As we came together there in the parking lot he said, "My name is Billy and God sent me here to pray for you today." Though quite surprised, I said, "Praise the Lord! Let's do it!" Billy took my hands and prayed a beautiful prayer for me and the whole congregation. I was struck by how loving, encouraging and peaceful his prayer and countenance were. As he finished the prayer, still holding my hands, before I could even say thank you, he looked me right in the eye and said, "Tell your people to keep their eyes on Jesus. Don't be discouraged. God is about to bless you."

Almost stunned by his words I said, "Thank you. I receive it!" How could this stranger have known that this particular Sunday was a very important one for our congregation as we were unveiling significant plans for the future? He turned around and started walking toward his cab. In the few seconds it took me to look up he was gone, vanished out of sight. I knew in that moment that this was an angel visitation. I shared the story of that encounter with the congregation during worship a little later that morning and it brought great encouragement. I do the same for you!

Whatever place you find yourself in life, "Keep your eyes on Jesus. Don't be discouraged. God is about to bless you." The purpose of this chapter is to encourage you to "live your best life" for as many days as God gives you on the Earth.

Thrive

We all desire to thrive in life not just survive. Your "best life" may look different than mine but I'm guessing we each have a pretty good idea of what we would like it to be. As I've shared in previous chapters, most of us would like to enjoy this 4th quarter of life in relatively good health and financial security, but most importantly, experiencing loving relationships with family and friends. If we are able to also enjoy hobbies and travel, and cross a few more items off our "bucket list," we will be doubly blessed. Couple these hopes and dreams with a growing faith and the opportunity to positively influence the generations that follow us and our picture of the next 10, 20 or 30 years comes into focus. Our Baby Boom generation still has much to live and much to give!

That's how a young "Boomer" felt back in the 60s who had worked for the railroad for several years and finally had an opportunity to be promoted to the job of Signalman which included a significant pay raise. He knew he had much more to give. For his interview he

Our Baby Boom generation still has much to live and much to give!

299

was told to meet the inspector at the signal box where he would be asked a series of questions to test his judgment.

The inspector said, "What would you do if you realized that two trains were heading toward each other on the same track?" The young man said, "That's easy. I would switch the tracks for one of the trains." Next the inspector said, "What if there was no response?" The young candidate said, "Then I'd jump down out of the signal box and use the manual lever over there to switch one of the tracks." So far so good… but the inspector pushed him further.

He said, "What if the manual lever had been struck by lightning and wasn't functioning either?" The young man said, "Then I would run back and phone the next signal box to let them know what was happening." The inspector continued, "What if the phone was busy?" The young man said, "Well in that case I would run to the public emergency phone at the crossing up there." The inspector continued, "And what if the public phone had been vandalized?"

The candidate said, "I would run into town and get my uncle." That answer really puzzled the inspector so he asked, "Why would you go get your uncle?" The young man answered, "He's always wanted to see a train crash!"

I don't know if he got the job but I would suggest that too many in our generation feel that rather than "thriving in life" we are headed toward a crash and there's nothing we can do about it. We may see that crash coming in our workplace or health or finances. We may perceive a disaster coming in our marriage or family or personal relationships. It's easy to look ahead in life and become paralyzed with fear and a sense of impending doom. We will all face set-backs and challenges, some of them serious? However, let's remember that Jesus has promised us an abundant life which is more than just surviving. It's thriving no matter what our age or stage. In order to do that we must claim our new normal.

Claim Your New Normal

You may find that in these years there are things you just can't do anymore that you loved to do when you were younger. This might include travel, running, working in the garden or around your yard, hunting, attending a sporting event, enjoying the theater and more. One of those items for me is ice skating. In Minnesota you learn to skate starting at about 3 years old. We are called the State of Hockey after all! My grandkids are all learning to skate, and Sam, my oldest grandson, is a very good hockey player.

When our family was all together this past Christmas we decided that a trip to the local ice rink would be a fun outing. I hadn't skated for years but figured it would be like riding a bike. I put my skates on and headed for the ice expecting to jump on and go. Not so! I looked like a 5-year old at his first skating lesson as I slowly made my way around the rink hoping not to fall and break anything. As crazy as it sounds, the thought actually went through my head, "Is ice slipperier today than it used to be?" That's how surprised and embarrassed I was. Could I have learned that skill again? Maybe. Instead, I told Colleen that as a result of that humbling experience I had crossed three things off my list of life skills; ice skating, snow skiing and water skiing. Instead I would focus on things I can still do fairly well like swing a golf club. It is my new normal!

As we age our physical abilities will change. What doesn't have to change is our zest for life. The Apostle Paul put it this way: **"Therefore we do not lose heart. Though outwardly we are wasting away, yet inwardly we are being renewed day by day" (2 Corinthians 4:16).** "Wasting away" seems a little harsh… but it should certainly be our desire to continue being renewed inwardly every day. That's what keeps us young at heart! Instead of focusing on "what was" or even "what is," if we want to live our best lives we need to focus on "what can still be." "Boomers" who are constantly saying "I used to…" and "I can't…" tend

> As we age our physical abilities will change. What doesn't have to change is our zest for life.

to not be very happy people. A better alternative is to focus on what we can still do and remain active and engaged to the best of our ability. I think this is a key to aging gracefully.

Remember how we used to laugh at the two old guys in the balcony on the "The Muppet Show" named Statler and Waldorf? From their high perch they were known for heckling the other Muppets. They had sarcastic, cantankerous opinions about everything. Funny? Yes, but not when we become them! I know too many people in our generation who have become old curmudgeons before their time, spending their days being down on everything in life; their spouse, their neighbors, the cost of living, their restaurant meal, the weather, the pastor's sermon, the politician's proposal. Nothing is right!

Many of us need to take a good look in the mirror and ask, "Is this the kind of person I want to be for the rest of my life; somebody who is always complaining and bringing others down?" We need to come to terms with the fact that life will not be exactly the same today as it was 20 or 40 or 60 years ago. While this is true, we can still embrace our new normal as an opportunity to live life to the fullest within the scope of our personal limitations. There may be a lot we can't do now… but as surely as God gives us breath there is a purpose for living and a reason to be positive and focused on what we can do. For starters, every morning we can get out of bed and declare: **"This is the day the Lord has made. Let us rejoice and be glad in it" (Psalm 119:118)!**

Why is it so easy for us to become increasingly negative as we get older? My hunch is that it's because we seek after happiness rather than joy.

Find True Joy

Joy is different than happiness. Happiness comes from "what happens." Happiness depends on our circumstances. If we get a letter from the I.R.S. stating that we owe $10,000 in back taxes we're not going to be happy. If we spend an hour sitting on the freeway in construction traffic and are late for an appointment we're not going to be happy. If our doctor tells us she wants to take a biopsy of that spot on our face we're not going to be happy. There can be hundreds of little things that affect our happiness every day. Sometimes we feel like such a roller-coaster of emotions that we have trouble just keeping it together.

Joy is different. It's constant. It goes deep. It is knowing that in every circumstance God is with us, God is for us and nothing can separate us from His love. That's true joy! As a matter of fact, I would say that joy is the foundation upon which happiness is built. In **Romans 14:17** Paul says: **"For the kingdom of God is not a matter of eating and drinking, but of righteousness, peace and joy in the Holy Spirit."** "Eating and drinking" refers to daily life and things that can make us happy. "Righteousness, peace and joy in the Holy Spirit" represent the true joy that is a gift from God and meant to be a constant companion in our lives!

Joy is therefore both a posture toward life and an attitude that must be practiced. Where there is no joy, there is no strength or will to live. No wonder we see so many of our fellow "Boomers" just limping through life feeling weak and defeated or shouting their insults from the balcony. Where there is joy there is also thanksgiving. I call it thanks-living!

Be Thankful

What is the basis of thanksgiving? Once again it is God's goodness, not our circumstances. King David wrote: **"Give thanks to the Lord for he is good. His love endures forever" (Psalm 107:1).** Do you know the hymn, "Now Thank We All Our God?" We used to sing it often at worship services near Thanksgiving in the U.S. It was written in 1636 by a German pastor named Martin Rinkart. That's going on 400 years ago! It begins, "Now thank we all our God with hearts and hands and voices. Who wondrous things has done, in whom the world rejoices."

Martin Rinkart wrote this hymn not in the midst of a peaceful religious setting but rather during a very troubled and dangerous time in history. Does that sound a little like today? Germany was in the midst of what came to be known as the "Thirty Years War." This war began in Europe in 1618 and continued until 1648. How did it start? It began when a new Pope was elected in Rome and demanded that all of Europe become Catholic.

At one point in history that kind of edict might have flown… but not anymore. The Protestant Reformation led by Martin Luther and others had begun approximately 100 years earlier in 1517, also in Germany. The Protestant countries in northern Europe now rejected any attempt by the Pope in Italy to exercise control. There were other factors that contributed to this war as well but religious division was the main one. The "Thirty Years War" became one of the bloodiest in history. Get this! There were a total of nearly 8 million deaths, too many to even count. Some were casualties of war, others from famine and disease. This represented about 20% of the total population in Europe at that time.

Pastor Martin Rinkart lived and served in the German city of Eilenberg. Refugees from the war streamed into his city causing overcrowding, famine, disease, suffering and death. At times he was the only pastor in this city of thousands doing funerals for up to 50 people a day, which at one point included his wife. Even so, he received abuse rather than encouragement from the city authorities saying that he wasn't doing enough.

Pastor Rinkart died in 1649, just one year after the war ended, totally exhausted and unappreciated. Now how could a person who lived through such a difficult time write such a beautiful hymn expressing thanksgiving to God? It was only because his thanks wasn't dependent on his circumstances but rather his enduring relationship with Jesus his Savior.

What circumstances do you find yourself in right now? Are you feeling exhausted and unappreciated by others? Are you battling grief, depression or disease? Take these words from Philippians to heart and they will show you how to experience peace, joy and thanksgiving in the midst of every circumstance: **"Rejoice in the Lord always. I will say it again: Rejoice! Let your gentleness be evident to all. The Lord is near. Do not be anxious about anything, but in every situation, by prayer and petition, with thanksgiving, present your requests to God. And the peace of God, which transcends all understanding, will guard your hearts and your minds in Christ Jesus" (Philippians 4:4-7).**

This is like a recipe for life! Start with 2 cups of rejoicing. Add 1 cup of faith and another of prayer. Add a generous portion of thanksgiving. Mix together every day and bake in the Spirit. Not only will your heart be protected against negative thinking but you will experience peace like never before.

Live Your Dash

There is a wonderful poem called "The Dash" written by Linda Ellis. If you've never read it I encourage you to check it out. The essence of the illustration is that someday, on the program at our funeral or the tombstone where we are buried, there will be our date of birth and our date of death. The dash in-between will represent the life we have lived. For those of us who are Christians we are called to "live our dash" for Jesus.

Life is like a race in the sense that there is a starting line and a finish line. Humanly speaking, Usain Bolt from Jamaica is the fastest man in the world. He is the World Record holder in the 100 meter dash at 9.58 seconds and a 9-time Olympic gold medalist. Do you know how fast that is? That's running 27.79 miles per hour which is like covering 30 feet per second. The only time I run that fast is between the couch and the refrigerator!

The key to living our dash is faithfulness, not speed! Some people like our grandchildren or great-grandchildren are just in the starting blocks of life or are beginning to pick-up speed. In terms of their relationship with

> The key to living our dash is faithfulness, not speed!

Jesus they are just getting to know Him and what it means to be His follower. They are choosing friends, determining values and dreaming of the future.

Others, like our children, are in the middle of the dash; raising a family, developing a career, growing deeper in their relationship with Jesus… or perhaps have been sidelined by injuries in body, soul or spirit. Others, like we "Boomers," are in the home stretch of our dash, running at full speed, leaning for the tape, celebrating life's blessings and wanting to leave a lasting legacy. No matter where we find ourselves in the race of life the key is to keep running all the way to the finish line.

In **1 Corinthians 9:24-26,** Paul says: **"Do you not know that in a race all runners run, but only one gets the prize? Run in such a way as to get the prize. Everyone who competes in the games goes into strict training. They do it to get a crown that will not last, but we do it to get a crown that will last forever. Therefore, I do not run like someone running aimlessly."**

Your dash represents the unique and precious life God has given you to live. Your crown will be the gift of eternal life celebrated in the presence of your Savior. What will be said about your dash at your funeral someday, or even more importantly, as you stand before your Creator? Let us not run aimlessly but with our eyes firmly fixed on Jesus!

Cause a Change Reaction

To live our "best life" we must embrace constant change and learn to respond to it. From the moment we are conceived in the womb until the moment we die our bodies are changing. Those of us with grandchildren marvel at the rate of change that happens in the first year of life alone. These wonderful gifts from God grow from helpless newborns into little personalities learning to walk, feed themselves and say their first words. How absolutely amazing! We could call it exponential growth. Physically, this growth continues at a rapid pace throughout childhood, the teenage years and into early adulthood. As we live our adult lives the change happens more slowly and yet as we look at old photos there is no doubt that we cannot stop the progression of time.

What doesn't slowdown is the rate at which the world is changing around us. Sociologists suggest that we experienced more change in the 20th century than in all 19 centuries before. Many also believe that in just the next 25 years the pace of change will double or triple again. That means that during the remaining years of our lives as Baby Boomers we are still going to experience more change than at any time in our past. If it's true that change gets harder as you get older we are in for a real challenge.

In order to live our "best lives" it is important that we don't just react to change but serve as agents of change. Together our generation can cause a "change reaction" for the better. We're all familiar with the concept of a "chain reaction." It's like the "Domino Effect" where one event sets off a chain of other events, just like a falling row of dominos. Chain reactions can have a positive or negative effect. The most strident example is that of nuclear fission. This chain reaction can either be used to power thousands of homes… or blow them to smithereens.

> In order to live our "best lives" it is important that we don't just react to change but serve as agents of change.

The same is true in human relationships. One act of love can lead to another and another. One act of hate can have the same effect. One person who stands for truth, justice and equality can begin a movement like the civil rights movement started by Dr. Martin Luther King, Jr. in the 60s. Another who stands for hate, violence and chaos can start a chain reaction like the protests we've seen recently that have resulted in death, property damage, disrespect of law enforcement and a general disdain for our public institutions and fellow citizens.

What kind of a "change reaction" are we to cause as followers of Jesus? Statements like the following may surprise and challenge us to think about our role in the world differently. In **Matthew 10:34-36** Jesus says: **"Do not suppose that I have come to bring peace to the earth. I did not come to bring peace, but a sword. For I have come to turn 'a man against his father, a daughter against her mother, a daughter-in-law against her mother-in-law – a man's enemies will be the members of his own household.'"**

Are we to intentionally bring division into our households? No! There are times, however, when sharing the Gospel even with loved ones will lead to division. Jesus is making the case that He must be our highest priority because the change He desires is heart-deep.

Positive "change reactions" need to happen in our own homes and families before we can expect to change the world. For example, I have a friend who came from a home where alcoholism had been an issue leading to divorce, abuse and financial stress for several generations. At a Promise Keepers event he came under deep conviction. He stood up and declared "No more! In Jesus' name I break this generational curse! It stops here!" It was a powerful moment. He is sober now and is leading his family and others in his family system to break free of addiction and establish a new legacy of health and wholeness.

The Bible speaks of a generational blessing for those who love and serve God. **Psalm 100:5** declares: **"For the Lord is good and his love endures forever; his faithfulness continues through all generations."**

I am so thankful to have experienced that generational blessing in my family heritage. My great-grandfather, Martin Pagh, emigrated from Denmark in the early 1900s to a small town called Luck, Wisconsin. He was a devout Lutheran Christian. My middle name is Martin and I have his Bible from 1901.

His testimony of faith continued in the life of his son and my Grandfather, Theodore Pagh. My oldest son Matt's middle name is Theodore, as Colleen and I chose to carry on the tradition of giving the first-born male grandchild in each generation the middle name of their great-grandfather. Matt has Theodore's Bible.

Matt's son, Sam, has Gary for a middle name. Gary was my dad and Sam's great-grandfather. Are you totally confused? If Sam chooses to continue this "naming tradition," he will someday give his first-born son the middle name of Gregory. No pressure, Sam!

Naming is one way to show honor to past generations. In the Pagh family line it is also indicative of a Christian heritage that can now be traced back at least 6 generations. Friends, we can't inherit our faith but this legacy, for which I am extremely thankful, is an example of the positive "change reaction" we need in every family today. Here's the good news! Regardless of your family history, it is never too late to break from the past and claim a generational blessing in Jesus' name for those who follow you.

Be Bold

Jesus came to save us from our "worst self" so that we can be our "best self" and live our "best life." Our "worst self" is rebellious toward God, lives in darkness and is in bondage to sin. This choice results in confusion, disillusionment and destruction. It is the road that many people are on today even though they may look like they have it all together on the outside.

> Jesus came to save us from our "worst self" so that we can be our "best self" and live our "best life."

By contrast our "best self" exhibits the Christ-like qualities of a transformed life. There is faith instead of rebellion. There is light instead of darkness. There is freedom instead of bondage. Jesus saves us from something… for something, which is to be bold as we live our lives for Him! When it comes to confronting the sin and evil in our world the next generations desperately need us as "Boomers" to stand in the gap for them.

There was a guy who arrived unexpectedly at the "pearly gates" of heaven. St. Peter quickly checked the Big Book to see if his name was written in it. After about a minute of intense searching he closed it, furrowed his brow and said, "I'm sorry but I don't find your name written here in the Book of Life."

The guy said, "How current is your copy?" St. Peter replied, "I get an upload every ten minutes. Why do you ask?"

The guy said, "I'm embarrassed to admit it, but I've always been the stubborn type. It wasn't until the moment of my death that I cried out to God, so perhaps my name just hasn't arrived yet."

"Oh I see," Saint Peter said. "A death-bed confession. We get a lot of those! While we're waiting for the update why don't you take a minute and tell me about a really good deed you did in your lifetime?"

The guy thought for a moment and said, "Hmmm, well there was this one time when I was driving down a country road and I saw a group of biker gang members harassing a pretty girl. I slowed down, and sure enough, there were about 20 of them surrounding her and taunting her with their foul mouths. Infuriated, I got out of my car, grabbed a tire iron out of my trunk and walked up to the leader of the gang.

He was a huge guy, about 6-foot-4 and maybe 250 lbs., with a studded leather jacket and a chain running from his nose to his ear. As I came closer the bikers formed a tighter circle around me and the girl and told me to get lost or prepare to suffer. So I ripped the chain out of the leader's face and smashed him over the head with my tire iron. Then I turned to the rest of the gang and yelled, "Leave this poor, innocent girl alone! You're all a bunch of sick, deranged animals! Head on down the road before I teach you all a lesson in pain!"

Saint Peter, duly impressed, said, "Wow! When did this happen?" The guy said, "About three minutes ago."

There is boldness in life, yes! There is also foolishness but which of us would not have done the same… or at least called for help! I love **1 Corinthians 16:13-14**. It says: **"Be on your guard; stand firm in the faith; be courageous; be strong. Do everything in love."**

We need bold, courageous leadership today in every part of society. We may feel like we're surrounded by overwhelming forces of evil but our God goes with us. As Baby Boomers we are called to stand-up for our faith and values regardless of the cost. We are called to stand in the gap for the weak, the vulnerable and the traumatized. We have the wisdom and experience to be bold in the face of every evil today and yet balance it with love. Some of us will become martyrs in the process like Christians all over the world who are facing much more than a biker gang. So be it. It's better to be a dead hero than a cowardly survivor! Our hope is in Christ! We can declare: **"The Lord is my helper; I will not fear; what can man do to me" Hebrews 13:6b)?**

Can you identify a place in your life right now where you need greater boldness to confront evil, to call-out sin, to stand-up for truth, to bring wise counsel or rescue someone in need? With God's help, we can all be heroes.

> It's better to be a dead hero than a cowardly survivor! Our hope is in Christ!

We can choose to say no to our "worst self," call forth our "best self" and live our "best life." All this is possible through a Savior who gave it all! **"Since we have such a hope, we are very bold" (2 Corinthians 3:12).**

Onward and Upward

Many people experience some sort of a mid-life crisis. I had mine when I turned 50. I thought, "Oh man! If only I was 30 again with the passion, knowledge and experience I have now. What a difference I could make for the Lord!" I didn't go out and have an affair or buy a candy-apple red Corvette… but I was kind of down. One day I was speaking to a Chamber of Commerce group about marketplace ministry over the lunch hour. Afterwards I was standing in the parking lot talking to a dear friend, Gary Borgendale, who is the Local Ministry Director for KKMS Radio, AM980 in the Twin Cities. I shared my struggles. Gary laid his hands on me right there and prayed that God would lift that burden. He declared that the next 20 years would be the best years of my life.

I claimed that promise by faith and everything changed. I stopped regretting mistakes and missed opportunities from the past. I decided to press on… to strain forward to the new things that God was calling me to do. Not long afterward I went to Africa for the first time. Then to Argentina. Then God gave me insights regarding what I still call a "Transformation Church" vision. This led me to write a number of Small Group resources for congregations including "Faith Beyond Belief" that was translated into two different languages and went viral in the underground church in China. I climbed Mount Kilimanjaro with a team to help launch the Global Day of Prayer. Our prayer and transformation movement in Elk River, MN became the foundation to launch and lead our statewide movement called Bless Minnesota. These past few months I've found tremendous joy in writing this book. Who knows what God will do next!

There's an old song entitled, "These Will Be the Good Old Days Twenty Years from Now!" That 20 years is just about over for me. I turn 70 in 2023. You know what? I'm going to re-up and ask God for a new 20 years. No regrets. No looking back other than to celebrate and give thanks for all of God's blessings.

Friends, each of us has our own unique calling to serve God. My dad always said, "Life isn't about being successful. It's about being faithful!" Baby Boomers, during this important season of our lives I encourage you to thrive not just survive, to claim your new normal, to seek true joy and be thankful for every day. I challenge you to live your dash with passion, become an agent of positive change in the world and be bold for Jesus. Remember, it is our Savior who says: **"The thief comes only to steal and kill and destroy; I have come that they may have life, and have it to the full" (John 10:10).** Because of this amazing promise our journey in Christ is always onward and upward until that day we meet Him face to face! In this next important season may you live your "best life" ever!

Questions for Personal Reflection or Group Discussion:

1. What are some elements that are important to you in order to live your "best life" during your 4th quarter?

2. Explain in your own words the difference between happiness and joy. How much do your circumstances impact your outlook on life from day to day?

3. What kind of "change reaction" would you like to see in your family or community? How might you contribute to that change?

4. Are you running your "dash" for Jesus? What would you like people to say about you at your funeral someday?

CHAPTER 20

Leave a Lasting Legacy!

I literally had a mountain top experience on May 27, 2007. By the grace of God I climbed Mount Kilimanjaro, the highest peak in Africa at 19,341 feet above sea level, to help launch the Global Day of Prayer. Our expedition was led by the founder of the GDP, Graham Power, from Cape Town, South Africa. This amazing man of God passed away in October of 2022 having made a great impact on the world. The climb was 4 days up and 2 days down. Only 4 out of our 40-member team were from the United States. As we prayed and declared God's blessings from the summit early in the morning on that Pentecost Sunday it had been documented that for the first time in history there were individuals or groups praying together from every nation in the world!

I had invited a friend from Kigali, Rwanda, Bishop Nathan Gasatura Kamusiimi, to join me as my tent-mate. After a week of ministry together in Rwanda, along with some final training, we flew to Kilimanjaro International Airport in Arusha, Tanzania. As we were riding from the airport to the town of Moshi, at the southern foot of Kilimanjaro, we were watching out the windows of the taxi looking for a glimpse of what is called the "bashful mountain" because it is so often shrouded in clouds.

At one point our local taxi driver shouted, "There she is!" We said, "Where? We don't see it!" He said, "Look up! Higher! Higher!" We did, and at first sight Kilimanjaro took our breath away! My thought was, "In a few days we're going to be up there? Only if God helps carry us!"

Leaving a lasting legacy for future generations can look like a mountain too big to climb. What can we really offer at our age, with our limited resources that could possibly make a difference in the world? How about our faith and values, love and prayers, time and talents, experience and wisdom? Could the issue be that our eyes are focused too low… primarily on the things of this world? Could it be that too often we overemphasize our problems and underemphasize our resources because we underestimate our Maker?

As we each live-out our unique 4th quarter, the Call of God will require that we "Look up! Higher! Higher!" Facing countless challenges, King David declared: **"I lift up my eyes to the mountains – where does my help come from? My help comes from the Lord, the Maker of heaven and earth" (Psalm 121:1-2).** That was my theme verse during those amazing days on "Kili" and I have continued to speak-out these words in faith many times since. When I "lift up my eyes," the Lord "lifts up my spirit." He carries me places I could never dream of going on my own. His promises never fail. Where in your life do you need God's help right now? Look up, dear friend! Higher!

> *Could it be that too often we overemphasize our problems and underemphasize our resources because we underestimate our Maker?*

Legacy that Lasts

What is legacy? Quite simply it is "what we leave behind when we're gone." The dictionary defines legacy as "something transmitted by or received from an ancestor or predecessor or from the past." Here are some examples of different ways we use the word legacy today:

- His legacy included the family business, house, property and stock valued at more than $2,000,000.
- He left his children and grandchildren a legacy of love and respect.
- The election left behind a legacy of corruption and cheating.
- Her legacy as a song-writer will live on for years to come.
- The legacy of their family is one of abuse, drunkenness and dysfunction.
- His greatest legacy will be his generosity.
- The children squandered the family legacy in less than a generation.
- His legacy was one of hard work and a tremendous drive to succeed.
- Her portion of her grandmother's legacy included a diamond broach.

You get the idea. We will each leave a legacy to those who follow us. The question is whether it will positive or negative. The things people will say about us when we're gone will be the result of the choices we make over a lifetime. While we most often think of legacy in terms of leaving money or possessions, our legacy will also be shaped by our faith, character, values, reputation and the example we set for others.

My dad, Gary, was not a wealthy man in a financial sense but oh was he rich in spirit as is my mom. At his funeral I spoke about his deep love for Jesus, God's Word, worship, his wife, children, grandchildren, great-grandchildren and so many dear friends. He left an amazing legacy of faith and family that I know will continue in these future generations. At one point in my message I said, "Legacy isn't about what you leave for someone nearly as much as what you leave in someone!" My dad left so much "in us" for which we are eternally grateful.

Ask yourself this question. "If I were to pass away right now, 25 years from now would I be remembered by my family and friends for anything other than the money or possessions I left behind?"

This question begs another. "What would I like people to remember about me?" I've joked that I'm going to pre-record my own funeral message so that nothing important about my life is left unsaid! In the end, all I really hope for is that others will say "he loved Jesus, loved his family and loved people." That will be enough.

> *"Legacy isn't about what you leave for someone nearly as much as what you leave in someone!"*

Christian songwriter and artist, Nichole Nordeman, in the chorus to her song, "Legacy,"[1] sings her heart to Jesus with these words:

> *I want to leave a legacy,*
> *How will they remember me?*
> *Did I choose to love?*
> *Did I point to you enough?*
> *To make a mark on things*
> *I want to leave an offering*
> *A child of mercy and grace*
> *Who blessed your name unapologetically*
> *And leave that kind of legacy.*

What kind of an offering will you leave? What kind of mark will you make on things, especially your family? How will you be remembered? As you know, the Apostle Paul, inspired by the Holy Spirit, wrote much of the New Testament of the Bible. He traveled widely in the 1st century sharing the Gospel and starting many Christian congregations. As he was nearing the end of his life he wrote: **"I have fought the good fight. I have finished the race. I have kept the faith" (2 Timothy 4:7).** In this one verse we find three important keys to leaving a lasting legacy for our families and generations to come. Let's take a closer look together. First...

> *To leave a lasting legacy requires that we live all of*
> *life on purpose.*

There is no such thing as retirement for the Christian. Our assignment doesn't end until the day we walk into heaven… and that day will be a promotion! Paul says, "I have fought the good fight." Are you willing to fight for your family? Are you willing to stand up for your faith and values in this increasingly godless culture? For this to happen we must live all of life on purpose, conscious of the tremendous calling God has given us.

Strong families are the foundation of a healthy society. They don't just happen by accident. They require an intentional commitment to God and one another. A lot of families are fighting hard today but are fighting the wrong battles. They're running the rat race as fast as they can but going in the wrong direction. When parents and grandparents are confused about their priorities it leads to confusion among the next generation and tension builds everywhere. Before long we're fighting each other rather than our real enemies, both seen and unseen, that threaten to tear our families apart.

In **Proverbs 22:6** it says: **"Start children off on the way they should go, and even when they are old they will not turn from it."** What begins with our children is meant to continue in each of us who are "children of God" for a lifetime. By our own testimony and example we show that "Jesus is the way." This is the beginning of a lasting legacy.

> There is no such thing as retirement for the Christian. Our assignment doesn't end until the day we walk into heaven… and that day will be a promotion!

To fight for our faith and values doesn't mean with clenched fists. As I shared in the last section of Chapter 14, we have been given spiritual armor with which to do battle. Some of our equipment is defensive in nature to help us hold the ground against evil. Some of it is offensive in nature to help us advance the kingdom of God, especially the **"… sword of the Spirit, which is the word of God" (Ephesians 6:17b).** Paul tells us to "stand firm." Love that wins the day is not squishy. Like the love of Jesus, it is willing to go all the way to the cross!

In addition to the battles we are called to fight for our families there are also battles to be won in society. Whether it be in business, education, government, the Church or some other area of culture, our goal must be to see the character and values of God permeate these institutions.

Roe vs. Wade may have been overturned by the Supreme Court in July of 2022 but the fight for a culture of life where there are no abortions continues. The battle against institutional racism has seen great advances during our lifetimes but there are still attitudes that must be changed and injustices that must be confronted. Whether the issue is ethics in business, corruption in government or hypocrisy in the Church, the Baby Boom generation has the opportunity to engage on these issues and bring about positive change. If not us, who? If not now, when? We have the experience and wisdom of years to see the big picture but also discern the steps that are needed to make lasting change. The truth is that we must "go big" before we "go home!" Second…

To leave a lasting legacy requires that we never give up.

In the second part of our verse Paul says, "I have finished the race." Yes, life is like a race. If the first phrase in 2 Timothy 4:7 refers to "purpose," this second phrase refers to "perseverance." Regardless of the obstacles that come our way in life we must never give up! One of my favorite stories is "The King's Race."

> *The truth is that we must "go big" before we "go home!"*

Once there was a king who organized a great race. All the young men of the kingdom were invited to participate. A bag of gold was to be given to the winner, an enormous amount of money. The finish line was within the courtyard of the king's palace. When the ram's horn was blown the runners took off following the designated route through the countryside, up and down hills, through woods and over streams. Along the way they were surprised to find a huge pile of large rocks blocking the road.

Anxious to reach the finish line first, the runners managed to climb over that pile of rocks or run around them and eventually they came to the courtyard of the palace. It soon became clear that all the runners had crossed the finish line except one, but still, the king wouldn't call off the race. After several hours that lone runner came through the gate.

He lifted a bleeding hand and said, "O great king, I am so sorry that I am late arriving at the finish line, but you see, I found a large pile of rocks and stones blocking the road and it took me some time and effort to remove them." Then he lifted his other hand and said, "But great king, I found beneath that pile of rocks this bag of gold." The king said, "My son, you have not only won the race, but you have already claimed the prize, for he runs best who makes the way safer for those who follow."

The Christian life is like this race, and Jesus, the "King of Kings," calls us to run it well… to persevere… to finish strong! Our real mission in life is to make the way safer for those who follow. This applies specifically to those of us who desire to leave a lasting legacy of blessings for our families today and future generations tomorrow. To finish well requires sacrifice. We may even get bloody in the process but there is a prize worth far more than gold hidden beneath all the rocks in our road. It is the prize of love and life and lasting joy awaiting us at the finish line!

Some of you may feel like you're at the point of quitting right now. That pile of rocks in your life may look too large to overcome. I know plenty of marriages where the love-light has gone out. I know too many families where parents and children have inflicted so many hurts, wounds and disappointments on one another that they have reached the breaking point. I minister to too many people who are living with depression, chronic pain and various addictions.

I want to encourage you. Don't give up! Finish strong! The King hasn't called the race yet because He believes in you. In Jesus Christ you are an overcomer! The man who won the king's race became legendary. His story taught future generations the importance of perseverance and sacrifice that makes the way easier for those who follow. When we serve Jesus with this same commitment, the

> *Don't give up! Finish strong! The King hasn't called the race yet because He believes in you. In Jesus Christ you are an overcomer!*

stories of our lives will become legendary to our children and children's children! Third…

To leave a lasting legacy requires that we always remain true to Jesus.

In the last part of our verse Paul says, "I have kept the faith." Paul isn't saying that he was perfect. None of us are. To "keep the faith" is to stand-up for it, guard it in the face of lies and confusion, and nurture it in your life and in the lives of others. To "keep the faith" is to so honor the Lord with our words and actions that we become a contagious witness for Jesus.

With the "woke" mob today trying to crush free speech, those who profess Jesus and declare His truth to others are increasingly being censored today. Expect this persecution to increase. It's been happening for centuries in other places around the world. There is coming a day when simply declaring the Gospel from the pulpit, workplace or coffee shop, let alone taking a biblical stand on social issues, will be considered "hate speech." It's already happening.

Jesus says: **"Whoever acknowledges me before others, I will also acknowledge before my Father in heaven. But whoever disowns me before others; I will disown before my Father in heaven" (Matthew 10:32).** Straight to the point, isn't it! We cannot fail to remain true to Jesus and His teaching during this critical time in our families, nation and world. We must always remember that Jesus is life! There is no other name by which people can be saved!

In the Old Testament book of Job one his friends named Shuhite came to him in the midst of his suffering. Nearly everything of value had been stripped away in Job's life; physically, emotionally and spiritually. It was a test of faith for the ages! In the midst of this traumatic season Shuhite gave Job this word of encouragement. He said, **"But if you will seek God earnestly and plead with the Almighty, if you are pure and upright, even now he will rouse himself on your behalf and restore you to your prosperous state. Your beginnings will seem humble, so prosperous will your future be" (Job 8:5-7).**

Other translations say, "Your latter days will be better than your former days." I declare to you again that every year you have lived so far in your life has been but a preparation for what God has in store next. It's so tempting to think that our season as "Boomers" is over. It's so easy to feel that we have done our part and deserve to ride off into the sunset and enjoy a life of leisure. Nothing could be a bigger mistake!

Are you a history lover? If so you might like this story. In 1874 a sociologist by the name of Richard Dugdale, who also served on the Executive Committee of the Prison Association of New York, did a study on two well-known family lineages. The purpose was to show how faith and values influence a person's legacy. The facts I'm about to share have been confirmed by numerous researchers as true.

> *I declare to you again that every year you have lived so far in your life has been but a preparation for what God has in store next.*

The first man was Max Jukes. He did not believe in God and married a girl who had the same opinion. From their union eventually came 1,026 documented descendants. The study showed that 300 of his descendants died at a young age, 100 were sent to prison for committing a whole range of crimes including murder, 190 sold themselves as prostitutes, 100 were drunkards, and all toll, this extended family eventually cost the State of New York $1,100,000, which was a huge amount of money at that time!

The second man in the study was Jonathon Edwards. He believed in God and married a girl who believed the same. Jonathon Edwards became one of the great revival preachers of the 1700s. He and his wife, Sarah, produced 11 children. 729 of their descendants were studied and they discovered that 300 became pastors or missionaries, 100 were lawyers, 80 were elected to public office, 75 were university presidents, 6 were authors, 3 were U.S. Congressman and 1 was Vice-President of the United States.

The legacy you leave behind will not entirely depend on you because every individual in every generation will make their own choices. However, there is no doubt that those who "keep the faith" and share it with each succeeding generation will be blessed and make a tremendous difference in the world. When we "fight the good fight and finish the race and keep the faith" God meets us right where we're at and is more than able to help us overcome every challenge. Can we change the trajectory of our legacy? Yes. To answer any other way would be to deny the power of God to work in us. Family legacies can be turned around when we live life on purpose, never give up and always remain true to Jesus. How will future generations remember you? Listen and let the Holy Spirit speak to you now!

Utilize G.P.S.

If we truly wish to serve God faithfully for all our days we must learn how to use G.P.S. – God's Positioning System. During these coming years He has promised to guide us from point A to B when we are exploring new territory, going "off road" to pursue the lost and hurting, or navigating our way through this world of "foggy" beliefs and values.

I have always been fascinated by the technology that guides the G.P.S. systems in our phones and vehicles. Ancient sailors used the constellations and stars in the sky to figure out where they were and where they were going. Today we use satellites. There are 30 navigation satellites strategically positioned around the earth at all times. Ground stations use radar to make sure the satellites are where we think they are.

The receiver built into your phone or car is constantly listening for signals from these satellites. Once it locks on to four or more of them it is able to triangulate and calculate your precise location, in most cases, within a few feet. In a similar way it has the ability to plot the best course on the ground to get you from one location to another. Without G.P.S. many of us would be lost today.

The same is true when it comes to God's Positioning System. Without it we are lost and likely to make many unnecessary detours in life. If you are a Christian you've been given a built-in receiver called the Holy Spirit. He is constantly listening for signals from the Father and the Son that are needed to guide your life. Sometimes the Spirit tells us to go left when we want to go right. Sometimes He takes us on a route in life that doesn't make sense. Sometimes the road ahead may even look dark and scary.

The question is, "Do we trust Him to get us to our final destination?" The One who created the stars to guide mariners of old is available to guide your life as well. As you consider the question, "What will I do with the rest of my life?" know that when you keep your receiver on, the Holy Spirit will show you the way forward to a life filled with adventure and untold blessings!

The Baby Changed Everything

Throughout this journey I have repeatedly encouraged you to consider the importance of a personal relationship with Jesus. I assume that many of you were not raised in a Christian home with Christian parents like me. I understand that many of you did not grow up attending church, participating in a youth group, going to a Christian college and seminary. Although this has been my life story, and I'm thankful for it, I want you to know that there have still been plenty of challenges in my life. I've made more than my share of mistakes. There have been many points along the way where I've had to pause and honestly look at "what I believe and why." Each time I have come to the same conclusion. The baby changed everything. Jesus' birth in Bethlehem, followed 33 years later by His death, resurrection and ascension, became the most pivotal events in all of human history. Emmanuel – God with us!

There is a wonderful short story called "The Luck of Roaring Camp." It was written by noted American author, Bret Harte, and was first published in August of 1868. You can find it online and enjoy it for yourself. It's the story of a prospecting camp called "Roaring" during the California gold rush and the birth of a baby boy to the only woman at the camp, Cherokee Sal. She died soon thereafter and this notoriously rough collection of miners decided to keep the baby and care for him themselves. They fed him with mule milk. At his christening they gave him the name Thomas Luck because it seemed that his birth had brought them good luck in their panning for gold. They were among the original "forty-niners."

Because of baby Thomas the whole climate of the camp began to change. The miners decided to give up their cursing and fighting. They couldn't disturb a sleeping baby! They stopped gambling and used their money instead to paint some of the camp buildings, hang curtains and plant flowers. They brought little baby "Luck" to the riverside during the day and placed him in a Rosewood cradle lined with silk they had purchased along with their other supplies from San Francisco. When they found pretty stones in the river they brought them up and placed them around the cradle as tokens of their love. In short, the baby changed everything!

Jesus has changed my life and I pray He has changed yours. Of this I am certain. We will all need fresh experiences of His love, grace and provision in our lives in order to "press on" during this next season. Yesterday's manna won't feed us today. If all we can talk about is what God did for us in the past we will miss out on what He wants to do in our lives in the future.

If you've never asked Jesus to be your Savior and Lord there is no better time than right now. Just pray, "Jesus, please meet me right where I'm at and make of me a new

> We will all need fresh experiences of His love, grace and provision in our lives in order to "press on" during this next season.

creation. I put my trust in you and ask you to lead me forward for as many years as I have to live. I want to make a difference in this world and leave a lasting legacy of faith for those who are following me." Remember, no fancy words are required… just a sincere heart.

Contribute to a Generational Legacy

Your legacy will be different from that of anyone else. Why? God has created you as unique in all the world with a special set of talents and abilities that belong just to you. Don't try to create a legacy that doesn't belong to you. Allow God to shape your own. However, when your gifts are combined with those of many others there can be a generational impact. As Baby Boomers we have this opportunity today.

Throughout this book I've lobbied for our generation born between 1946 and 1964 to stay engaged in the world and in partnership with others. I've encouraged us to "re-fire," not just retire. I've asked that we would "rise-up," not just "ride-it-out." You see, if we can spend our 4th quarter as "Boomers" having as much impact as we have had during the first three, anything is possible! We must each do our part.

When I was in Africa one time I heard this story. There was a tribal chief who decided to throw a big harvest celebration in his village. God had blessed his people with abundant crops that would more than see them through the winter. He asked that each family contribute a jug of wine into a large vat in the center of the village for the community celebration. As they all came together for a meal they would each draw-out a cup of wine to drink as a symbol of their unity. Some thought, "No one will miss my wine. I will pour water from my jug instead." The day came for the great celebration. The tribal chief drew out the first ladle of wine to toast the members of his village. Much to his embarrassment the vat of wine was so diluted that it was nearly worthless."

To leave a generational legacy we need everyone to contribute with passion and generosity, not holding back. Without it our message and impact will be watered down. It's the difference between fulfilling our "duty" or pursuing our "destiny." One is "have to." The other is "want to." One is our responsibility. The other is our privilege. Duty is motivated by the Law. Destiny is motivated by the Gospel!

> To leave a generational legacy we need everyone to contribute with passion and generosity, not holding back.

You see, God gives us each a "measure of faith" to exercise in fulfilling our mission here on Earth. When we use it, it grows. When we neglect it, it diminishes. In **Romans 12:3** Paul says: **"For by the grace given to me I say to every one of you: Do not think of yourself more highly than you ought, but rather think of yourself with sober judgment, in accordance with the measure of faith God has given you."**

When it comes to utilizing our gifts to impact this world in partnership with others my hunch is that most of you are like me. Your problem isn't excessive pride. It's excessive humility, even false humility. Couple this with fear of failure and both undermine our ability to respond to God's Call. Excessive pride overshoots. Excessive humility undershoots. Both miss the mark. There is a better way! It involves all of us! In **Colossians 3:17** we find this beautiful and challenging summary of our calling. Paul says: **"And whatever you do, whether in word or deed, do it all in the name of the Lord Jesus, giving thanks to God the Father through him."**

Twice Mine

There was a young boy who lived in a small Midwestern town in the U.S. who loved to build things with his dad who had quite a shop in their garage. One week his dad was out of town on business. The boy came home from school and decided to build a toy boat with some leftover scraps of lumber. He cut and nailed and sanded for three days and even added a rudimentary mast and sail and rudder. He painted the boat and was quite proud of his creation. It was time to test it out.

He went to a safe landing on the river that ran through his town, attached a long string to the boat and let it out for a test run. It floated beautifully but as the wind hit its sail it got caught in the current, the string broke and it was gone. About three weeks later the boy was walking down Main Street of his town on the way to the bakery for donuts when he looked in the window of a second-hand store and there was his boat.

He ran inside and announced, "That toy boat you have in the window… it's mine!" A rather gruff older man behind the counter responded, "Well it's not yours anymore! Somebody found it and brought it in. If you want it back it'll be three bucks!" The boy ran home, took the plug out of the bottom of his bank, and counted out three dollars in change. He quickly ran back to the store, put his money on the counter and went to the front window to collect his treasure. As he walked out of the store he looked down at his toy boat and said, "There! First I made you. Then I lost you. Now I bought you back for a price. Now you are twice mine!"

I believe that's what God our Father says to each one of us. "First I made you – a unique creation unlike anybody else. Then I lost you – lost you to sin or pride or ambivalence. Then I bought you back for a price – the life of My very own Son, Jesus. Now you are twice Mine!" This is how Jesus has taken hold of each one of us with His love, forgiveness, grace and generous gifts. He has promised to never let go… and neither should we!

What Will We Do With the Rest of Our Lives?

The question that faces "each of us" and "all of us" in our Baby Boom generation is "What will we do with the rest of our lives?" What, if in fact, we have 10, 20 or 30 more years to live? Will we use this season to make a real difference?

Every chapter in this book has been written to help us weigh our options and seek answers to this question that ultimately only God can give. Along the way we've considered the importance of taking stock of our current situation but continuing to dream big dreams. We've recognized again the importance of mending and tending to key relationships in our lives, starting with our own relationship with God. We've looked at the various world views operating in culture today and seen how they can keep us wrapped-up in lies about ourselves and the world around us. We've considered marriage, parenting, work, recreation, money and more and have asked, "How can we live our best lives?" Throughout this journey we've talked about legacy and what we hope to leave those who come after us.

I pray that you have been encouraged and challenged to consider the "much more" that God has prepared for you in this important season of your life. I sincerely believe that God is about to write a new chapter in the story of our world. He's asking each of us if we would like to be a part of it. Regardless of our past, through Jesus we can experience a brand new beginning. I am saying, "Yes, God! I'm all in!" Fellow Baby Boomers! Please join me and let's change the world!

Questions for Personal Reflection or Group Discussion:

1. Reflect on the statement, "Legacy isn't about what you leave *for* someone nearly as much as what you leave *in* someone!" How might this realization change how you approach the rest of your life?

2. As you run your race for King Jesus, what rocks are currently inhibiting your path to the finish line? What blessings are you discovering in working through them?

3. What "measure of faith" has God given you to help fulfill your mission here on Earth? Are you willing to use it and ask God to grow it?
4. What is the legacy you would like to leave the world and the generations of family that will follow you?

Notes

1. Nichole Nordeman, Song *"Legacy,"* (Woven and Spun Album, Sparrow Records, 2002).

Made in the USA
Monee, IL
01 March 2023

f280f470-df5f-47fc-801c-b8be1f2c9daeR01